T0333436

The PEST DETECTIVES

The definitive history
of **RENTOKIL**

The
PEST
DETECTIVES

Rob Gray

HARRIMAN HOUSE LTD

18 College Street

Petersfield

Hampshire

GU31 4AD

GREAT BRITAIN

Tel: +44 (0)1730 233870

Email: **enquiries@harriman-house.com**

Website: **www.harriman-house.com**

First published in Great Britain in 2015.

Hardcover ISBN: 978-0-85719-507-4

eBook ISBN: 978-0-85719-508-1

British Library Cataloguing in Publication Data

A CIP catalogue record for this book can be obtained from the British Library.

CONTENTS

Every owner of a physical copy of this edition of

The PEST DETECTIVES

can download the eBook for free direct from us at Harriman House, in a DRM-free format that can be read on any eReader, tablet or smartphone.

Simply head to:

ebooks.harriman-house.com/pestd

to get your copy now.

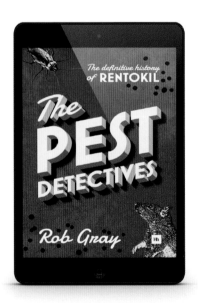

FOREWORD

For many people, Rentokil means pest control. It is by far and away the strongest pest control brand in the world, enjoying an unrivalled global leadership position as the most international business of its kind – today operating across more than 60 countries.

The story of Rentokil's rise to pre-eminence is a compelling one. You don't get to be top dog by plodding along. It takes bravery, purpose, originality, expertise and determination. These qualities shine through time and time again in the history of the Rentokil brand.

More than anything it has been Rentokil's exceptional people who have made the difference over the years, from the scientists who have delivered brilliant R&D breakthroughs, to frontline technicians and surveyors bending over backwards to provide outstanding customer service – often in challenging environments. All the more so in the early years, when there was not the technology that we can call upon today. They are highly-skilled pest detectives – searching for clues to how pests might be entering a building or where pests are living – looking at the evidence and acting to protect people.

The evolution of Rentokil from those early days into a global powerhouse brand I hope makes for great reading. There are plenty of revelations along the way – some of which will surprise even Rentokil insiders.

Rentokil unquestionably has a fascinating past. I can also say with confidence that a bright future lies ahead.

Pest control is a very attractive industry, with annual worldwide revenues of around £10bn. Market growth is projected to top 5% per annum globally over the next few years. Future prospects look good across both developed markets and the emerging higher-growth regions of Asia, Latin and Central America, Africa and the Middle East.

Rentokil's expertise really comes into its own for those businesses and organisations where there is a zero tolerance towards pests, such as in food processing and pharmaceuticals. Today we offer the kind of pest control products and management information tools which often give organisations a licence to operate. I can only see the importance of the pest control industry growing in the face of climate change, urbanisation and the expanding middle class of emerging economies.

Already there have been cases of dengue fever and West Nile virus in North America and southern Europe. And even in the temperate climes of the UK, NHS data reveals that every year over 5,000 people in England go to hospital due to insect bites and wasp stings.

This book sets the stage for Rentokil's next ten years, when the business will celebrate its centenary. Over the next decade I expect there to be significant changes in pest control as we 'reinvent Rentokil'. But we mustn't forget our past. Ours is a rich heritage –

and it's our people who made it happen and continue to go the extra mile for customers every day.

They are the Rentokil brand.

Andy Ransom

CHIEF EXECUTIVE OFFICER
RENTOKIL INITIAL

SUPPORTING MALARIA NO MORE

James Whiting, Executive Director, Malaria No More UK with Maureen Odhiambo and her family in Kenya.

For every copy of this book sold, Rentokil will donate £1 to Malaria No More, a young and ambitious charity with a mission as transparent as its name: to end one of the world's oldest killer diseases; to make malaria no more. Malaria is a horrific disease but entirely preventable. And treatment is cheap. It costs less than £1 to save the life of a child with malaria.

www.malarianomore.org.uk

THE BIRTH OF A PEST CONTROL POWERHOUSE

What a year was 1925.

F. Scott Fitzgerald published *The Great Gatsby*, Benito Mussolini seized dictatorial power in Italy and Kristiania became Oslo. The fez was outlawed in Turkey, water skis were patented, Louis Armstrong made his first record under his own name and the Nobel Prize in Literature was awarded to George Bernard Shaw.

Walt Disney got married, and released the black-and-white short animated comedy *Alice Rattled by Rats* in which a group of boisterous rats play havoc with a cat (some things never change!), a full three years before Mickey Mouse took his debut bow. It was the year that saw the birth of Margaret Thatcher, Malcolm X, Richard Burton, Sammy Davis Jr, Peter Sellers, Bill Haley, Pierre Boulez and Paul Newman. And to top it all, it was the year in which the Rentokil brand came into being.

In the pages that follow, we chart the many twists and turns in the development of this remarkable brand and share some entertaining stories from the people who have made Rentokil Initial a great place to work and an outstanding success. As this book celebrates the 90th anniversary of Rentokil – and the forthcoming 90th anniversary in 2017 of the formation of British Ratin, which bought Rentokil in the 1950s before rebranding itself under the Rentokil name – inevitably the main focus is on the Rentokil side of the business. But of course this is not in any way intended to downplay the significance of other businesses within today's diverse multinational company. Initial, for example, has its own illustrious history and a name that pre-dates Rentokil, beginning life in 1903 as a supplier of monogrammed towels before expanding into other laundry and business services, eventually coming together with Rentokil in one of the major UK corporate mergers of the 1990s.

As with all great brands, people have clear opinions on what Rentokil stands for. Yes, for many it is a byword for market leadership in pest control. But of course there is far more to it than that – both in terms of the services delivered and the values that make Rentokil, the business and brand, utterly unique. Genuine concern for people and a passion for customer service run through the company's DNA. These values have remained constant in a fast-changing world. Despite the passing of the decades, the appetite to be the best and go above and beyond in meeting customer needs has remained. Indeed, it is keener than ever. The Rentokil brand encapsulates all of that.

Yet while staying true to its core values, Rentokil has evolved. After all, it's impossible to keep ahead of the field by standing still. By and large the pests have remained the same, albeit some have developed immunity to what was once effective, necessitating new approaches. But the biggest driver of all behind transformation in the business is the degree to which the world has changed and continues to change. Customers are increasingly demanding; regulations have been tightened; business is more global; time frames get ever shorter.

In an age of instant access to information and super-fast automated processes, customers now take it for granted that their business partners will respond swiftly to meet and surpass their expectations. Companies cannot afford for production plants to stand idle or wait an age for hotel bedrooms to be made fit for guests once again. Rentokil's well-equipped and highly motivated employees take pride in ensuring that business-critical problems such as these are resolved with the minimum of fuss and maximum efficiency. Rentokil employees are the best ambassadors of all; the reason why the brand is so widely recognised and admired.

That's always been the case. It's just even truer now than 90, 50 or even ten years ago. The way we work and live in the 21st century has raised the stakes, but also generated opportunities on an almost unimaginable scale. Today there are between 15 and 20 million hotel rooms globally and people criss-cross the world in enormous numbers on business and for pleasure. According to the International Air Transport Association, scheduled flights carry an astonishing 3.3 billion passengers per year on around 50,000 routes. They also transport around 50 million tonnes of freight. That's a lot, although it's only a tiny fraction of the goods and resources transported by sea. The world shipping fleet has the capacity to carry 1.7 billion tonnes – that's at any one time, not over the course of a year – and is growing steadily, with global capacity 4% higher in 2014 than in the previous year. Demand for pest-controlled environments is ever expanding.

The amount of food processed to be sold in supermarkets and convenience stores is also on the rise. Euromonitor research finds that 1.8 trillion units of food packaging are made every year. All of the food packaged in this way must be produced in hygienic, pest-free environments to meet exacting food standards. Through hard work, innovation and attention to detail, Rentokil makes that possible.

Hotels, restaurants, ships, warehouses, offices, factories, retail units: operators of these and other types of facility all need Rentokil's expertise. So, too, do homeowners.

Through the decades, generations of householders have turned to the company to protect their cherished living spaces from the ravages of damp, dry rot and pests of all kinds, from the largest rodents to the smallest bed bugs. Rentokil has been a pioneer in this field since its early days, pushing the boundaries with scientific breakthroughs. The business set the bar high then and still does by employing talented people and training them to become experts in the essentials. In 2014, 66,000 courses were undertaken globally though the U+ in-house university, sharing technical knowledge, developing leadership skills and embedding best practice on health and safety. Rentokil's reputation is based on the technical expertise and commitment of its people.

Read on for the fascinating story of how the business got to this point. There follows an account of outstanding individuals – a few of them larger than life – shrewd deals, smart innovation, pragmatic solutions, international growth, ground-breaking assignments, marketing and PR flair, consistent values and occasional outbreaks of tragedy, comedy and the simply bizarre. This is a story that begins with a gifted Imperial Entomologist, an important scientific breakthrough in Denmark and a formidable entrepreneurial woman who strove to build a brand and deliver excellent service at a time when female business leaders were thin on the ground. This is a story that takes in the Palace of Westminster and royal residences, that stretches from the Sydney Opera House to the magnificent stave churches of Norway, from the Petronas Towers in Kuala Lumpur to the sewers of Brussels, from desert sands to the capital of Iceland, from the Olympic

Games in Atlanta and Beijing to the 2014 FIFA World Cup in Brazil, from a modern twist on the Pied Piper to the ancient art of snake-charming, from work on humble dwellings and ordinary business premises through to demanding assignments such as cathedral restoration and crucial roles in massive infrastructure projects, right the way through to the preservation of cultural artefacts, historic ships and works of art including many masterpieces. This is a story about solving problems, applying expertise, surpassing expectations and delivering unbeatable service.

Above all else, and like all fascinating tales, this is a story about people: the people who made Rentokil great, and those whose work is making Rentokil greater still.

'I knew we shouldn't have brought those two woodworms.'

CHAPTER ONE

Dangerous Experiments

Entomology – n. The scientific study of insects

The Rentokil story begins with a brilliant life cut tragically short.

Harold Maxwell-Lefroy was born on 20 January 1877 in the Hampshire village of Crondall, the middle child of seven. His father, Charles, was a country squire who served as an officer in the 14th King's Hussars, one of the most esteemed cavalry regiments of the time, and the family could trace its ancestry back to the Huguenots. With a long tradition of military service and respectability, the Lefroys resembled the kind of characters found in the novels of Hampshire writer Jane Austen, the famously perceptive observer of manners and morality.

That they did was no mere coincidence. Harold's great-great-grandmother Anne, wife of Reverend Isaac Peter George Lefroy, was a neighbour and mentor to the youthful Jane Austen, encouraging her early endeavours as a writer and sharing a love of literature. But there was also love of the romantic kind between the Austens and Lefroys. When Anne and Isaac's nephew, Thomas Langlois Lefroy, came to visit them at Ashe House in the winter of 1795–96, having recently graduated from Trinity College, Dublin, he soon became the object of 20-year-old Jane's attentions.

The romantic attachment ended when Tom departed Ashe early in 1796, but there has been plenty of speculation through the years that he inspired some of the author's greatest literary creations, including Mr Darcy in *Pride and Prejudice*, which Austen began writing soon after the dalliance ended. A 'sexed up' version of the relationship provided the basis for the 2007 biopic *Becoming Jane*, in which James McAvoy played the part of Tom Lefroy opposite Anne Hathaway. In real life, Tom went on to become an MP and eventually Lord Chief Justice of Ireland. But it was by no means an end to the ties between the families. In 1814, Jane Austen's niece, Anna Austen, married Tom's cousin, Benjamin Lefroy.

Considering his colourful and accomplished background, young Harold Maxwell-Lefroy had a lot to live up to. Educated at Marlborough College, today still one of the UK's most prestigious public schools, he was admitted to King's College, Cambridge, in 1895 to study Natural Sciences. At Cambridge, a lifelong passion for insects was nurtured and he excelled academically. After achieving a first-class degree, he went on to complete his masters. Maxwell-Lefroy's avid curiosity and fast-growing expertise quickly led him to exotic outposts of the British Empire, where he was able to conduct field research and offer practical advice on dealing with pest problems.

First he spent four years in the Caribbean, lecturing on economic entomology in Barbados in 1899 before assuming the role of Entomologist at the Imperial Department of Agriculture in the West Indies. A devastating hurricane had brought death and destruction to large areas of the Caribbean in autumn 1898, and as part of the economic reconstruction efforts landowners were diversifying their crops and needed advice on how best to protect them from pests. Maxwell-Lefroy travelled extensively across the islands, studying pests such as the sugarcane moth borer, and while in the Caribbean met his future wife, Kathleen. Then in 1903 he took the opportunity to move to the other side of the world, swapping West Indies for East Indies as Entomologist to the government of India.

Professor Harold Maxwell-Lefroy.

IMPERIAL ENTOMOLOGIST

During the best part of a decade in the subcontinent, Maxwell-Lefroy's standing in the scientific community grew in leaps and bounds. In 1905, he played a significant role in the foundation of the Indian Agricultural Research Institute (IARI) at Pusa, in the state of Bihar, overseeing the creation of a large entomology department. The IARI came into being at the behest of Viceroy and Governor General of India, Lord Curzon, and thanks to a £30,000 grant from American philanthropist, Henry Phipps. In the 21st century, now headquartered in New Delhi, it remains India's premier institute for agricultural research, development and education, employing over 3,500 people. Unfortunately the original buildings and most of the early records were destroyed by a devastating earthquake on 15 January 1934.

While still in his 20s, Maxwell-Lefroy followed in the footsteps of Charles Darwin in becoming a fellow of both the Entomological Society and the Zoological Society of London. Before long, his diligence and eminence in his field were recognised when he became the first person to be given the job title of Imperial Entomologist. His reputation was further cemented by the publication of ground-breaking books *Indian Insect Pests* (1906) and *Indian Insect Life* (1909), the latter an exhaustive, monumental work weighing in at just under 800 pages.

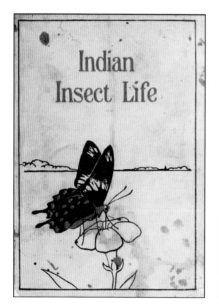
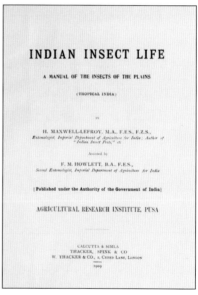

Maxwell-Lefroy's Indian Insect Life *is a scientific tour de force, weighing in at just under 800 pages.*

All of this took place at the time of the British Raj, a couple of generations before the birth of an independent India, and it's tempting to picture the gifted young Cambridge scientist discussing the weighty issues of the day with his imperial contemporaries beneath the big fans of a well-appointed colonial club, while the monsoon rains lashed down outside. Or sitting on a veranda observing a glorious tropical sunset, gin and tonic in hand. In his line of work, Maxwell-Lefroy would have understood better than anyone the anti-malarial properties of the quinine in his tonic water!

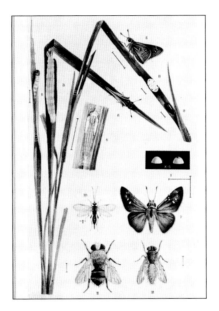

The rice skipper, a beautifully illustrated plate from Indian Insect Life.

The reality, however, was harsh, as a profile of Maxwell-Lefroy that appeared in the December 1988 edition of *Hampshire* magazine makes abundantly clear: "In 1910 Lefroy reluctantly decided that he must leave India. Two of his children had died from fly-borne diseases. He did not want to risk the life of his surviving son."

Thankfully, despite the death of his elder son Denis and daughter Gladys, his remaining son, Cecil, was to be spared – enjoying a successful career as the General Manager of Burmah Oil and living until the age of almost 90.

RETURN TO ENGLAND

Shortly after the death of Denis at the age of four in November 1910, a devastated Maxwell-Lefroy applied for home leave for the first time since his arrival in India. Early in January 1911, the professor, his wife and Cecil set sail for England, where they moved into a house on the Thames at Strawberry Hill, Twickenham.

Maxwell-Lefroy was initially granted 'privilege leave' for three months, to which 18 months' furlough was added. Although it had boosted his career, India had taken a severe toll on his family. However, the professor's reputation and prodigious knowledge of insects presented him with opportunities in academia back in his homeland. He began lecturing at Imperial College in South Kensington, where his inaugural lecture caused quite a stir.

In it, Maxwell-Lefroy set out a compelling case for the importance of applied entomology – studying the effects insects have on man. He explained:

> "It is only lately that the significance of the insect world has become apparent... The opening up to agriculture of new tropical countries, the increasing competition in the cultivation of tropical products, the discovery of the part played by insects in disseminating human disease, have brought entomology to the front and have shown that, far from being a science concerned solely with the minute classification of interminable varieties and species, it is a science which has great significance for man, and one which requires to be developed in serious earnest if we are to be in a position to harvest our crops, to cope with disease, and to populate tropical areas successfully."

His lecture also cited the role of the mosquito in causing malaria epidemics and the rat flea in spreading bubonic plague.

This and subsequent lectures added to Maxwell-Lefroy's already considerable standing in the scientific community and gave impetus to the argument that the status of entomology as a field of study should be enhanced. In 1912 he was appointed the first Professor of Entomology at Imperial College. At the time Imperial enjoyed a high profile, having been created just five years earlier after the Board of Education recommended the amalgamation of the Royal College of Science, the Royal School of Mines and the City & Guilds College into a single institution that would act as a world-class hotbed of scientific excellence. When construction began on a new university building in 1909, the foundation stone was laid by King Edward VII.

An enthusiastic and mercurial educator, Maxwell-Lefroy was popular with his students. Evelyn Cheesman, who went on to become a renowned butterfly expert, wrote in her 1957 autobiography, *Things Worth While*: "Lefroy was an erratic teacher, but his lectures had the merit of being unusually interesting."

By 1913, the energetic academic was combining his position at the university with honorary positions as curator of the new insect house at London Zoo and Entomologist to the Royal Horticultural Society at Wisley. Given his renown as an expert on pests and Imperial College's burgeoning reputation for scientific breakthroughs, it was no great surprise that the government should seek him out when one of the country's most splendid buildings was found to be at risk.

WESTMINSTER HALL IN PERIL

The structure in question was Westminster Hall, the oldest building on the parliamentary estate, dating back to 1097. Its beautiful hammer-beam roof, commissioned by Richard II in 1393, is the largest medieval timber roof in northern Europe and is generally considered a masterpiece of design and engineering. This great building has also been the setting for numerous momentous events in English history. Here Henry VIII granted clemency to the Evil May Day rioters; it was the location for the trial of Guy Fawkes and the other Gunpowder Plot conspirators; and for the trial of King Charles I.

Fortunately, Westminster Hall escaped destruction during the devastating fire of 1834 that destroyed much of the rest of the Palace of Westminster. Lord Melbourne, the Prime Minister of the time, personally directed the fire engines to douse the roof with water in a frantic effort to preserve the structure for the nation. By this point, the medieval Palace of Westminster housing the Lords and Commons, had already burnt to the ground (construction of the famous replacement building by architect Charles Barry, with its tower housing Big Ben, began in 1840).

The loss of so much historical heritage meant the preservation of Westminster Hall assumed enormous importance. When it came to light in a report by architect Frank Baines, Director of the Office of Works, that the roof beams of this fine building had suffered significant damage due to a deathwatch beetle infestation, resolving the problem became a matter of urgency. In 1914, Baines contacted Maxwell-Lefroy for assistance. The professor set to work formulating the first chemical fluids specifically designed to control wood-boring insects. In a letter about the restoration published in *The Times* on 22 May 1914, Baines wrote appreciatively:

"All other methods of exterminating *Xestobium tessellatum* [deathwatch beetle] having failed, I called in the assistance of Professor Maxwell-Lefroy and he invented a spray which is constituted thus – 50 per cent tetrachloroethane, 6 per cent cedarwood oil, 2 per cent solvent soap, 2 per cent paraffin wax and 40 per cent trichloroethylene. The first is a perfect insecticide and is so dangerous that those who handle it must use gas masks – this was done on Saturday and Sunday. The cedarwood oil protects the wood against future attacks and the scent impregnates the timber and keeps the beetle away."

Westminster Hall's magnificent hammer-beam roof was threatened by deathwatch beetle.

Courtesy of Adam Wolfitt/Robert Harding Picture Library.

The formula was refined as work on the beams progressed and proved to be highly effective. Success in treating Westminster Hall brought Maxwell-Lefroy a good deal of favourable publicity and he began thinking of the commercial potential of his new fluid. We can therefore tentatively trace the first inklings of the business that was to become Rentokil to this point in time.

THE FIRST WORLD WAR

Yet this being 1914, darker events were unfolding, forcing Maxwell-Lefroy to put his entrepreneurial aspirations on hold. Following the outbreak of the first world war, the Entomology Department at Imperial College focused its work on insecticides as part of the war effort to keep troops healthy and safeguard food supplies. The British Government sent Maxwell-Lefroy back to India to assess the viability of reviving the country's silk industry. But simultaneously he applied himself to alleviating the misery of British troops. In a letter to the *British Medical Journal* (published 13 February 1915), Maxwell-Lefroy lamented the "pitiful situation" of many soldiers affected by pests such as lice and revealed he had received an "unexpected flood" of 1,100 letters requesting details of remedies he had referred to in his pre-conflict books.

Having completed his three-volume report on the silk industry, Maxwell-Lefroy continued his family's military tradition when given the rank of acting lieutenant colonel in the Mesopotamian Expeditionary Force. There was a desperate need for his pest control expertise in the searing heat and terrible conditions of the Middle East and the professor journeyed there from India to throw himself into improving hygiene, particularly for the wounded, by poisoning flies and vermin. His valuable practical and scientific work in the theatre of war in what is now Iraq formed the basis for a book, published in 1917, on fly poisons for outdoor and hospital use. He was then sent all the way to Australia due to concerns over weevil infestation of the huge stores of bagged wheat in Sydney awaiting shipment to the UK.

> "Within a few weeks of his arrival in Sydney he had discovered that the temporary warehouses were not sufficiently protected from rain blown in from the sea. Ideal conditions were thus created for weevils to flourish in damp softened grain, in bags too closely stacked."
>
> – HAMPSHIRE (*THE COUNTY MAGAZINE*), DECEMBER 1988

Before embarking on the epic sea voyage home, the intrepid entomologist gave his recommendations for improving storage and devised a method for 'cleansing' contaminated grain.

After the war, Maxwell-Lefroy was able to return to Imperial College and resume his lecturing and experiments with gusto. He also contributed to several early black-and-white documentary films on insects that were part of a pioneering science and wildlife series called *Secrets of Nature*. The series made ground-breaking use of techniques such as time-lapse and microscopic cinematography that have become so familiar to viewers of David Attenborough programmes and other nature documentaries. Maxwell-Lefroy is known to have been directly involved with at least two *Secrets of Nature* documentaries: *The Wasp* and *The Tiger Beetle*. It's unclear whether any copies of these films survive, however the BFI has released a compilation DVD featuring several of the other films in this trailblazing series.

Work also recommenced on the restoration of Westminster Hall – which was eventually reopened by King George V and Queen Mary amid much fanfare in 1923. In his excellent 2015 biography of Maxwell-Lefroy, *The Entokil Man*, Laurence Fleming writes: "A magnificent building, of great historical importance and enormous architectural value, had been saved, with all its unique, irreplaceable carvings. A beetle had been studied, its grubs in all probability already present in the original timbers, and a liquid invented which sealed its death warrant. For his work at Westminster Hall, Mr Frank Baines was offered, and accepted, a knighthood. If Professor Maxwell-Lefroy was offered one at the same time – there is a legend in the family to this effect ... he politely refused it."

EARLY TIMBER FLUID MARKETING

The publicity around his involvement with the restoration meant custodians of other threatened old buildings began beating a path to Maxwell-Lefroy's door. Fully aware of the commercial possibilities of his timber fluid, he began targeting a market of architects, builders, furniture makers and antique dealers. With business taking off, it became clear that the combined demands of academia and commerce were too much for one person. Consequently, Maxwell-Lefroy brought in a young woman from London called Elizabeth 'Bessie' Eades, initially on a freelance basis, to help out with billing clients and bookkeeping. Eades took to the role like a duck to water and before long was running the commercial side of the business.

As demand for the product grew, Maxwell-Lefroy set about establishing a company to better exploit the business possibilities of his timber fluid. On 29 September 1924, Disinfectants and General Products Ltd came into being, described as a disinfectant manufacturer. The generic nature of the name had some advantages but brevity, originality and memorability were not among them. To help with the marketing of the insecticide fluids, what was called for was a brand name that stuck in the mind.

Maxwell-Lefroy and Eades were keen on the name Entokil – from the Greek word for insect, *entomon*. Unfortunately, there was an objection to the use of that trademark. The pair didn't want a name too far removed from their original intention and played around with the word by adding various letters. It's safe to assume that Sentokil or Wentokil would have been quickly dismissed as being too brutal so soon after the horrific war. Rentokil, on the other hand, had a catchy ring to it and tripped easily off the tongue. So it was that in 1925 a great, highly versatile brand name made its quiet entrance. Nowadays we might say it came in under the radar, but this was a time more than a decade before the acronym RADAR had even been coined. And more than 80 years before Rentokil would launch a hi-tech mousetrap bearing the RADAR name.

AN UNTIMELY END

Sadly, Maxwell-Lefroy was not to see either his business or the new brand name grow and prosper. He was dead before the year was out, the victim of one of his own insecticide experiments gone terribly wrong. It was certainly not the case that the scientist was unaware of the risks he was taking with his research. In March the previous year there was a narrow escape when testing an insecticide on flies. While the flies were apparently unharmed by the toxin, Maxwell-Lefroy inadvertently breathed in the poisonous fumes and began choking. Unable to wrench his laboratory window open, he was almost overcome. Luckily, in this instance he was able to stagger into a nearby room and alert some colleagues, who saved his life by promptly administering oxygen for an hour.

But on Saturday 11 October 1925, the professor's luck ran out. Due to the inherent dangers of his work, Maxwell-Lefroy generally took the precaution of conducting his experiments alone. Once again he was testing an insecticide gas, this time on house fly larvae. When he failed to come home for dinner, his concerned wife Kathleen went to Imperial College to discover the professor lying unconscious on the floor. He died four days later in St George's Hospital, without regaining consciousness.

The accident and subsequent death of such a prominent scientist made headlines across the United Kingdom and further afield. Newspapers including *The Times* paid tribute to his knowledge, courage and public service.

> "The achievements of his comparatively short life were great. He was the true heroic enthusiast. While apparently reckless, in spite of more than one serious warning, of the dangers to which he exposed himself in his experiments with deadly poisons, he had in fact a juster knowledge of them than anyone else, as was proved by the care he took that no one except himself should be exposed to them."
>
> – OBITUARY, *THE SPECTATOR*, 25 OCTOBER 1925

Maxwell-Lefroy's friend, Francis MacLean Scott, told the inquest into his death how he had seen the entomologist staggering around on the Saturday of the incident and complaining of having inhaled the vapour. "The little beggars have got the best of me," he had been heard to remark. Although clearly feeling unwell, Maxwell-Lefroy was determined to return to his laboratory, where he succumbed.

As the *Aberdeen Journal* reported, "The post-mortem showed that the professor's condition was compatible with the continual inhalation of gases. The coroner, in returning a verdict of 'death through misadventure', said the professor was a brilliant research worker who lost his life in trying to benefit the human race."

Tributes to the man and his achievements flooded in. Writing in *The Times*, Professor Edward Stebbing, an eminent expert on forests who worked with Maxwell-Lefroy in India, said: "Without exception he was the keenest and most enthusiastic man I have ever met. In his nine years in India he revolutionised all previous methods of studying the insect pests of agricultural crops... there was none abler or more of a 'live wire' than Lefroy."

A separate obituary in *The Times* bearing the headline 'A Great Economic Entomologist', celebrated the professor's pre-eminence and tremendous success in dealing with insect pests at both administrative and practical levels. It included a passage written by an old friend which was very revealing about Maxwell-Lefroy's impatient character and obsession with scientific research. Accepting a lift with this "ardent and dangerous" motorist was not for the faint-hearted:

"It was an experience to be driven by him in a car whose battered wings gave little confidence, as fast as the car could go, through London traffic, in company of a biscuit box of noxious living insects, a few glass bottles of poisons, and a cylinder of some lethal gas. In revenge for such a trip, I once took him from Regent's Park to St Paul's and back in a very fast car with quick acceleration, intending to 'show off' a little. Lefroy took not the slightest notice of the risks but continued to describe a new method of cooking the goose of the red boll weevil, drawing diagrams on the back of an envelope and thrusting them on the driver's attention. Lefroy was not only a great investigator, but a wholly delightful personality."

As a mark of respect, the College of Pestology introduced a commemorative gold medal in Maxwell-Lefroy's name to be awarded annually for the best essay on a pest-related theme.

The talented professor was dead at the relatively young age of 48. Yet 90 years later, the brand he created is stronger than ever.

The College of Pestology – an entomological society at its height in the 1920s – introduced a commemorative gold medal in honour of Maxwell-Lefroy.

ROYAL ENTOMOLOGICAL SOCIETY LIBRARY

Maxwell-Lefroy, Harold, **Indian Insect Pests**, 1906

Maxwell-Lefroy, Harold, **The Bombay Locust** (*Acridium Succinctum*): *A report on the investigation of 1903–1904, Memoirs of the Department of Agriculture in India*, Entomology Series Volume 1 (1), 1906

Maxwell-Lefroy, Harold, and Howlett, F.M., **Indian Insect Life**: *A Manual of the Insects of the Plains (Tropical India)*, 1909

Maxwell-Lefroy, Harold, **Mulberry silk rearing in the United Provinces**, 1910

Maxwell-Lefroy, Harold, and Ansorge, E.C., **Report on an inquiry into the Silk Industry in India**, *vols I–III*. 1916–7

Maxwell-Lefroy, Harold, and Jackson, A.C., **Some fly poisons for outdoor and hospital use**, Bull. ent. Res. 7: 327–335, 1917

Maxwell-Lefroy, Harold, **Manual of Entomology with Special Reference to Economic Entomology**, 1923

THE ESSENTIALS

1877 – Harold Maxwell-Lefroy is born in Hampshire.

1895 – Maxwell-Lefroy is admitted to King's College, Cambridge, where he studies natural sciences.

1899 – Travels to the West Indies.

1906 – Publication of Maxwell-Lefroy's highly regarded book, *Indian Insect Pests*.

1912 – Becomes first ever Professor of Entomology at Imperial College.

1914 – Office of Public Works invites Maxwell-Lefroy to help preserve the magnificent wooden hammer-beam roof of Westminster Hall, which had suffered deathwatch beetle damage.

1917 – Deals with pests in arduous conditions near the frontline in the Middle East during the first world war.

1923 – Reopening of Westminster Hall by the King and Queen.

1925 – Creation of the Rentokil name... and the untimely death of Maxwell-Lefroy.

CHAPTER TWO

The Early Years of Rentokil

The nascent Rentokil could very easily have died with Harold Maxwell-Lefroy but the formidable Bessie Eades had other ideas. She took control of the trading company she had formed with the late professor and bought the rights to the timber fluid from his widow Kathleen – it is said she paid £90 (around £5,000 in today's money). The first world war had triggered far-reaching change in British society and brought about new opportunities for women in the workplace, but commerce was still an overwhelmingly masculine preserve. It's worth remembering that the act giving women the same voting rights as men only came into law in July 1928, by which point the trailblazing Eades had been calling the shots as a businesswoman for nearly three years.

Coincidentally, summer 1928 also saw the first statutory meeting of a new company, Rentokil (Sales) Ltd, which Eades set up with Elsie May Lanstein in Hatton Garden, London. The latter was appointed to the position of General Manager, Sales Manager and Organiser at an annual salary of £250 (equivalent to £14,000 today), allowing Eades to devote more time to research and development. By far the most important strategic decision Eades made in this period was to start selling directly to members of the public. Rentokil fluids had previously been sold in drums of one gallon or larger, with trade customers to the fore. Switching to smaller containers and putting marketing emphasis on the long-lasting nature of the timber fluids allowed Rentokil to target the consumer market.

Bessie Eades, the formidable entrepreneur who ran Rentokil for 30 years.

A 1930s promotional leaflet titled *Will it Break Out Again?* promised to protect wood against attack from furniture beetle and deathwatch beetle because it had been compounded and used by the greatest entomologist of his time, namely Maxwell-Lefroy. "Not one case of re-infestation since it was discovered 10 years ago," trumpeted the leaflet. Product packaging also referred to the fact that the timber fluid followed the original formula developed by the late professor. An advertisement for a newly developed beetle powder from the same decade, headlined *Death Comes in the Night to all Kitchen and*

Bakehouse Pests, encouraged product trialling beneath an image of a large arrow-of-death smiting a bug. "It's so simple," read the copy. "Just sprinkle around overnight and next morning bodies of beetles, cockroaches and crickets are lying around ready to be swept up. Try it yourself by sending 4½d for TRIAL TIN."

A pre-war Rentokil advertisement.

The company moved to new premises at 171 Bermondsey Street, London, SE1 in 1933 and Eades was proving herself an adept businesswoman, expanding the product range and building sales through advertising. Eades was certainly no slouch when it came to closing a deal. Whenever a salesman came to call, if time allowed she would invite them in and listen to their pitch before turning the tables to plug the wonders of her pest control products. On more than one occasion it would be the visiting salesman who made a purchase rather than her, leaving the Bermondsey building content but a little bemused that a Rentokil product or two was in their hands.

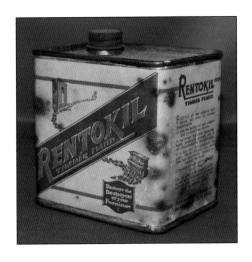

Early Rentokil timber fluid packaging, bearing the slogan "Destroys the Destroyers of your Furniture". Text on the side of the can includes the claim that the product is made "From the original formula of the late Professor H. M. Lefroy".

Eades also proved adept at generating publicity on a shoestring. She penned an article for *Musical Opinion* magazine in response to concerns among its readership about woodworm infestation in pianos. Inspiration on how to open the piece came on a visit to St Mary-le-Bow church, which in the early 1930s was undergoing extensive renovation, including to beams ravaged by deathwatch beetle. Incidentally, the centrepiece of the project – the restoration of its famous bells – was paid for by brash retail magnate Harry Gordon Selfridge. But Eades' motif was wood borers and her piece began by evoking thousands of "Cockney" deathwatch beetles, all born within the sound of Bow Bells.

In the decade of the Great Depression, it was far from plain sailing for Rentokil. Growth was slow and there were times when the figures made miserable reading. In the year ending 31 August 1934, Rentokil made a net loss of £64 (the equivalent of £4,000 today). The outbreak of the second world war in 1939 inevitably brought more challenges, not least during the Blitz, when the company premises in Brixton were destroyed following a direct hit from a Luftwaffe land mine. "That was one of the hardest blows – to see all our work destroyed," Eades was to recall over a decade later in an interview with furniture trade magazine *The Cabinet Maker*. Yet there was nothing for it but to carry on. "We set up our office in the ruins," Eades continued. "Sometimes we worked in the snow. People loaned us typewriters. One of our typists worked her own machine from her home. We took the mail from the postman in the street. Then we got a lock-up shop in Stockwell Road, and then another lock-up shop and then a house, and we carried on."

In the tough environs of bomb-damaged Stockwell Road, opposite a tatty used car dealership, the indefatigable Eades overcame one hurdle after another, determined to keep her aspirations for Rentokil alive.

AN EYE FOR TALENT

Despite the obvious hardships, wartime was a period of rapid development for Rentokil, with annual profits leaping to £18,000 by the end of the conflict (roughly £700,000 today). In 1944, Eades showed she had a good eye for talent by recruiting Dr Norman Hickin, who became a key figure in driving the business forward.

Prior to joining Rentokil, Hickin had been at Dunlop Rubber Company for a number of years, most recently working on an important project to develop self-sealing aircraft fuel tanks, designed to reduce the risk of planes exploding when hit by enemy fire. However, when it came to the subject of flight, Hickin was in truth much more an expert on winged insects than he was on fighters and bombers. After graduating from Birmingham Central Technical College (today Aston University) in 1936 with a BSc in zoology with special entomology, he obtained his PhD as an evening student with the University of London. He wrote his thesis on wood-boring beetles (*Ptinidae*) which needless to say made him very well-qualified to work at Rentokil. As with his predecessor, insects were a passion. Spotting a recruitment ad in the *Daily Telegraph* for the position of Entomologist, Hickin decided it was time to move into the field that truly fascinated him.

A bomb landed close to the Stockwell Road building a few days before the job interview, smashing several windows. So it was that one January day Hickin found himself quizzed by Eades on entomology in a dingy little office where cardboard had temporarily replaced window panes. The setting may have been dismal but the pair hit it off immediately. Hickin was impressed by the tall, genteel lady in the white coat, judging that she possessed "an extremely agile wit and dogged perseverance". For her part, Eades liked what she saw sufficiently to offer Hickin the job at a starting salary of £475 per annum – £50 more than he was earning at Dunlop. He accepted happily but was not in a position to start full-time until December, when permission came through from the Central Register – during the war, scientists were unable to change employer without the say-so of this body.

At this time, the company's top-selling product was an oil-based insecticide called Kilit, later renamed Rentokilit, which was packed in a tall, round-shouldered bottle which bore a bright blue, green and yellow label. Other products included a moth treatment, timber fluids (of course), furniture cream, insect powders and a couple of innovative sidelines, one of which was Sprazone, a germicide for telephones. The other was a damp extractor mainly aimed at the piano trade!

 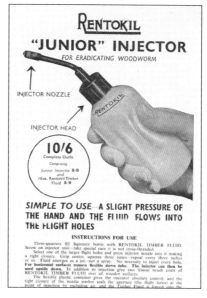

(Left) Promotional leaflet for the Fetcham Injector (early 1950s). (Right) Rentokil 'Junior' Injector for eradicating woodworm (early 1950s).

Hickin soon proved himself a worthy heir to Maxwell-Lefroy, throwing himself into entomological experiments and compound development in the lab and rising to the position of Scientific Director. The pest control market was becoming increasingly competitive and professional, as evidenced by the formation in 1942 of trade body the Industrial Pest Control Association, forerunner of the British Pest Control Association. One of Hickin's earliest innovations was to develop an applicator to push timber fluid into the flight holes made by beetles. This eventually came to be known as the Fetcham Injector. These injectors made the treatment more effective and the design was fine-tuned several times before receiving a British patent in 1948. Following further design modifications including evolution from metal canisters to easy-squeeze plastic containers, by the late 1950s over 1 million injectors had been sold.

With the second world war at an end, Eades and Hickin were well aware that in a fast-changing business environment more would have to be done to enhance Rentokil's reputation to ensure its survival and prosperity. Fortunately, in addition to being an accomplished scientist, Hickin was a skilful writer and eloquent public speaker with a natural flair for publicity. His lecturing and technical journalism for publications such as *Cabinet Maker*, alongside a modest amount of press advertising, were the foundations on which the Rentokil brand was built at this time.

DDT, which sprung to prominence during the war and was widely touted as a wonder pesticide, was added to the Rentokil product portfolio shortly after the end of hostilities. As part of its post-war expansion, the business also moved into rodent control for the first time with the launch of Rentan, a rat poison based on the organo-sulphur compound ANTU (alpha-naphthylthiourea).

WHEELER-DEALING TO GET BY

Although the business was on an upward curve, there were still times when Eades and Hickin were flying by the seat of their pants. Improvisation and wheeler-dealing were often the order of the day. As Hickin wrote in his unpublished autobiography, which bore the glorious title *My Life with Woodworm*:

"One great problem, however, which did not become resolved for some years was containers. For some months we were reduced to going around the local rag and bone yards to find bottles and we literally kept up our output of 'Kilit' and 'Mothproofer' by sending out in all sorts of bottle sizes. The women at the Stockwell factory cleaned them up [so] that they looked like new crystal glass. We made a few pounds on the side, so to speak, by cleaning up and selling several gross of bottles embossed with well-known trademarks, so anxious were the companies concerned to get them."

Tough it may have been, but a spirit of make-do-and-mend was serving the company well. By 1947 it had grown to a point where additional premises were required. An old dance hall at Fetcham near Leatherhead in Surrey seemed to fit the bill – but in order to secure permission to begin manufacturing there, Rentokil had to agree to plant a belt of trees to minimise the impact of any noises and smells on local residents. After a day's work at Stockwell, Hickin and Foreman 'Mac' McConnel would load up their cars – a 1936 Ford 8 and an old Wolseley – with chemicals, containers and equipment and transport it all down to the new site. This went on for three months. Meanwhile, Rentokil's ingenious chemist, Charles Nichols, applied himself to converting war surplus junk into manufacturing equipment, and he and Hickin worked wonders in converting the building internally to create a second floor. Improvisation extended to using Morrison Shelters as packing tables – these were a kind of fortified steel table distributed during the war under which people could take shelter indoors during air raids. When production finally began on site, Alice Wake relocated from Stockwell to oversee filling and labelling. But the building remained a work in progress for some time, so in order to meet growing demand production continued at Stockwell for the best part of two years.

Bessie Eades lays a foundation stone at Rentokil's new Fetcham site, 1947.

In 1947, Hickin was rewarded for his immense contribution to multiple aspects of the business with a seat on the board. Versatile, ingenious and dependably accomplished he may have been, but there was one area of pest control above all others he pursued with evangelical enthusiasm: woodworm. Granted, the creatures were one of his scientific passions. Yet his analytical mind also identified woodworm infestation as being a huge growth area for the business. Received wisdom used to have it that once woodworm – the larvae of wood-boring beetles, but in particular those of the common furniture beetle – had taken up residence in wooden furniture, the problem could not be cured. Cabinet makers and antique dealers took the view that pieces of furniture with woodworm holes were beyond redemption and should be burnt to prevent the pest from spreading. With the treatments now at his disposal, Hickin considered this to be absurd. A fabulous business opportunity was presenting itself.

On his travels across the UK to lecture and give product demonstrations, Hickin was frequently invited to survey buildings for woodworm infestation. The amount of damage he saw from woodworm and dry rot further persuaded him that the time was ripe to mount a major campaign alerting homeowners to the problems and that Rentokil needed a new approach. Eades concurred. First, from 1948 onwards greater care was taken to advertise both the effectiveness of the timber fluid and the damage woodworm caused. Instead of displaying beautiful furniture in mint condition there were images of wood damaged by the unmistakeable flight holes of woodworm. No-nonsense slogans such as "Rentokil Timber Fluid – the woodworm destroyer" and "Rentokil Timber Fluid kills woodworm" were introduced. Sales flourished, aided by the opening of the Woodworm and Dry Rot Centre at 23 Bedford Square in central London. An advisory bureau and showroom for the public and building trade, this Bloomsbury location also replaced the old Stockwell Road address as Rentokil's London office. It was officially opened in May 1951 by Norman Denbigh Riley, Keeper of Entomology at the nearby British Museum. Then on 30 October 1952, Rentokil took a huge step forward by forming a new company called Woodworm and Dry Rot Control Ltd (WDRC).

There was now a twin-pronged business strategy. WDRC was very much a service business, treating buildings on behalf of professional clients and homeowners. Meanwhile, a separate Rentokil team, headed up by Sales Manager Willie Sproat, was responsible for retail sales of products such as the 4oz and 8oz bottles of timber fluid. As awareness of what was possible spread, demand for Rentokil products soared. Antique furniture and houses that had been unsellable were, after treatment, valuable and desirable once more.

Norman Hickin (second from left) and Bill Holmes (second from right) in scientific discussions at the Woodworm and Dry Rot Centre, Bedford Square, in the 1950s.

Norman Hickin's lectures on wood-borers were vital in developing the Rentokil brand during its early years.

W. E. Peto, who joined WDRC as the first full-time member of its office staff in 1952, and was allocated a "small corner" at Rentokil's

Fetcham headquarters, recalled the early days of the venture in a 1959 piece for the company newsletter:

> "To cover the whole of the United Kingdom we had two surveyors, Messrs Rex Beeching and K.J. Course, and a supervisor/surveyor, Mr Arthur Eaton. The surveyors travelled in their own antique cars and many is the time when one or other of them would come on the telephone from their home in London and say sadly, 'Can't get to Llanrwst for the 10 o'clock appointment this morning – had to put the car in for a new rear axle and gear box last night'."

It may not have been the most auspicious of starts, but the company was definitely onto something. Enquiries snowballed. As business grew, so did the workforce.

By 1953, the company had well over a hundred employees. Government contract work had increased and Rentokil brand products were sold over the counter in almost 20,000 retail outlets. As well as timber fluid, the product range at this time encompassed insect powder, mothproofing fluids, fly spray and dry rot treatment. Building contractors, in the main those specialising in home and church restoration, were a key target audience. Eades' standing in the industry now was such that she was the subject of a full-page profile piece published in the 13 June 1953 edition of *The Cabinet Maker*, under the headline 'A Woman Pioneer'. The profile said:

> "Miss Eades passes much credit for the success of the firm to her 'family' of 130 employees, in relation to which she thinks of herself as mother. Through discriminating recruitment and encouragement for good work she has built up an enthusiastic and most competent staff with the greatest regard for their governing director."

The maternal nature of her management style – what today in a business context we might refer to as softer skills such as empathy, communication and the ability to motivate others – undoubtedly served both Eades and Rentokil well. Further evidence that she was ahead of her time comes from the fact that she was an active member of the Business and Professional Women's Club and that through Rentokil she supported the Cheam Church of England Home. In fields such as networking and corporate responsibility, she was incredibly forward-thinking. She was also an accomplished marketer. And as the business grew, she made sure marketing activity became more ambitious and sophisticated.

PROMOTING EXPERTISE

A mobile exhibition unit toured county shows and horticultural events to promote Rentokil's expertise in wood preservation and insecticides. Meanwhile, Hickin further advanced his own reputation, and that of Rentokil, with the publication of two books. First, in 1952, there was an account of the biology of the British caddis fly. Then came *Woodworm: Its Biology and Extermination* (1954), a classic of its genre. His aim was to produce "something like a textbook for the layman" and he hit the mark by tackling his subject in impressive detail while writing in a style that was easy to understand. The book featured an introduction by Bessie Eades in which she wrote:

"I have been associated with Norman Hickin since he came from Birmingham to join my Company in its ceaseless battle against woodworm. I recognised in him then, a young man of sound scientific knowledge, a born entomologist so well informed on the subject of wood borers as to be regarded an authority.

"Considering the extensive damage caused by wood-eating insects from time immemorial, it is surprising that such little published information is available to the general public. Valuable research by the late Professor H. Maxwell-Lefroy has been greatly extended by Dr Hickin and is recognised by timber authorities as being of the utmost value to the community."

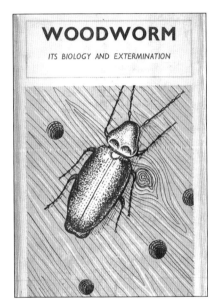
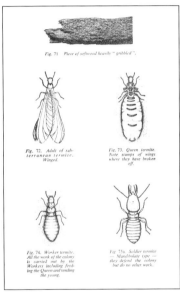

(Left) Cover of Norman Hickin's 1954 classic Woodworm: Its Biology and Extermination.
(Right) Norman Hickin was a gifted artist who illustrated his own books, as was the case with these images of termites.

Not only was Hickin a lucid writer and great authority on his subject, he was also a talented artist and applied his creative skills to illustrate the book using the scraperboard etching technique. Hickin went on to write almost 20 books in his lifetime, about pests and on more general natural history subjects – with titles including *Beachcombing for Beginners* and *African Notebook: The Notes of a Biologist in East Africa*.

His meticulous original artwork was often integral to the books, so much so that he became a member of the Society of Wildlife Artists.

Even today, his books are revered. Rentokil's current Entomologist, Matt Green, holds Hickin up as one of his heroes and was an admirer of his work long before joining Rentokil in 2008. Incidentally, he also has a tenuous connection to Maxwell-Lefroy, having spent a year at Imperial working on his master's degree before moving on to Brunel to complete a PhD in wood-boring insects. However, it is the work that Rentokil did in the post-war era, with Hickin leading the way in terms of scientific advances, that most impresses Green.

"We used up a lot of timber in two world wars, particularly in the first world war for making trenches," says Green. "The Forestry Commission was formed in 1919 to manage timber resources. We started using cheaper, faster-growing timber which in turn led to more wood-boring pests. So Rentokil steps in in the 1940s and 50s, selling woodworm killer spray in early targeted marketing towards housewives who were spending much of their time at home and didn't want woodworm in the back of their wardrobes. It did fantastically well and became a household name. The rest of the industry is defined by standards Rentokil put in place 50, 60, 70 years ago."

The Rentokil mobile exhibition unit, 1955.

(Left) Rentokil furniture cream leaflet, 1953.
(Right) Dry rot fluid leaflet, mid-1950s.

After retiring from Rentokil in the early 1970s, Hickin remained a consultant to the company until his death at the age of 80 in 1990. But that is to take a big jump forward in our story. Back in the mid-1950s, Hickin and Eades were focused on the expansion of the business. And with that in mind, in February 1956 they recruited Bill Holmes, who had extensive experience in the building sector, to the position of General Manager at WDRC with a brief to boost sales. That he did with aplomb, increasing turnover at WDRC from £60,000 to £100,000 (£1.4m to £2.3m in today's terms) during his first year in charge. WDRC was now a healthy business with almost 40 staff, including four surveyors, a foreman-cum-contracts manager, 20 operators working in teams of two based in Fetcham and a further dozen operators located at the old Stockwell Road site in Brixton.

(Left) A bottle of Rentokil timber fluid, produced circa 1950.
(Right) Rentokil timber fluid leaflet, early 1950s.

Overall, the prospects for Rentokil were bright. It was a growing company with a portfolio of effective products and in WDRC it had a business with an excellent reputation both for customer service and delivering results in wood preservation. A series of product field tests held overseas in association with laboratories and government departments was also creating some export demand. Among the noteworthy places to benefit from Rentokil products was the Colonial Williamsburg historical village in Virginia and remote locations such as St Helena, the Falklands and Fanning Island in the South Pacific. There's a story that the company once received a letter from Uganda apologising that the effectiveness of Rentokil products used to treat a gate at the edge of Lake Victoria could not be judged – because the gate had been destroyed by a hippopotamus. Yet despite its increasing reach, what Rentokil did not have at this time was a substantial national UK sales operation.

The company's many plus points, together with its relative lack of scale, made it an appealing takeover target. It was in this context that Hickin received a lunch invitation in 1956 from Stuart Hedgcock, a long-serving executive at the rival British Ratin Company. In the clubbable working atmosphere of the 1950s, invitations to dine with competitors were far from unusual. Indeed, Hickin had previously enjoyed a gourmet meal, fine wine and a good cigar at British Ratin's grand headquarters, Felcourt. This time, however, he had an inkling that as well as lunch there was to be an offer on the table.

Hickin and Eades talked it over and despite some misgivings – Eades had, after all, been running her own show for three decades – they decided Hickin should go ahead with the lunch meeting. Eades, at nearly 60, was receptive to offers for the business in a way that would not have been the case a few years earlier.

Hickin's intuition had served him well: over lunch at a hotel in Surrey it emerged that British Ratin was indeed interested in acquiring Rentokil. Soon negotiations began in earnest. Rentokil was on the verge of entering the big time.

THE ESSENTIALS

1928 – Bessie Eades forms new company Rentokil (Sales) Ltd three years after creation of the Rentokil name.

1940 – Brixton head office destroyed during the Blitz.

1944 – Dr Norman Hickin joins the business.

1945 – Introduction of timber fluid injector.

1947 – Head office, plant and product stocks relocated to new building in Fetcham, near Leatherhead, Surrey.

1951 – Opens Woodworm and Dry Rot Centre to showcase expertise at 23 Bedford Square, London.

1952 – Woodworm and Dry Rot Control Ltd set up to provide service for professional clients.

1957 – Rentokil acquired by British Ratin Company.

CHAPTER
THREE

Parallel Beginnings -
The British Ratin Story

For an alternative starting point to the Rentokil story we should go back to the beginning of the 20th century. The modern age was dawning but, as remains true today, even in developed countries people still faced some of the same horrifying threats to health and life more typically associated with medieval times. In the year 1900, there was a significant international outbreak of bubonic plague. Cases were reported as far apart as San Francisco and Sydney, Glasgow and Osaka, Beirut and Bombay. Public health officials across the globe struggled to halt its spread by imposing strict quarantine measures on shipping and affected ports. There were over 500 plague deaths in Australia alone in the early years of the century.

Due to the pioneering work of scientist Alexandre Yersin of the Pasteur Institute in studying a plague outbreak in China, it was established in the 1890s that the disease was caused by a bacterium – subsequently named *Yersinia pestis* in his honour. The bacterium is transmitted from rodents to humans through the bites of infected fleas. Given that between a quarter and a third of Europe's 14th century population was wiped out by the 'Black Death' caused by the disease, the international outbreak of 1900 gave impetus to research into rodenticides. The race was on to find new ways to stop disease-spreading vermin in their tracks.

We now move to Aalborg, Denmark in 1902. Here pharmacist George Neumann found a bacterium that was part of the salmonella group when conducting tests on the urine of a person with cystitis. He created a broth culture of the bacteria and, when he administered it to rats and mice, observed that it triggered gastroenteritis, leading to death by septicaemia. A powerful new pest control weapon had been discovered, and importantly it appeared to be relatively safe for humans. Neumann named his discovery Ratin. Although fully aware of the potential of his rodenticide, Neumann failed to secure the financial backing he needed to turn his breakthrough into a viable commercial product. In 1904 he gave up trying and assigned his rights in Ratin to a group headed by another Danish scientist, Dr Louis Bahr, who had himself been hunting for an anti-rat bacillus for several years.

Bust of Ludvig Elsass, Managing Director of Sophus Berendsen.

Courtesy of Elsass Foundation

Bahr's group, A/S Bakteriologisk Laboratorium Ratin, began production of the rodenticide in Copenhagen. Just as Neumann before him, Bahr understood that if Ratin was to succeed in the marketplace it would need the support of a large commercial partner offering experience of the business world that the scientists lacked. Bahr approached Ludvig Elsass, Managing Director of Danish corporation Sophus Berendsen A/S, who was to become a pivotal figure in the Rentokil story – indeed, three generations of the Elsass family have had important roles to play.

The Sophus Berendsen business had ridden the construction boom of the previous half-century, importing iron girders and glass from countries such as the UK and Belgium, and more recently steel. This long track record in import-export meant the business had the scale and capabilities to exploit a product such as Ratin. Ludvig Elsass, who became Managing Director in 1897 following the death of the company founder's son, Albert Berendsen, took a little persuading that investing in pest control would be a sensible move as it was outside his company's traditional areas of business. But the problems rodents caused at docks and construction sites were familiar to him and the closer Elsass looked into it, the more the potential opportunities presented themselves. The demand for pest control was evident. With a promising product now at hand, why couldn't building a business on the back of Ratin prove a lucrative venture? Together with his colleague Viggo Petersen, Elsass secured Sophus Berendsen the sales rights for Ratin across Denmark and several other European countries, including the UK and a large chunk of the British Empire.

Sophus Berendsen's prominence in its domestic market ensured Ratin was a success in Denmark from the off. A London sales office was opened in 1906 but the product did not at first fare quite so well in the UK. Undeterred, in the 1920s Sophus Berendsen made a second attempt to crack the UK market. This was a better-resourced venture. On 1 October 1927, The British Ratin Company Ltd was formed with nominal share capital of £2,000 and a mission "generally to contract for the destruction of all classes of vermin". An ambitious young Danish businessman by the name of Karl Gustav Anker-Petersen was put in day-to-day charge of the company and given a small equity stake. It was an inspired appointment. With his determined if sometimes autocratic leadership style, Anker-Petersen was to build British Ratin into a pest control powerhouse.

Danish businessman Karl Gustav Anker-Petersen, the driving force behind British Ratin.

Born on 4 May 1898 in the Danish town of Hillerød, Anker-Petersen was the son of a savings bank director. He attended the famous Niels Brock Business College in Copenhagen and after his studies worked briefly for a bank and as bookkeeper at a steam mill. Early in the 1920s he spread his wings with a move to Paris, working first for prestigious department store Grands Magasins du Louvre and then as an Assistant Director of Compagnie de la Plume du Nord. During his time in France he met his first wife, Madeleine Claire Bourgeois.

They married in April 1925 and the following year the couple moved to Copenhagen, where Anker-Petersen took up a position as Head of Sales at Ratin. The energetic young man made such a good impression in the role that he was the obvious choice to be entrusted with cracking the UK market.

Anker-Petersen's boss, Viggo Petersen, who assumed the role of Governing Director, remained in Copenhagen, allowing the young man plenty of decision-making autonomy. The Ratin bacillus was registered as a trade name, as was Ratinin – a rodenticide derived from the powdered bulbs of Mediterranean plant red squill. Bottles of Ratin manufactured in Copenhagen were shipped over to a small basement warehouse and Anker-Petersen set up his office at 109 Kingsway, in Holborn. Alf Ridgwell, who since 1920 had been working for the Ratin sales agency in London, became the company's first Treatment Advisor – a technician in today's terms – while a man called George Coates looked after the warehouse. Together with typist Elizabeth Jones, that was the extent of the British Ratin workforce in the early months.

A small telephone directory advertisement of the time, some of the first advertising undertaken by the company, described British Ratin Co. Ltd as: "Distributors of Ratin, the 100% Rat and Mouse Exterminator. Officially adopted by the Governments of Denmark, Sweden, Norway, Germany and Finland. Safe, sure and economical in use."

FROM HUMBLE BEGINNINGS

To be sure, these were fairly humble beginnings. But Anker-Petersen had ambitious plans and expansion was very much on the cards. In 1928, he hired two salespeople and split responsibility for the north and south of the UK between them. Fellow Dane, Sophus Jensen, was given charge of the South (gaining extra support the following year when ex Royal Artillery sergeant-major Bill Tenniswood was brought in to focus on the vital area of East London, with its rat-infested Docklands and sprawl of small factories); Jim Wilkinson, the North and Scotland. The same year also saw the beginnings of a service business culture that generations later, though much evolved, remains integral to the way Rentokil does business today.

An early example of British Ratin advertising.

In the field in London Docklands, with Tower Bridge in the background.

At work on the wharves in London Docklands.

As a product, Ratin had a relatively short shelf life – and its shelf life was further reduced once the bottle was opened. Customers who paid no attention to this when using the product unsurprisingly found it to be less effective than billed. Fearing that the disappointing results experienced by those customers could very easily compromise product reputation, Anker-Petersen decided to reposition the business towards more of a service model, pushing the advantages of having teams of trained experts carry out the treatment. Continuous contracts were introduced, to be renewed annually, which clients could terminate by giving three months' notice.

The service was built around the Ratin System: the use of Ratin and Ratinin in carefully timed synergy. In the company jargon of the day, technicians spoke of these rodenticides as "ones" and "twos". Rats and mice were put down with a powerful one-two combination.

Adopting a service model meant hiring more staff, with an inevitable increase in overheads. But the move put the business on a strong footing. Whereas in 1928 the company made a loss, the figures for 1929 showed a net profit of £503 (£28,000 in today's terms) on turnover of £5,460 (£310,000 today). The continuous contracts model fuelled rapid growth, taking the company to another level. British Ratin also began branching out beyond rodent control, signing contracts that included control of cockroaches, silverfish and other insects. An early customer secured by Jim Wilkinson was the Nottingham head office of Boots.

Preparation of bait for use in an agricultural setting.

Bait being laid on farmland.

Press advertising of the era was to the point. For instance, under the headline *Getting Rid of Rats and Mice*, one advertisement urged readers to send for a book that showed how British Ratin was serving hundreds of big London firms. The ad copy began:

"It is a difficult job. Probably you have tried this, and you have tried that; and yet the foulness remains.

"Now comes the British Ratin Co. whose Service is based on Science – on the researches of Dr. Louis Bahr, the eminent Danish bacteriologist.

"Ratin is the stuff that kills the things and keeps them killed. We do not say so. We *show* so in a book which you can have *FREE*."

Prospective customers of the time were doubtless reassured that once killed the critters stayed killed, rather than rising up again as rodent zombies. As it happened, British Ratin was not slow to take some cues from the new fad for horror movies. The cover of its booklet,

The Menace of the Death Rat, featured a monstrous rat of King Kong proportions towering over terrified people, giant teeth and claws at the ready. Subtle it wasn't, but it got the message across. And it was part of a well-thought-out approach.

Smart use was made of direct mail to push the underlying message that British Ratin's service provided cleanliness and peace of mind. Marketing mailshots were sent out to almost 35,000 businesses in 1929 to 1930. More than a thousand replied to request an information booklet. Anker-Petersen made certain that every single respondent not only received the booklet but was called on by a member of his salesforce. The tactic worked a treat. Sales leapt and more staff were taken on, both to service clients and generate yet more new business.

Among the early customers were Ringers tobacco factory in Bristol, Kent brewery Fremlins, Southampton Harbour Board and Armstrong Siddeley Motors in Manchester. British Ratin was enjoying fast-track growth. When in 1934 it secured the rodent control contract for the royal residence at Sandringham, its prestige shot up too. Emboldened by success, expansion into Ireland followed with the Irish Ratin Company incorporated in Dublin on 12 July 1935.

THE RATS HAD NO IDEA

Advertising at the time featured the tag-line "The Scientific Suspicion-Allayer", playing on the fact that rats could have no inkling of the danger posed by the "deliciously scented" bait because death came nine days after consumption. A 1935–6 advertising campaign in the satirical magazine *Punch* carried headlines such as, "Doomed – but unsuspecting" and, "Due to natural causes – think the rats". The advertisements promoted British Ratin's rodent control service delivered through a burgeoning branch network using language that sometimes veered to the excessive:

> "Ratin, the scientific suspicion-allayer, has met with tremendous success in destroying the foulest and filthiest menace with which man has ever had to contend."

One suggested that if every person in the UK were to kill a rat, it would save the country £99m a year. "Not to mention the benefits to health by removing the carriers of such diseases as bubonic plague and nematodes." A touch heavy-handed it may have been, but the message was well-received.

By 1937, the company had 110 staff, a fleet of 36 motor vehicles and was generating £62,000 in annual turnover – over ten times more than in 1929, and equivalent to £3.8m today. Servicemen, what today we would call technicians, were paid around £2 per week.

	British Ratin 1937	Rentokil Initial 2014
Number of colleagues	110	28,000
Number of motor vehicles	36	16,000
Annual turnover	£62,000	£1.8bn

A typical day would begin in Drury Lane, which is where the small central London 'store' operated, having originally been in Lamb's Conduit Street. From around 8am servicemen would congregate to cut up squares of dried bread, soak these in Ratin and wrap them up individually in newspaper to make sure they stayed moist. Then they headed off to carry out treatments, lugging suitcases filled to bursting with roughly packed portions of bait. Territorial General Managers

(TGMs), given the incentive of commission, were proving very adept at drumming up new business from their designated regions.

From a business standpoint, there was a lot to be optimistic about. But the storm clouds of war were gathering again. As the international crisis mounted, Anker-Petersen wisely took steps to safeguard the future of the business. Reasoning that if war did break out the supply line from Denmark would swiftly be cut, he arranged for one of the scientists from the Copenhagen lab to come to the UK and pass on the finer points of making Ratin. Stuart Hedgcock was chosen as the ideal man to learn the manufacturing process – the same Stuart Hedgcock who two decades later would open the negotiations on buying Rentokil over lunch with Norman Hickin.

This forward planning meant British Ratin was in a position to be entirely self-sufficient when war was declared in September 1939. Germany's invasion of Denmark in April 1940 proved the wisdom of taking these steps. Shipments from Denmark ceased entirely once the country was under German control.

INVASION OF THE NETHERLANDS

Sophus Berendsen A/S was sufficiently impressed by the performance of British Ratin Company that in 1936 it sent Anker-Petersen on a visit to Holland to look into how sales there could be significantly improved. As a result of his recommendations, the Dutch Ratin company (De Nederlandsche Maatschappij) was reorganised and British Ratin acquired a stake in the business in return for a £1,300 investment (around £82,000 today).

To further beef up the Dutch operation, in July 1938 Danish national Henning Franzen was brought in to manage the business. Two years later, Holland had been overrun and was under German occupation.

"One day two German officers entered the office and claimed to take over the business as we were a British firm," Franzen recalled in a 1960s interview. "I had foreseen that and had altered the books in time so that the name of British Ratin had disappeared. I claimed that we were 100% a Danish firm and as they could not prove the contrary, they disappeared."

When German forces first occupied the country in 1940, the Dutch business had just two operators. By the end of the war this had risen to 12. "It was not because the business had grown that much," said Franzen. "Most young people were sent to Germany for work. But when employed by us they could get a permit to stay. And so we saved young people from slavery in German factories."

In the chaotic aftermath of the war, a friend in the Allied military called Franzen and asked if he and his team could exterminate the rats that were adding to the misery across large swathes of the country. The problem was that Franzen only had limited supplies of Ratin. So eight military trucks were despatched to collect large stocks of the poison from Copenhagen, with Franzen riding along to ensure everything was done to plan.

"As I could get no permit from the military authorities, I was put into a Dutch soldier's uniform – and I passed all frontiers. We arrived safely back to Holland with our preparations. We also got military trucks for our work, and we got a staff of about 30 operators to do the job. It was done – and properly too – and we were paid about £20,000 for the whole campaign, which covered about a quarter of the whole country."

Germany's invasion of Denmark had ramifications for British Ratin that went far beyond the supply chain. At a stroke, the British government re-designated Denmark as an "enemy occupied territory". Given that British Ratin was Danish-owned, an extraordinary general meeting was called at the behest of the government's Custodian of Enemy Property department, which was headed up in England by the mandarin Sir Ernest Fass. At the meeting, Viggo Petersen was removed from office to be replaced as a director by George Harris, a former auditor to the company whom Anker-Petersen put forward as an acceptable choice. Additionally, former Minister of Supply, E. L. Burgin, was appointed to the board to protect the interests of Sophus Berendsen A/S and Viggo Petersen for the duration of the conflict.

From that point onwards until the end of the war, Anker-Petersen was free to do more or less as he pleased with the business. As one of his former colleagues put it: "The occupation of Denmark by Germany from 1940/5 meant that Sophus Berendsen was unable to exercise a restraining hand on AP's ambitions. Sir Ernest Fass allowed AP far more freedom of action than Sophus Berendsen would ever have done."

Twice British Ratin switched the location of its UK production facility during the war – a laboratory in Croydon was deemed too high-risk after bombing raids began on the nearby aerodrome, a major fighter station during the Battle of Britain. Yet danger and disruption aside, the war brought with it enormous business opportunities. Both turnover and profit more than trebled during the course of the hostilities. Pest control was considered by the government to be vital to the war effort. So much so that it was given 'reserved occupation' status – this meant that British Ratin employees were exempt from being called up for military service. New legislation also helped the business flourish. The Ministry of Food's Infestation Order of 1943 tightened the responsibilities on farmers, food manufacturers and retailers to protect food from rodent and insect damage and required local authorities to provide information on the presence of rats in their area. Work of this kind was made to measure for British Ratin.

When it became clear that potential business had been lost due to a lack of insect control capabilities, British Ratin snapped up the six-year-old Chelsea Insecticides Ltd in 1941 for £145. With a broader range of expertise and treatments at its disposal than ever, the company was well-placed to win important state and military contracts and achieved great success here.

Dramatic advert for Chelsea Insecticides, a business acquired by British Ratin in the 1940s.

Jeff Gauntlett, who had responsibility for the West Country, helped get the ball rolling when called in to Portsmouth Dockyard to help the Mines Design Department deal with a problem at the Gosport shore establishment *HMS Hornet*: mice were eating vital technical drawings. Successful treatment led to a wave of business from the Royal Navy. More than 50 warships were treated by British Ratin while in dock being refitted, among them the famous battleship *HMS King George V*. There was also work from the army, Royal Air Force, the Canadian Air Force's headquarters in Bournemouth and even the Bank of England.

During the war years, it's fair to say Anker-Petersen kept only one eye on the business. As a prominent member of the Free Danish Council, he played an important role in supporting Danish exiles in the fight against the Nazi occupiers of his home country. It's rumoured that he helped coordinate and support special undercover operations in Denmark from his home in the UK – Brambletye Manor Farm in Forest Row, East Sussex. On more than one occasion, locals spotted a Westland Lysander plane in the vicinity of Anker-Petersen's farm. The Lysander was particularly well-suited for clandestine operations because it could land on bumpy ground and had a comparatively short stopping distance. In light of the stealthy missions that supposedly went on, it's ironic to discover that the land is now used for simulated-combat Ultimate Laser Games, with customers directed to reach the site by looking out for "a large wrought iron sign on the left side of our drive reading Brambletye Manor Farm".

FUNDRAISING FOR SPITFIRES

What's known for certain is that during the war Anker-Petersen was a formidable fundraiser. He went on a lengthy visit to the USA in 1941 to raise money to buy Spitfires that would be flown out of the UK by expatriate Danish pilots. Elizabeth Jones, who had been recruited as a humble typist but after 13 years at head office knew the workings of the business as well as anyone, kept the plates spinning in his absence. After pressing the flesh and schmoozing relentlessly with potential donors across the Atlantic, Anker-Petersen returned to the UK having secured vital money for the cause.

As the Air Ministry News Service Bulletin released on 10 April 1942 reported:

"At an aerodrome in the South West today, three Spitfires which had been subscribed by the Free Danes were presented to a squadron to which the first two Danish pilots had been posted. Mr K G Anker-Petersen, Chairman of the Spitfire Funds Committee of the Free Danish Council, in making the presentation told how one of these first two Spitfire pilots took eight months to escape from Denmark to Britain where he was accepted into the Royal Air Force."

It must have been a very proud day indeed for Anker-Petersen.

Unfettered from the need to justify his decisions to Sophus Berendsen, Anker-Petersen also made some interesting moves a little wide of the company's core business. "We had a hefty investment in farms," says Ken Bridgman, who joined the business in 1953 as part of the finance team and served on the board for the best part of 30 years, from 1964 to 1992. "AP seemed to imagine that as a true born Dane he must, perforce, be a successful farmer. And so the end of the war saw the company owning three or four farms in the East Grinstead area, in one of which, Brambletye, AP lived. One other farm was in Cambridgeshire, Dry Drayton Estate, which the company owned and managed. It was not a commercial success."

When the fighting was over, British Ratin was able to resume contact with its parent company in Denmark. Viggo Petersen and Ludvig Elsass were still active at Sophus Berendsen and Ludvig's son Adam had recently joined the executive team, where he was to play a key role for decades. Although the Copenhagen laboratory had remained operational and unscathed during the war, Anker-Petersen decided not to jettison the production expertise British Ratin had acquired. Consequently, Ratin continued to be manufactured under licence in the UK – with production switching back to Cherry Orchard Road in Croydon now that the skies were clear of danger once more – with supplementary supplies shipped in from Denmark.

There was plenty of work to do on the home front. For instance, extensive bombing of the East End of London had driven many rats into the more upmarket West End. Understandably, affluent property owners in Mayfair, St James's, Belgravia and Kensington did not take too kindly to an influx of rats and turned to British Ratin for a solution. But the biggest challenge for the business in the immediate post-war years came from, of all places, Iceland.

SUCCESS IN ICELAND

In 1946, Reykjavik was overrun with rats. Investigation of almost 5,000 properties in a specified zone found a horrifying 84% were infested. In desperation, Reykjavik City Council approached British Ratin for a solution to its epic rodent problem. Once terms were agreed, a British Ratin team went to Iceland and met with great success. Subsequent feedback, taking in nearly all the target properties, found them free of rats. The city council wrote to Anker-Petersen to express its appreciation that British Ratin had carried out its work to the letter and revealed it had received no complaints of accident or illness among people or pets. The campaign was an unqualified triumph, adding greater lustre to the British Ratin name.

THE MOVE TO FELCOURT

Steady expansion continued and as the 1940s drew to a close it was evident the company needed much larger premises, not to mention better lab facilities. In 1949 British Ratin acquired Felcourt Manor, a grand Edwardian building from 1909 located in 13½ acres of land on the Surrey/West Sussex border near East Grinstead. It had previously been the English country home of construction tycoon Sir Robert McAlpine,

Borgarstjórinn í Reykjavík

Reykjavík, **Nov. 5th 1946.**

J/17.

K.G. Anker-Petersen, Esq.,
The British Ratin Company Ltd.,
London, S.W.1.

Dear Mr. Anker-Petersen,

At a meeting of the Executive Committee of
the Town Council of Reykjavik held on the 25th of
October, a statement from the town's auditor, concern-
ing your report on the rat-campaign in Reykjavik and
Seltjarnarnes, was discussed. The campaign was performed in accordance with your offer, dated 25th May,
and the Town Council's acceptance, dated 20th June.
The Committee found that you had in every way fulfilled
your obligations, according to the contract.

Taking the opportunity I want to state the
following:

1. When the campaign started in the middle
of July, 3905 of a total of 4858 properties in the territory specified in
the contract were infested with rats, i.
e. 84% of the total. After the campaign
declarations had been given from 4726
properties, i.e. 97.3% of all properties
in the territory, that they were free
from rats.
This result was obtained after three
treatments on the territory. Your
employees state, that after the first
treatment, when Ratin was used, rats
disappeared in 80% of the properties,
in which the preparation was used; after
the second treatment, when Ratinin was
used, rats disappeared in 16%, and after
the third treatment, when Ratin-Supplement
was used, in 4% of the properties.

2. I take particular pleasure in informing
you that no complaints of accidents or
illness in people or domestic animals,
in connection with the campaign, have
received by my office.

Confirming the before mentioned results, I
express my thanks for the cooperation, which has been
most satisfactory in every way.

With kindest regards,

Letter from Reykjavik, Iceland 1946

*1946 letter from Reykjavik town council thanking British Ratin for
its successful campaign in Iceland.*

and during the second world war Canadian troops had been billeted in this splendid setting. As those marketing the property in the 1940s would have it, the "old-fashioned house" on this freehold residential and sporting estate was "approached by a carriage drive guarded by an ornamental stone and gabled lodge". The lodge and stable block pre-dated the Edwardian manor house, having been built in the 1850s. However, historical records pertaining to the estate stretch back many centuries. On the dissolution of the monasteries from 1536–41, the manor of Felcourt was granted to Sir John Gresham by King Henry VIII. Gresham would go on to become Lord Mayor of London.

Felcourt, a grand country house setting for the company headquarters.

Felcourt still stands to this day (albeit having been converted into luxury flats in 2006). Back in spring 1949, when staff moved in after some sprucing up of the interior, it made for an excellent headquarters. The place became such an intrinsic part of the business that for a time the employee newsletter was called *Felcourt*. Post-war austerity was on its way out and the magnificent pile and extensive grounds made an eloquent statement about the status and aspirations of British Ratin.

Counting machines at Felcourt.

A serviceman hands in his report.

Customer cards.

Together with his appetite for hard work, Anker-Petersen was a true *bon viveur*. At Felcourt he seemed to the manner born, imperious yet charming as he directed company affairs in a plush environment of oak panelling, elegant furniture and feature fireplaces. A team of gardeners kept the lawns in immaculate condition, first-rate chefs were hired to ensure the executives feasted on *haute cuisine* at a magnificent table in the directors' dining room (a separate large canteen for staff would be introduced later). The great cooking the directors were treated to was made all the better by the fact that fresh fruit and vegetables were picked daily from a carefully-tended kitchen garden. A housekeeper lived on site, and kept an eye out to make sure junior employees were not shirking. As an *aficionado* of the finer things, Anker-Petersen carried a box of expensive cigars around with him and had a penchant for a good drop of white wine. He also had a flamboyant sense of occasion. Formal company dinners were a regular occurrence and the dress code was rigid: white tie and tails.

When the company marked its 25th anniversary in 1952, all employees with 20 or more years' service were invited by Anker-Petersen to a week-long celebration in Denmark. Extravagant it may have been, but there was genuine pride in how far the business had come. Elizabeth Jones, who started as a typist in 1928 and had capably filled a management role when her boss was on his Spitfire fundraising tour in 1941, was the employee with the longest service. But a dozen more from England had clocked up two decades with the business: Sophus Jensen, Jim Wilkinson, Tommy Weston, Len Coombes, Bill Tenniswood, Eddie Paine, Charlie Ridley, Allan Stanway, Eddie Sargeant, Jeff Gauntlett, Bob Fisher and Miss M. Cole. Other guests included Benny Aston and Victor Hamilton, respectively from the firm's Irish and Scottish operations. Company Director George Harris, whose involvement with British Ratin stretched back to his time as auditor in 1928, was one of the hosts. Activities included a visit to the Ratin Laboratories but for the most part the trip was a luxurious celebration embracing excursions to Elsinore Castle, the Tuborg brewery and a night at the Royal Theatre for a performance of the Tchaikovsky opera *Eugene Onegin*.

In his unpublished 1974 history of Rentokil, Hugh Barty-King wrote:

"The climax of the celebration was the banquet on May 10 at Solyst served by waiters in blue livery with silver buttons under the direction of a major-domo who clapped his hands at the end of each course in what had once been a royal hunting lodge. There was turtle soup, cold salmon, roast duck, asparagus, liqueur ices and a 1934 Chateau Montrose. A high spot was the bringing in of figures carved in ice.

"Karl Anker-Petersen was at the head of the top table, flanked by George Harris, Ludvig Elsass, Adam Elsass and other Danish directors. The guests included Marius Rasmussen, Robert Jorgensen, Aage Dyssegaard, Henning Franzen, Paul Tillge, Stuart Hedgcock and the veteran Dr Louis Bahr, the 'father' of the Ratin virus from whose development of the Neumann bacillus the whole enterprise derived."

A COMMITMENT TO SCIENCE

Despite the partying, hard work remained paramount. The most significant event of 1952 was not the anniversary festivities but the opening of a new laboratory at Felcourt under the stewardship of Laboratory Controller Bob Farmer, who had previously worked in the research department at Boots. By making this investment in scientific research, British Ratin demonstrated that it was a heavyweight committed to breaking new ground and making improvements.

Inside the laboratory at Felcourt.

More thought was also being given to how the company positioned its services in the marketplace. The Chelsea Insecticides name had attracted criticism for seeming too local. So in 1953, this part of the organisation was rebranded as Disinfestation Ltd. Customers were urged to "Call in the D Service now!" in advertising of the period, which broke the service down into the three Ds: detection, diagnosis and destruction. Yet with rodents in mind, how the business delivered the 'destruction' part of its service was about to change.

In 1953 Chelsea Insecticides was rebranded as Disinfestation. A decade later the business changed name again, becoming Rentokil Laboratories.

A new class of rodenticides was emerging. The anticoagulant warfarin, nowadays best known as a medicine prescribed to prevent blood clots in people, was first used as a rodent poison in the late 1940s. Amid growing evidence of warfarin's effectiveness and mounting concerns that rat colonies were building immunity to Ratin, the company began trials of the anticoagulant. In places where Ratin had failed, warfarin produced excellent results. The writing was on the wall for the product around which the company had built its name. At a board meeting in June 1954, the decision was made to use warfarin more widely. Like so many rats that had eaten it, Ratin was on its way out. Before the end of the decade, the company stopped using it altogether.

This was a period of diversification, with numerous new avenues being explored. A timber fluid had been developed at Felcourt by Bob Farmer and his team in 1952 when a business opportunity came to light – a customer asked a surveyor in Cheshire whether the company undertook woodworm treatment. But in 1954, British Ratin abandoned in-house production after signing a deal with Cuprinol. Under the terms of the agreement, the Disinfestation subsidiary bought timber fluid from Cuprinol, which in return pointed all enquiries related to treating wood borers in the direction of Felcourt.

Preparing for a big day.

(Left) The rodenticide Ratin broth was added to the bread used as bait.
(Right) Bait packed in special containers, which operators took to the
scene of infestation.

Technicians (at the time called servicemen) arrive at a major pest
control operation carrying cases filled with bait.

The 1950s were not without setbacks, however. Midox, a foray into manufacturing horticultural pesticides, turned out to be ill-advised. But for the most part it was good news on the business front. The amount of marketing and technical material now being produced led to the creation of a photography department at Felcourt in 1955. And a decade on from the triumph in Iceland, British Ratin's exemplary reputation earned it another large overseas contract. This time it was not slightly south of the Arctic Circle, but south to the desert sands of Bahrain.

An entire lab was shipped out to the Gulf at the beginning of 1956 to be followed by a British Ratin team, which spent five gruelling months dealing with a massive rodent infestation in oppressively hot conditions in the densely populated bazaar areas of Bahrain's major urban centres. This was the same year as the Suez Crisis and there was unrest throughout much of the Middle East. Against an unsettling backdrop of anti-British riots and a clampdown by the authorities, the British Ratin team earned respect and appreciation from the local population for reducing the rat population by 90%. A letter of appreciation from the government of Bahrain's public health department thanked the company and its staff for being very successful, efficient and tactful, adding – in an admirably understated manner – that they "overcame unexpected difficulties". Some of the work in Bahrain was filmed on an old Kodak cine camera and a short film was shown to managers. It went down so well that another film was made on the research laboratories at Felcourt and this early dabbling eventually led to the creation of a Film Unit.

Anker-Peterson had flown out to Bahrain himself for a week to oversee the beginning of the operation. On his return to the UK, a potential acquisition was soon on the agenda. Executives at British Ratin had been considering how best to grow business in the woodworm and dry rot sector, and the activities of a company called Rentokil had caught their eye.

After tentative overtures regarding a takeover went well, a meeting was arranged between Anker-Petersen and Rentokil's Dr Norman Hickin. The British Ratin boss was impressed with Hickin and what he had to say, in particular about international expansion. Anker-Petersen asked Hickin to write a report for him setting out his views on the future of the wood preservation and pest control industries, and the go-ahead was given to study the viability of the acquisition in more detail. Hickin, for his part, considered Anker-Petersen to be a "kind and appreciative gentleman" during the delicate negotiations that were the prelude to the takeover. Bringing the two companies together seemed to stack up. Rentokil might have been the smaller, but its outstanding reputation would make it an admirable addition to the fold. The projected purchase was discussed at a British Ratin board meeting on 23rd October 1956. It was to be the last board meeting for Anker-Petersen. Less than a month later, following a short illness, he was dead at 58. His untimely passing was an unwelcome bolt from the blue for the business he had moulded with intensity and aplomb.

One former long-serving employee, who joined the company a few years after Anker-Petersen's death, says colleagues who had worked with the driving force behind British Ratin "remembered him as an irascible and forceful entrepreneur who was prone to sudden outbursts of temper. He did not sound like a man to be trifled with, but he certainly had a great eye for a business opportunity."

Ken Bridgman, a colleague at Felcourt for three years, recollects Anker-Petersen as a "larger than life" person with contradictory character traits. On occasion he could be autocratic, dogmatic and overbearing, but he was also enthusiastic, charismatic and generous. "Like most Danes, AP's English was almost flawless," says Bridgman. "Only when heard from a distance could you tell that the intonation was that of a foreigner. But one word always seemed to elude him: Ipswich came out as 'Ispwich' – a transposition of consonants which I found curiously infectious!"

The contradictions in his nature and actions made for a fascinating mix. Here was a man who relished the high life yet applied himself unstintingly to securing donations that would pay for Spitfire production. Here was a profit-seeking businessman who kept the company wage bill under firm control – in the early 1950s British Ratin operators were paid around £6 per week (£140 in today's terms) – yet who nonetheless was noted for his generosity. In the run-up to Christmas, he took great pleasure in instructing that every member of staff at Felcourt should queue up outside his office, to be invited in one at a time to receive festive greetings and an envelope containing the Yuletide bonus – equivalent to a week's salary. Maybe these apparent paradoxes aren't so strange. Many a hard-nosed entrepreneur intuitively grasps that from time to time some Santa-style largesse is exactly what's needed to lift morale and strengthen loyalty. And while his management style may on occasion have been abrasive or distant, he was no slouch when it came to business thinking. He commanded huge respect.

Starting pretty much from scratch, through an appetite for hard work, force of personality and commercial nous, Anker-Petersen built a strong national organisation with an exciting future. With turnover approaching £1m (£22m in 2015) and profit above £100,000 (£2.2m today), he left the business in a solid financial position. At the time of his death, his holding in the business was worth £23,306, a not inconsiderable sum for the time – around £500,000 today. In line with the instructions in his will, the stock was held in trust for the benefit of his heirs. As the business grew in size, so too did the scale of the trust fund. According to High Court documents, at 5 April 1996 the fund's net assets stood at £181,883,250.

It's genuinely a pity Anker-Petersen did not live to see the completion of the Rentokil deal. But through his single-mindedness, sometimes spiky charisma and flair for spotting and developing opportunities, it was he above anyone else who made it possible.

THE ESSENTIALS

1927 – Formation of British Ratin Company Ltd.

1934 – Rodent control contract for the royal residence of Sandringham.

1940 – UK manufacturing of Ratin poison begins.

1941 – Purchase of Chelsea Insecticides Ltd.

1946 – Huge contract from Reykjavik town council to clear the Icelandic capital of rats.

1949 – Head office moves to Felcourt.

1953 – Chelsea Insecticides rebranded as Disinfestation Ltd.

1954 – Successful trials of warfarin lead to the gradual phasing out of Ratin.

1956 – Death at 58 of Karl Anker-Petersen.

CHAPTER
FOUR
The Road to Flotation

The death of Karl Anker-Petersen inevitably sent shock waves and consternation through British Ratin.

Having called the shots with distinction for three decades, his was an unusually tough act to follow. Fortunately, there were talented executives in-house able to step up to the mark. At the beginning of 1957, the triumvirate of Bob Westphal, Teddy Buchan and Stuart Hedgcock took up positions on the board. They were keen to push on with buying Rentokil and offered the target company a couple more months to mull the offer over in light of the changed circumstances. At Rentokil, Eades and Hickin were satisfied with the terms and in mid-February indicated they would accept.

On 1 March 1957, all shares in Rentokil Ltd and its sister company Woodworm and Dry Rot Control Ltd were transferred to British Ratin. The cost of the acquisition was £100,000 – around £2.2m today.

As soon as the transaction was completed on 1 April 1957, Eades ceased to play a decision-making role. Out of respect for her achievements she was invited to attend formal occasions such as Royal warrant holders dinners in an honorary capacity, but her presence within and influence on the business were at an end. Just as with Anker-Petersen, hers was an outstanding legacy. Sometimes against the odds, she had kept Rentokil going, nimbly changing tack when circumstances demanded it. Paying tribute to her canniness, Hickin wrote: "If business was failing in any particular line, she was quick to regroup, make changes and reapply energy and enthusiasm."

But the younger generation's time had come. At the apex of the new corporate entity, Buchan and Westphal made up the dynamic executive double act that was to steer the business adroitly deep into the 1970s, delivering massive growth along the way. The brutal truth of the matter was they had no room in their plans for Eades. However, Hickin and Bill Holmes – both considered by their new employers to be exceedingly useful and able – were tasked with bedding in best practice in treating woodworm and dry rot, which soon led to the creation of a force of Timber Infestation (TI) Surveyors who operated separately from the Pest Control team. In short order, the TI force leapt from seven to 35 staff.

British Ratin and Rentokil may have had very different origins but their values were remarkably similar. Both organisations cherished scientific knowledge and technical expertise and shared a deep-seated commitment to customer service. This common ground made integrating the two businesses a relatively straightforward task.

At the boardroom table Westphal and Buchan were joined by Chairman Pat Burgin and British Ratin veterans Stuart Hedgcock and George Harris. The latter, you may recall, was called into emergency corporate action during the war. There's a charming profile of Harris in an old company newsletter. It reads: "George Harris, for all his quiet retiring ways, sometimes startles us with his love for the unusual – he drives a *red* Jaguar, and wears a *white* tuxedo." The italics are in the original. Although noted for his steady dependability, it seems Harris was partial to some flamboyance.

THE WESTPHAL-BUCHAN DOUBLE ACT

Yet despite Harris's proto-James-Bond wardrobe and penchant for sports cars, it was Westphal and Buchan who were moving fast. The duo had great mutual respect, having flown combat missions during the war: Westphal as a navigator with Bomber Command, Buchan piloting the *Fairey Swordfish* torpedo-bomber from Royal Navy carriers. Both had joined British Ratin in the same year, 1950, and initially worked in the field before moving into management positions under Anker-Petersen. Together they set about taking the business to another level.

Teddy Buchan (left) and Bob Westphal, the dynamic double act that oversaw strong UK growth and massive international expansion.

"It was not generally recognised that a new style of management was required if the company was to grow and prosper," says Ken Bridgman, who joined the business in 1953 and was promoted to the board in 1964. "The real driving force behind the company's subsequent expansion was Australian lawyer Bob Westphal, who under AP had rejoiced in the title of Branch Controller. A tough, strong character himself, he would not have deferred to AP's autocratic management style indefinitely. His appointment as one of three Executive Directors was to prove critical to the company achieving its international potential." Buchan's contributions were similarly vital and there was the added factor that he had a strong connection with the Elsass family: in 1948, the year after Buchan married Jenny Kirkland Wilson, Adam Elsass tied the knot with Jenny's sister Elaine.

The new regime grasped the nettle in dealing with several issues that were holding back growth and profitability. Out went the farms that Anker-Petersen had snapped up during the war. Joining them on the chopping block were the old-style contracts that had also put District Managers in a position to make hay. Under the old contracts, District Managers often didn't draw a salary but could be lavishly rewarded as they were entitled to 50% of the profits from their area. Using his legal skills, Westphal made sure contracts were renegotiated to be more favourable to the company. He also gave customers of Disinfestation peace of mind by drafting a warranty. This confidence-boosting approach played a major role in lifting turnover at the Woodworm and Dry Rot business.

The biggest issue, however, was transforming the business into an international concern.

Plans for overseas expansion were taking shape but came under threat of being derailed when an unexpected obstacle emerged. It appeared that the Aalborg Consortium, a group of Danish investors separate from Sophus Berendsen, owned some rights to international operation that the directors of British Ratin had previously been unaware of – and truth be told, struggled to fully understand. Danish lawyers were consulted and confirmed that this would indeed be a hindrance. Negotiations began and the consortium was persuaded to sell its rights for a reasonable fee. The path to international expansion had been cleared.

With the company growing strongly, communication with employees needed to be carried out with greater professionalism and regularity. The first issue of *The Felcourt Newsletter*, which would evolve into *Rentokil Review*, was published in August 1958. Bill Holmes edited the despatch and it featured an article from Bob Farmer that looked at a new weed control service and thermal vaporising units for fly control – at the time being tested in the offices of executives at Felcourt. In 1955, Farmer had written the company's first pest control manual, which became a mainstay. It was quickly evident that other areas of the business would benefit from such an approach. Holmes and Alan Farrington were tasked with developing a timber surveyors' manual, with Norman Hickin's early books figuring large among the source material. The business was increasingly a repository of technical knowledge.

Several more UK acquisitions were made before the 1950s drew to a close. The purchases of Fumigation Services Ltd, Insecta Laboratories Ltd and Scientex Ltd brought additional expertise in specialist fields such as fumigation for the food sector, maritime pest control and bird repellents. Given how fast British Ratin was expanding and diversifying, it made sense to organise a unifying event. Consequently, the first group-wide conference was held in Brighton in May 1959. But there was sad news a few weeks before this event took place, with the death of Ludvig Elsass. The Sophus Berendsen leader's belief in Ratin as a product and willingness to invest in it had been instrumental in the inception of British Ratin and its transformation into a substantial business. Fortunately, Ludvig's son, Adam, who had been actively involved with British Ratin since the 1940s, was to prove himself similarly committed.

Adam Elsass succeeded his father, Ludvig, as head of parent company Sophus Berendsen.

As the group grew in size, it was able to support a full-time Publicity Manager. Frank Jefkins, the first to occupy the role, began courting the media and exploring other PR opportunities. He worked out of the new Dry Rot and Pest Advisory Centre opened at 16 Dover Street, Mayfair on 5 November 1959. This superseded the old Rentokil advice bureau in Bedford Square, which had been the first centre of its kind when it opened nearly a decade earlier. A useful service offered to businesses and householders was pest identification, and by 1972 the centre had answered its 10,000th enquiry of this kind – the pest in question was a wharf borer (*Nacerdes melanura*). Jeff Gauntlett took charge of Dover Street which, in addition to informative displays on rot and pest problems and the methods provided to resolve them, featured an upstairs cinema. The high-quality documentary films the company had recently begun making had been identified as an important communications tool.

The Woodworm and Pest Advisory Centre opened at 16 Dover Street, Mayfair, on 5 November 1959.

Interior of the Advisory Centre in Dover Street.

By 1960, annual turnover had broken the £2m barrier and with the stumbling block against international growth overcome, the company was casting its eye further afield for suitable acquisition targets. Dr Norman Hickin had travelled extensively in East Africa at the end of the 1950s, sizing up the local pest control businesses and was keen to see the international growth plans he'd outlined during the takeover talks come to fruition. On his recommendation, a business in Kenya was snapped up. So began a dynamic period of international growth that saw Westphal and Buchan regularly taking to the skies with takeovers in mind.

A GROUND-BREAKING POLICY

Another key move in 1960 was the launch of the UK's first woodworm insurance policy. Before a policy could be issued, properties needed to be surveyed by one of the company's timber infestation surveyors. These surveys were done for free – and the fact that they were free was an intrinsic part of marketing the insurance product – but of course, if any woodworm was found, that area had to be treated before homeowners could get cover. The model proved an astute one, with treatment charges and insurance premiums producing twin revenue streams.

However, the most momentous decision of 1960 was still to come. With Ratin the rodenticide phased out and the word 'British' no longer representative of a business that had ambitious international plans, the British Ratin name was, despite its respectable history, beginning to seem more like an irrelevance or a liability than an asset.

Rebranding discussions took place internally and advice was sought from a firm of management consultants. A wonderful, great-sounding brand name was to be found right under their noses. The name Rentokil still had a catchy ring to it, a laudable pedigree, enjoyed widespread recognition and presented itself as a very versatile option.

Naturally there were some among the British Ratin old guard who resented the choice, aggrieved that a dominant company that swallowed up a comparative minnow should just a few years later wave goodbye to its name... and replace it with the name of the minnow. But the arguments in favour of the change were compelling.

On 1 December 1960 British Ratin Company Ltd was renamed Rentokil Group Ltd. Stuart Hedgcock, who had given staunch service over the years, chose this moment to retire, which left Westphal and Buchan as the two Executive Directors on the board. Even though they had selected a tried and trusted brand name, there was no shadow of a doubt that this was a new era for the business. Rentokil was going places.

In his festive message on the cover of the December 1960 edition of *Felcourt Newsletter*, Rentokil Group Chairman Pat Burgin hoped "after the rigours of this memorable and exciting business year" readers would find relaxation and refreshment over the Christmas holidays. "This year," he wrote, "I am immensely proud to know that my personal good wishes will be read by nearly one thousand readers scattered not only throughout the United Kingdom, but in Eire, on the Continent, in East Africa and even in America where we now have business associates."

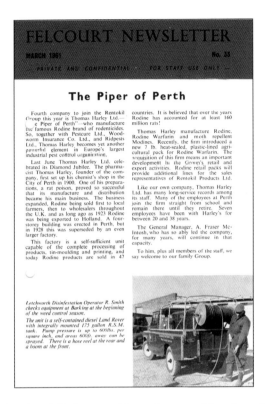

The final Felcourt Newsletter, March 1961.

Inside the newsletter, as a counterpoint to expansion news, tables ranking Rentokil's top sellers and a 'Photo Guide to Group Promotions', the centre spread was taken up by 'Dr Hickin's Christmas Quiz'. One guinea book tokens were on offer to the ten readers submitting the "most meritorious" set of answers. Given the depth of his knowledge, it's perhaps not surprising that the 40 questions set by Hickin were fiendishly difficult. Here's a flavour:

- To what order of mammals does the mole belong?

- How is *Tribolium confusum* identified from *T. castaneum*?

- What is a C X T figure?

- Give the Swahili for an insect.

- If a gallon of fluid is allowed to spread evenly over 200 sq. ft. what is the resultant thickness of the film in mm?

It's hard to imagine there were many perfect scores. In any case, not everyone took the challenge entirely seriously. In response to the question, "What is *Nomen nudum*?", one joker answered, "An all-female nudist colony". A definition more likely to stick in the minds of non-biologists than the real one: a species which has been named, but without an accompanying description.

April 1961 saw the lavish staging at the Grand Hotel, Brighton, of the Pest Control Conference of the Rentokil Group, attended by surveyors, sales representatives and all the top UK management. Unsurprisingly, Hickin was among the speakers – his topic, 'An Introduction to the Study of *Anobium punctatum*' (aka the common furniture beetle). A packed programme included sessions on pest control in both Holland and California, woodworm insurance, rising damp, weed control, techniques in evaluating pest control products, protecting timber against fire, marketing a new product and pest control in shipping.

In his presentation, 'The Growing Menace of Woodworm', WDRC General Manager Adrian Tyrer was able to cite data from the 10,426 property surveys carried out by his division in 1959 and explored the rising infestation in residential properties "against the background of the historical context of timber usage". Tyrer's figures showed that *Anobium punctatum* was far and away the biggest source of wood-boring infestations, responsible for 83% of incidences – with *Xestobium rufovillosum* (deathwatch beetle) a distant second on 5.64%. Blaming the rising use in recent decades of inferior-quality softwood timber with a greater sap content, his paper warned of "a high potential *Anobium* infestation susceptibility factor in the future unless pre-treatment is made the rule rather than the exception."

SCARECROW STRIP

Meanwhile, Disinfestation Technical Director Miles Price spoke about the successful trials of a new bird repellent called Scarecrow Strip in his presentation, 'The Role of Resins in Industrial Pest Control'. "We had to find a material which would make the perching bird feel uncomfortable and insecure," he explained. "Such materials must have 'give' or elasticity and have just the right amount of holding power or 'tack' – sufficient to create a sense of panic or discomfort, but not enough to hold even a sparrow. At the same time, the repellent should have little or no 'string', which might entangle the bird and adhere to its flight feathers."

Price explained to delegates how this stable gel composed of a combination of new synthetic plastics was applied using a caulking gun and did not freeze or melt. Trials carried out over the previous ten months had proved to be 100% effective, with pigeons and starlings cleared from those buildings where Scarecrow Strip had been applied.

"The earliest treatment carried out was at the British Home Stores, Croydon, on 6 August, 1960," Price continued. "Here a very considerable flock of pigeons used to perch on all the ledges along the face of the building, where they could watch the street market across the way. The results of the treatment were spectacular – the whole flock moved across the street and took up residence on Carters the Drapers. Carters complained but, of course, there was nothing we could do about it except treat Carters. Carters accepted our terms and are delighted with the results."

In between sessions, the Brighton programme included a visit to the Royal Pavilion and a company cricket match. The climax of proceedings was an extravagant banquet containing too many calories to bother counting – there was no chance of delegates escaping unnourished.

In June 1961, Rentokil Review replaced the Felcourt Newsletter. Issue one was a special edition focusing on the Brighton Conference.

In June 1961 the *Felcourt Newsletter* was replaced by *Rentokil Review*. The company was taking its branding more seriously than ever and was increasingly looking to present consistent messages to employees and customers alike. It was no coincidence that this first issue contained the announcement that 1 January 1962 was to be "an historic date" on which group subsidiary Disinfestation Ltd would be rebranded as Rentokil Laboratories Limited. Change was happening thick and fast.

A key element of that change was a continuation of the buying spree. The most notable of several acquisitions in 1961 was the purchase of 61-year-old Scottish business Thomas Harley Ltd, which had made its name with the Rodine rat poison. The company bore the nickname "the Piper of Perth" and, from beginnings as a single chemist shop at the turn of the century where the eponymous Mr Harley had a knack for knocking up rat poison for the locals, had grown into a multinational selling its products in 47 countries. As well as Rodine, the company produced Rodine Warfarin and moth repellent Modines. Its 'self-sufficient' factory could carry out the whole production process from product processing to tin moulding and printing. Clearly, Rentokil was now in a position to buy up highly sophisticated rivals.

Thomas Harley's respected General Manager, Angus Fraser McIntosh, was to play an important role in Rentokil and more widely in the pest control industry until his retirement at the end of 1974. He served six terms as President of the British Pest Control Association and became the founding President of the Confederation of European Pest Control Associations (CEPA). His diligence and commitment to protecting the interests of the sector earned him an OBE for services to pest control.

SECRETED IN THE VAULTS

Much like the closely guarded recipe for Coca-Cola, for many years Thomas Harley kept its formula for Rodine safely under lock and key in a bank vault. In the Rentokil archive there's a receipt from Union Bank of Scotland dated 16 June 1933 for the safe keeping of the sealed envelope containing the formula. More intriguingly, there's the envelope itself. On its front, typewritten above four signatures it reads: *This envelope contains the details of the Formula and Method of Manufacture of Rodin Rat Poison and other Proprietaries.* Turn the envelope over and there are two wax seals. Pristine, unbroken. Over the years, people have shown a lot of self-restraint.

It would be stretching it to say the same for the major Rentokil advertising campaign that ran in June 1962 to promote the Rentokil Woodworm Killer product, available to the general public through hardware stores and other retailers.

As part of a concerted effort under the banner of 'National Rentokil Week' (25–30 June), press advertising developed by agency WJ Southcombe Advertising in conjunction with Rentokil's in-house publicity department appeared in 200 national and local newspapers. The message behind the campaign was that treating woodworm with Rentokil products was child's play. But pushing the analogy to its limits resulted in a slightly odd campaign. Under a large picture of a girl and boy contentedly cradling their pet bunnies appeared what, at first glance, was a nonsensical headline: *Rabbits are kids' stuff with woodworm.*

On reading the opening lines of the body copy, the message began to make sense. "Finding woodworm wasn't supposed to be part of the game at all. It was just that the paper dart flew into the cupboard under the stairs..." where alert brother and sister noticed the tell-tale signs of woodworm damage. Their reward for bringing the infestation to dad's attention on his return home from work was, as you may well have surmised by now, "two handsome rabbits". PR activity in support of the campaign included sending out to target publications an editorial article penned by Frank Jefkins, which told parents how their children could become "home detectives" hunting for woodworm holes. (Presumably the sort of thing kids used to do before computer games and mobile phones came along.)

At the same time as the Thomas Harley deal, Rentokil was giving serious consideration to a move into damp-proofing, which promised to be a good fit with its other property services.

In 1960 the company had been approached by Peter Selby, who was marketing Hungarian inventions to potential commercial partners in the UK. One of these was a revolutionary new technique for electroosmotic (EO) damp-proofing developed by a Hungarian man called Miklos Lipcsey. Bill Holmes was so taken by the possibilities of EO that he taught himself Hungarian to immerse himself in the available technical literature and travelled to Hungary to meet the inventor. Once Holmes was satisfied EO was all it was cracked up to be, a deal was signed allowing Rentokil to use it under licence. In 1962, Rentokil launched the UK's first EO service for preventing rising damp (and penetrating damp not under hydraulic pressure). A 20-year warranty was offered, and the service quickly found favour among householders and local authorities. It was the cornerstone on which strong growth of a new Damp-proofing division was built until cheaper chemical damp-proofing courses using silicone came onto the market in the 1970s.

"EO was very expensive but in its day it was revolutionary," says Rentokil Property Care UK Technical Services Manager Nicholas Donnithorne. "It settled out the electrical potential in a wall. You needed to chase out the mortar course to run a thin metal strip – which could be copper or, later on, platinum – loop it in and out of the holes, then join it together using a fusion technology so it literally fused the metal strips together to give a proper bond. Then you needed to check with your circuit meter that you had the right earth potential back against the earth rod that you'd driven into the ground. Our system was a passive system that did not require electricity, but a lot of the opposition ones that came out later did. If you switched off the power by accident, they stopped working."

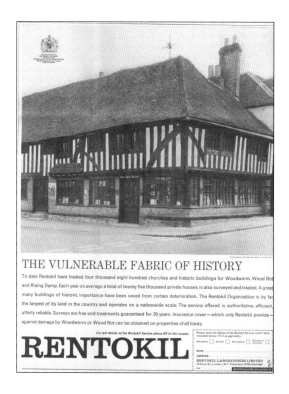

Advertising campaign from 1966 highlighting Rentokil's role in protecting vulnerable historic buildings.

Among Rentokil's most prestigious contracts during the 1960s was bird control work at Buckingham Palace.

The rise of local authority home improvement grants in the late 60s to early 70s helped fuel strong growth in the damp-proofing market. Meanwhile at a grander level, Rentokil's work for the royal residences, which stretched back to the 1930s, was gaining ever wider recognition. At the beginning of 1964 the company was able to add the Royal warrant for woodworm and dry rot control to the warrant for rodent control that had been bestowed six years earlier. It was welcome news not just in and of itself but because in the mid-60s the company was enveloped in a couple of crises.

CRISIS STRIKES: THE SMARDEN INCIDENT

Perhaps the lowest point in the company's entire history occurred in 1963 when spillage of chemical residue at Rentokil's factory at Smarden in Kent contaminated adjacent agricultural land, causing the deaths of around 20 farm animals. The toxic substance, fluoroacetamide, was used both as an insecticide for famers and gardeners and, in a more concentrated form, as a rodenticide. Rentokil cooperated fully with the authorities throughout the crisis and acted responsibly in dealing with what became known as the Smarden Incident.

The Smarden Incident hit the headlines and was debated in parliament. On 3 February 1964, Minister of Agriculture, Fisheries and Food, Christopher Soames – as it happens, Sir Winston Churchill's son-in-law – made a statement to the House of Commons about the affair. According to *Hansard*, while facing questions from MPs about the contamination, Soames said:

"The accident did not result from the use of the chemical as an agricultural product, but as a consequence of an accident at the factory. Somewhere there was a seepage of this very concentrated poison. I fully realise that there are many important lessons which we must learn from the accident... I have no evidence that any animals have suffered in any way from the proper use of this chemical as an insecticide. Had that been the case we would, naturally, have taken action before in the interests of the country as a whole as well as of agriculture. But this was an industrial accident and as such does not, in my view, put at issue the very real protection which lies in the hands of the Poisonous Substances Committee, of which most eminent people – doctors, veterinary surgeons and scientists – are members, advising the Government on the proper use of chemicals."

There is no good moment for an event like the Smarden Incident, but the timing was particularly unfavourable as it coincided with the emergence of a new environmental awareness. Rachel Carson's influential 1962 book, *Silent Spring*, brought the damaging effects on the environment of certain pesticides to wider public attention and moved ecology issues up the agenda. Against this background, it was inevitable that Rentokil would face added public scrutiny.

"We tried to do the right thing," recalls Rentokil's former Publicity Manager, Peter Bateman. "We had an open air press conference at Smarden and we made sure everyone knew we had all the public health insurance cover in place and that we had gone to see the affected famers to let them know they'd be compensated. I was there as you can imagine. The Chairman, Pat Burgin, was interviewed on the news because it was such a big story as it was the first pest control poisoning incident here after the publication of *Silent Spring*. Paradoxically, if there was an upside, it gave me press contacts it would have taken me years to make otherwise – like the fantastic broadcast journalist John Timpson, who went on to present the *Today* programme on Radio 4."

To fully clean up the contamination, around an acre of topsoil behind the factory at Smarden was removed, deposited in 40-gallon oil barrels, encased in concrete and transported far out into the Bay of Biscay for disposal deep at sea, beyond the Continental shelf, in much the same way as radioactive material. A Fisheries Protection escort attended and all possible precautions were taken to ensure there was no danger to marine life.

On guard for further environmental issues, Rentokil opted to voluntarily discontinue its use of organochlorine insecticides DDT and dieldrin in 1964 following publication of a UK government report by the Advisory Committee on Poisonous Substances used in Agriculture and Food Storage. The *Review of the persistent organochlorine pesticides*, often referred to by the punchier title of the

'Cook Report', recommended that these organochlorines should not be used for pest control because residues of these substances could be found in bird eggs and elsewhere in the natural world. This chimed with the concerns expressed in Carson's *Silent Spring* and by the blossoming environmental movement. Carson had been moved to write her influential book by a letter from her friend Olga Huckins, who owned a private two-acre bird sanctuary in Massachusetts. At the time crop-dusting with pesticides was generally considered progressive and was rife – film buffs will call to mind the famously tense sequence in the Alfred Hitchcock classic *North by Northwest* (1959), in which Cary Grant runs for his life while pursued across fields by a crop-dusting plane. In their efforts to deal with insect pests, the US authorities were indiscriminately spraying gardens and other open spaces whether the people affected wanted them to or not. When her land was sprayed against her wishes with the aim of killing mosquitoes, Huggins was outraged to discover birds showing symptoms typical of DDT poisoning. In anger and desperation, she wrote to Carson asking for help, and it was this letter that convinced Carson to write the book that did so much to change attitudes. DDT was beginning to be seen in a different light. With a view to preserving both a healthy eco-system and its good name, Rentokil took a unilateral decision to cease using DDT and dieldrin in favour of more biodegradable alternatives – switching to lindane in its timber-preservation fluids – long before any legislative restrictions were introduced. In fact, DDT was not banned in Sweden until 1970, the US in 1972 and in the UK as late as 1984; a full 20 years after Rentokil had exited this market.

FIRE AT FETCHAM

Adding to Rentokil's challenges, a major fire – said to be the worst in the area since the war – caused severe damage to the factory at Fetcham in April 1964.

Despite having worked at Felcourt since shortly after the takeover, Norman Hickin still lived nearby. On seeing the conflagration from his garden, he dashed to the scene. It took 11 fire engines to get the blaze under control. Afterwards, on inspecting the devastation, a sombre Hickin recalled the ingenious work that went into transforming the building back in 1947:

> "When we first inspected the dance hall it did not escape our notice that it was very lofty and could easily accommodate another floor. Charles Nichols went out one day and bought a Bailey bridge at a sale of surplus war equipment and we used it to construct a framework on which to support another floor. The existing walls were not used as supports but we built an entirely separate steel framework which we bolted together like a Meccano set. The architect whom we brought in to pass our handiwork as a sound structure was satisfied that we could drive a train over it! Sixteen years later when the building had been gutted by fire, I stood with Nichols surveying the desolate site. He and I could take a little pride that our steel erection withstood the test of fire. When everything else had vanished in the flames, our handiwork still remained."

The fire at Fetcham led to consolidation of production in the UK with the almost immediate opening of the Rentokil Laboratories factory in Kirkby, Merseyside, which initially employed around 60 staff. Once the new facilities at Kirkby were fully operational, Fetcham and the old Thomas Harley works in Perth were closed. Alan Deutsch, who took over running the Fetcham factory from Charles Nichols in the early 1960s, when Nichols moved to the Dover Street Publicity and Information Office, played a key role in identifying the site for the new plant in Webber Road, Kirkby and getting production up and running. Transport Manager Doug Edmonds and Processing Foreman Albert Penfold moved up to the North West with Deutsch, who eventually took on the Production Director title, but for the most part staff were hired locally. One extra installation required at the new Kirkby site was a plant for decanting 20-tonne cylinders of hydrogen cyanide and methyl bromide into smaller units for use by the Marine and Fumigation division, based mainly on Merseyside.

Rentokil exploited the medium of film to showcase its scientific expertise.

Among the other employees to move up to Kirkby was Bob Farmer, who was appointed Production Director, and then Technical Director, with responsibility for the manufacture and quality control of all the formulations at the new plant. In addition to his noted expertise in the lab, Farmer was doing wonderful directing work for the Rentokil Film Unit, which he set up in 1959. He was, one might say, the Hitchcock of the cockroach.

Like the master of suspense, Farmer was painstaking in striving to meet high standards. When making *The Intruders*, it was decided that there must be shots of a cockroach egg-case hatching and a cockroach moulting. Poised over the camera, members of the production team mounted a round-the-clock vigil, working in four-hour shifts. Finally, at 1.45am on the fifth night of waiting, Farmer got the shots he wanted.

The Rentokil Film Unit picked up a number of awards and was noted for the high quality of its productions.

The setbacks of Smarden and the Fetcham fire notwithstanding, things were going well. Investment in domestic and overseas acquisitions, training, production and research were taking Rentokil to a position of world leadership. Jim Nelson, editor of US trade magazine *Pest Control*, was so impressed by what he saw of the business in the mid-60s that he said, "Your company undertakes far more research and has better facilities than any other company in the pest control field that I know of."

Observing the rise of luxury tourism in the Caribbean, the company decided this region of tropical paradise islands was ripe for growth. On top of this, Rentokil's visibility was growing on the back of positive stories.

PIED PIPER PUBLICITY COUP

With publicity opportunities uppermost in mind, in 1965 Rentokil signed a ten-year contract to eradicate rats from a small German town. That town was Hamelin – or Hameln, as it is called in Germany – on the picturesque river Weser in Lower Saxony.

Of course, Hamelin is the location for one of the world's most famous folk tales, the story of the Pied Piper.

Legend has it that in 1284 a mysterious figure clad in a coat of many colours appeared in the town and pledged to rid it of rats in return for payment. Beguiling rats and mice with enchanting music from his pipes, he lured them to their doom in the river. When the city fathers then reneged on their agreement to pay for the musical massacre, events turned ugly. The Pied Piper returned to Hamelin to exact his revenge. This time he captivated the town's children with his spellbinding melodies, leading them helplessly away... never to be seen again.

Rentokil gained huge PR exposure from its pest control contract with Hamelin, dubbed Operation Pied Piper.

The Pied Piper is a resonant tale that has been retold many times since the Middle Ages. Back in the 1960s, while visiting the West German Rentokil subsidiary, Bob Westphal had caught sight of a road sign bearing the Hamelin name and saw the publicity potential in an instant. Rentokil's rodent eradication contract with Hamelin was the first of its kind since the legendary one signed with the Pied Piper.

As a public relations exercise, it was a masterstroke. Taking care to milk the opportunity for all it was worth, Rentokil made a film, *The Modern Pied Piper of Hamelin*, in which sequences showing the contemporary pest control methods used in the town were intercut with scenes depicting the original Pied Piper story. As Rentokil delivered the pest control goods, this time the burghers of Hamelin were more than happy to pay up.

The Contract

The famous contract Rentokil signed with the town of Hamelin.

"I went over for the press conference," remembers Bateman. "We had children dressed up as rats and the burgomaster, townspeople and other children paraded along dressed up in period costume. It was a PR manager's dream because pretty much every nation has heard, if only vaguely, of the Pied Piper of Hamelin. We were getting cuttings from newspapers as far away as the *South China Morning Post*. And the publicity did enable us to get a lot more rodent control work for local authorities – which was a big market in the UK in those days." The BBC gave the story four minutes on its *Tonight* programme and even *Time* magazine took the PR bait.

Rentokil's General Manager for Germany, Heine Jonker, added a theatrical flourish at the press conference held in Hamelin Town Hall when referring to the company's previous successes at clearing whole towns of rodents. Holding up two stuffed rats for the audience to see, he said: "This one is the last rat from Reykjavik in Iceland. The other is the last rat from the sands of Bahrain. The third specimen will be the last rat from the beautiful town of Hamelin."

A rodent control unit was set up at an office in the town's waterworks from which technicians pulled in from Rentokil operations in Hamburg, Bremen and Baden-Baden set to work. After the rats had been cleared, Rentokil hired a local man to maintain its service on the spot.

There were several publicity coups in the UK as well. First, a rather strange though very worthwhile collaboration with offbeat comedian Spike Milligan – *Goon Show* member and, as it happened, author of a much-loved silly verse on woodworm.

Milligan was a passionate conservationist and spent a year, having first secured permission from the Ministry of Public Building and Works, renovating The Elfin Oak. This 900-year-old tree stump located in Kensington Gardens was decorated by the work of sculptor Ivor Innes. His carvings of 'little people' such as pixies, elves, gnomes, witches and woodland creatures made in 1929–30 had been damaged by deathwatch beetle and wet rot. Rentokil timber technologist John Evans met with Milligan in Kensington Gardens and explained how the little people could be saved from decay. Badly damaged wood was hacked away and the massive stump was drilled and irrigated with Rentokil woodworm killer. All told, 50 gallons were used. Once Milligan's painstaking restoration work was at an end, the finished tree was further protected with a coating of Rentokil Clear Water Repellent. Several years later, the Elfin Oak appeared on the inside cover of Pink Floyd album *Ummagumma* – guitarist David Gilmour posing in front of the tree – and in the 1990s it was declared a Grade II listed structure.

Rentokil was also busy at the seat of government. A 1965 cover story in *Rentokil Review* flagged up the work Rentokil was doing at the Houses of Parliament, such as installing the Scarecrow Strip repellent to cut down on bird fouling and other avian damage to the statuary and various magnificent architectural features. "It is not normally permissible to publicise commercial treatment of the Palace of Westminster," the piece explained, "but when your company is using a fire engine's 100ft turntable ladder to apply a pigeon repellent in New Palace Yard, people are bound to notice it."

Politicians need pest control as much as anyone. The Houses of Parliament were another prestigious Rentokil customer.

Hard at work on the façade of the Palace of Westminster.

Rentokil installed its Scarecrow Strip bird repellent at the Palace of Westminster to reduce fouling and avian damage to architectural features.

Success here helped the bird repellent team add another landmark building to its client portfolio the following year: Buckingham Palace. There was also a visit to Kensington Palace for Sid Long of the Pest Control division, who brought with him three gallons of woodworm fluid and had the honour of instructing Lord Snowden himself on its proper application to vintage furniture using a Fetcham Injector. Perhaps this reverence for elegant chairs and sumptuous tables rubbed off on Snowden's son, Viscount Linley, then a young child, who went on to become one of the most famous furniture designers in the world.

There were times when Rentokil made sure its work at places less grand than palaces was noticed too. For example, when the business acquired an old drill hall on the banks of the river Leith for use as an Edinburgh office, the dry rot fungus that riddled the building was actually nurtured for two months – until 300 local government officials, private architects and estate agents were invited over to witness a demonstration of state-of-the-art dry rot treatment in action. Further smart thinking was applied when the World Health Organization in Geneva was invaded by cockroaches. Rentokil rode to the rescue and used the contract as a springboard to open a Swiss office.

In some of its advertising in the 1960s, Rentokil made great play of its role as a protector of period buildings. One 1966 print advertising campaign which appeared in *The Times* featured a large picture of an attractive half-timbered Tudor building above the headline 'The Vulnerable Fabric of History'. The ad copy announced that to date Rentokil had treated 4,800 churches and historic buildings for woodworm, wood rot and rising damp. The company was on average surveying and treating 25,000 private houses a year in the UK. The advertisement trumpeted: "A great many buildings of historic importance have been saved from certain deterioration. The Rentokil Organisation is by far the largest of its kind in the country and operates on a nationwide scale. The service offered is authoritative, efficient, utterly reliable. Surveys are free and treatments guaranteed for 20 years. Insurance cover – which *only* Rentokil provide – against damage by woodworm or wood rot can be obtained on properties of all kinds."

PROFITS TOP £1M

In 1966 group profits topped £1m for the first time (the equivalent of £16.6m today). The achievements of Buchan and Westphal, both in their mid-40s, were gaining wider attention. A four-page feature by W. G. Norris in the June 1967 issue of the Institute of Director's (IoD) *The Director* magazine profiled the pair, noting their success in internationalising the business and broadening its UK operations. At this point, the company employed around 2,300 people. Pest Control accounted for £1.5m in UK turnover, but Woodworm and Dry Rot had larger revenues at £2.4m. Damp-proofing with £500,000 and Manufactured Products at £400,000 also delivered significant turnover. On top of which, the Hermeseal acoustic and weatherproofing business acquired in 1965 added a further £250,000.

A strong sales culture was fostered by setting ambitious targets and publishing the monthly sales records of individuals and teams. Servicemen and surveyors were actively encouraged to cross-sell services from elsewhere in the group and stay alert for new business opportunities. Woodworm and Dry Rot surveyors on site might enthuse to homeowners about the fabulous draft-proofing services available from Hermeseal. "If a division can't see how it will reach its target everyone in it is encouraged to think up new services Rentokil could give," Westphal explained in an interview. "That is why we are now in pest control, weed control, damp-proofing, insulation, draught-proofing, bird control, woodworm and dry rot control, timber pre-treatment and so on."

Buchan himself liked to say that Rentokil's strong growth was not down to any magic but simply due to the systematic application of common sense. The expertise and skill of frontline staff was the key to success. As the IoD journalist noted: "Rentokil's achievement is to take ordinary workmen – carpenters and so on – and turn them into experts not only in their job but in selling their services, sometimes to very difficult and fussy customers. Not that they are encouraged to oversell."

There's a strong sense that this was a business very much at ease with itself and increasingly trusted by its customer base. At the outset of the decade, Rentokil pest control vans bore no brand livery and travelled incognito. There was a residual feeling in some quarters that pest infestations were a source of shame.

Woodworm division supervisors with their vehicles, at Felcourt in 1959.

Westphal and Buchan decided to blow this outdated notion out of the water and decreed that the entire 1,000-strong fleet of vehicles should be repainted to showcase the Rentokil brand name and Royal warrant. Some frontline staff initially disapproved of the move, believing that residential customers might feel uncomfortable that their neighbours could so easily see they had called in Rentokil. But the directors stuck to their guns, taking the view that showing neighbours you were taking care of your home could only be a positive.

Rufus, Rentokil's knightly brand emblem.

With its fleet sporting company colours criss-crossing the country, Rentokil's visibility shot up. Together with the company logo and Royal warrant, brochures and promotional material sported the brand emblem known as Rufus: a standing knight clutching a lance in his right hand and a large shield in his left. The shield represented the protection the company offered its customers and was decorated with a simple red 'R' for Rentokil. Group Marketing Director Alan Farrington and Publicity Manager Peter Bateman beavered away on further spreading the word. Part of the £100,000-a-year budget they had at this time was spent on external PR agency, Advice & Action, who placed stories in the press about new treatment techniques, prominent clients and the numerous lectures, presentations and film showings that the company undertook. The scope of these events encompassed everything from small talks at local Women's Institutes to national conferences with public health officials. What remained consistent was the depth of expertise and quality of information Rentokil could call upon. Up at Kirkby, Robert Farmer continued to produce informative films to exactingly high standards.

Entomologist Dr Peter Cornwell served as Technical Director and held additional responsibility for a number of overseas businesses.

Moreover, the tremendous scientific expertise on hand in the Felcourt labs was utilised not only for R&D and analytical purposes but to position Rentokil as the leading authority in multiple areas. A deal was struck with publisher Hutchinson to develop a series of books known as the Rentokil Library. It goes without saying that Scientific Director, Norman Hickin, already an eminent author, was one of the writers. But a new wave of scientific talent had joined the company, notably Dr Peter Cornwell, an entomologist with a PhD from Oxford who arrived in 1963 as Chief Biologist and was soon promoted to the position of Technical Director. Cornwell's books on cockroaches were widely regarded as definitive works. Curiously, like Hickin, he was also a talented artist – although in his case, watercolour paintings were his preferred medium.

This was a time of modernisation, avid exploration of new business opportunities and cutting-edge scientific work that was on a par with what was happening in academia. Yet paradoxically there was also a slightly cosseted, timeless air to life at Felcourt. Husband-and-wife team Jack and Gladys Vaughan had arrived in 1954 to live at the "little bungalow" which in later years became part of the sales ledger function. While Jack served as head gardener, Gladys was cook for the directors. The couple were still at Felcourt in the mid-1970s when they became great grandparents. Regular sporting events in which employees participated, like the Rentokil Golf Competition held at Tandridge Golf Club in Surrey, helped foster a good *esprit de corps*.

OPEN TO IDEAS

Allied to a strong sense of continuity at the company, the directors were very receptive to new ideas. "Teddy Buchan and Bob Westphal, as far as I was concerned, were the company, driving it forward," recalls Peter Bateman. "They were delightful. You've got this dour Scot with all the Scottish attitudes of courtesy and consideration and so forth and this wild Australian. I distinctly remember when I first joined Bob Westphal at Felcourt and he said: 'Look, my door will always be open. If you come up with an idea, even if it sounds crazy or ridiculous, come in and let me know.' That was his attitude."

Although UK management was firmly in control of day-to-day decision-making at Rentokil, the Danish parent company, with the

Elsass family to the fore, continued to wield power on major issues. As recognition for the many years he had spent helping build the business, in 1968 Adam Elsass was honoured with a CBE for his role in fostering Anglo-Danish relations. His investiture took place in Copenhagen, with the British ambassador conferring the honour on behalf of the Queen. With pleasing symmetry, Rentokil Chairman Pat Burgin was made Knight of the Danish Royal Order of the Dannebrog that same year. Anglo-Danish relations were in fine fettle.

The Australian business expanded quickly through a combination of acquisitions and organic growth. Note the kangaroo designed to resemble Rufus, the knightly Rentokil brand icon of the time, on the cover of this issue of Rentokil Review.

Having set up in Australia in 1965 – with an operation run by Bob Westphal's brother, Fred – Rentokil scaled up 'down under' in one fell swoop with its largest overseas acquisition of the 1960s: the purchase in 1968 of quoted Australian company Houghton & Byrne Holdings. That the Rentokil Group was on an exciting upward trajectory couldn't be disputed. Turnover more than doubled from £2m to over £4.5m between 1960 and 1965. And then was to triple again over the next half-decade to top £15m. Profits likewise surged. A business doing this well couldn't escape the notice of a predator indefinitely. All the more so as Westphal and Buchan took pride in their openness about company performance to employees and competitors alike.

Ken Bridgman (centre) and Data Processing Manager John Divall inspect an ICT 1901 computer, installed at Felcourt in 1968. The machine was capable of reading 300 characters a second.

A batch of termite fluid produced in Fetcham and destined for Bermuda.

As the 1960s headed towards a close, the Sophus Berendsen board received an approach from across the Atlantic. A fast-expanding corporation headquartered in Atlanta, Georgia named Rollins Inc. – which had begun life in 1948 as the owner of a radio station – had identified pest control as an area for rapid growth. In 1964 it made the bold step of buying the Orkin Exterminating Company. This deal is often said to be the first major leveraged buyout in US history. Rollins paid $62 million for the business, nearly seven times its own revenues. Unafraid to take risks and pursuing expansion at dizzying speed, now it had Rentokil in its sights. Adam Elsass and Steen Langebæk (who both sat on the Rentokil Group board) and the other members of the Sophus Berendsen board had some serious thinking to do.

"We understood that a price had been provisionally agreed," says former Company Secretary Ken Bridgman, one of the four UK-based directors on the Rentokil Group board at the time. "The English directors were thoroughly unhappy. What would happen to their own holdings in the company? Wouldn't rule from the US be far more restrictive than the benign loose rein that Copenhagen allowed? The Danes were persuaded that they would receive far more if they floated Rentokil shares on the London Stock Exchange. And so it proved."

NEW PINS APLENTY ON THE MAP

During the 1960s Rentokil grew strongly in the UK, both organically and through buying other businesses. But the eye-catching expansion story of the decade was the transformation of the company into a truly international concern. New subsidiaries sprang up faster than

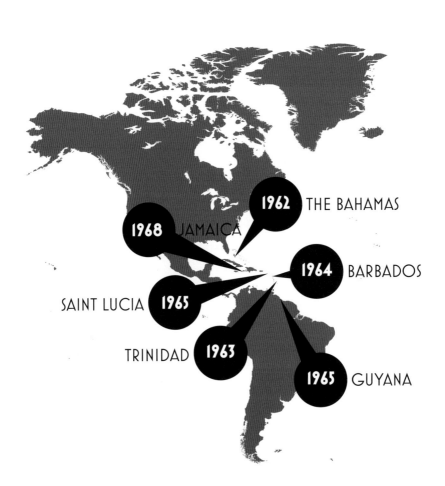

1962 THE BAHAMAS

1968 JAMAICA

1964 BARBADOS

SAINT LUCIA 1965

TRINIDAD 1963

1965 GUYANA

mini-skirt hemlines and while Beatles hits proliferated, so too did the hits Rentokil was putting out on beetles across the globe. It may have been the Cold War era, but Rentokil enjoyed a hot streak of overseas growth.

Rentokil vehicle in Malaysia in the 1960s, complete with the Rufus knight logo.

Ship & Shore Fumigation, an acquisition in Singapore.

Operators from Rentokil's German subsidiary at an East-West border checkpoint in Berlin at the height of the Cold War.

Rentokil entered the market in Guyana in 1965.

THE ESSENTIALS

1957 – Rentokil bought by British Ratin for £100,000.

1958 – Granted Royal warrant of Elizabeth II for rodent control.

1960 – British Ratin Company Ltd changes its name to Rentokil Group Ltd.

1961 – Launch of Woodworm Insurance Co. Ltd, offering protection policies for homeowners.

1962 – Disinfestation Ltd rebranded as Rentokil Laboratories Limited.

1964 – Production switches to Kirkby.

1965 – Following in the footsteps of the Pied Piper, Rentokil gets to grips with pests in Hamelin.

1966 – Bird repellent contract for Buckingham Palace and pest control work at the newly opened Post Office Tower (BT Tower), which at the time had a revolving restaurant open to the public.

1967 – Purchases of wood-preserving business Celcure and fire-retardant paints company Albi-Willesden.

1969 – Rentokil has over 3,100 employees in 53 operating companies spread across 27 countries.

CHAPTER FIVE

Life as a PLC

The trans-Atlantic takeover approach set the wheels in motion for a flotation on the London Stock Exchange (LSE). Yet it would be wrong to view the move as an entirely defensive measure. The business was in tremendous shape and growing at pace, which is why it caught the eye as a tasty acquisition target in the first place. Group turnover rose from £6.9m to £8.8m between 1967 and 1968, with net trading profits jumping 17%. There was no need for the company to be swallowed up. Actually, this was the perfect moment to go to the City in search of a massive injection of capital that could fund further expansion.

By the time of the flotation, Rentokil had a network of 44 regional offices across the British Isles. If not quite an A–Z, it was a geographically comprehensive A–S: from Aberdeen, Alton, Ashford and Aylesbury to Sheffield, South Shields, Stirling, Stoke-on-Trent and Swansea – with plenty in between. The Woodworm and Dry Rot division was treating over 24,000 properties a year, the majority of them (85%) residential. Meanwhile, technicians in the UK Pest Control Division were servicing 41,400 contracts, mainly for private sector customers but also for local authorities and hospitals.

The other UK divisions at the time were Damp-proofing, Hermeseal Insulation, Wood-preserving, Export and the similar sounding Production and Products divisions. The former was responsible for the manufacturing at Kirkby of products used by the group, while the Products division was in charge of marketing products bearing the Rentokil brand name and other registered trademarks such as Rodine and Insectrol. The wave of overseas expansion during the 1960s meant Rentokil was now a truly international business operating in 27 countries spanning Europe, Australasia, Africa, Southeast Asia and the Caribbean. Although the UK was still delivering the lion's share, with each passing year the overseas businesses, which were principally focused on pest control, termite eradication and fumigation services, were growing their proportion of turnover and profit.

The firm's initial public offering (IPO) was underwritten by Westminster Bank, which the following year would become NatWest. The bank agreed to subscribe for 2 million new shares, as well as buying 3.6 million shares from Sophus Berendsen. Although this diluted its ownership, Sophus Berendsen still maintained a controlling interest in Rentokil Group, with 55% of the equity. The continuation of its involvement was perceived very positively within the Square Mile. Institutional investors understandably found the stability reassuring.

Under the headline 'Rentokil Goes Public', a 7 March 1969 press release highlighted the company's sound management, successful expansion, seven major UK divisions and exports to 85 countries. "The group's growth rate has averaged over 20% per year for the past 10 years and on the 1968 turnover of £8,820,000, pre-tax profits amounted to £1,535,000", the release added.

*(Left) Rentokil debuted on the London Stock Exchange in 1969. The
offer was underwritten by the forerunner to NatWest.
(Right) How* Rentokil Review *reported on the flotation.*

One tenth of the shares were reserved for Rentokil's directors, UK
staff and overseas managers. All of the 344 employees who applied
were allocated shares. Demand from external investors once again
underlined what an exceptional business Rentokil had become.
The public offering, one of the largest new issues on the LSE for
several years, was four times oversubscribed. Investors were falling
over themselves to grab a piece of the action. Needless to say,
when Rentokil made its LSE debut, its share price took off like the
proverbial rat up a drainpipe.

Also in spring 1969, a new 4,000 sq. ft laboratory block opened at
Felcourt, underlining the company's commitment to scientific rigour
and R&D. A team of biologists, entomologists and chemists busied
themselves studying pest behaviour, developing safe, economical
and effective pesticides and perfecting techniques for property

maintenance and improvement. Expansion necessitated taking on further space beyond the boundaries of Felcourt – some employees were housed in offices previously occupied by Hall & Co in Garland Road, East Grinstead, while the accounts and wages staff moved into a nearby house on St James Road. These premises would be quickly outgrown. In the year of Apollo 11 and "one giant leap for mankind", Rentokil was making huge strides of its own, albeit terrestrial ones, moving into the hygiene sector with the purchase of Rashbrooke Chemicals. Two further hygiene acquisitions in 1973 showed Rentokil Group's serious intention to build business in this sector. As the 1970s wore on, new services such as Catercleanse were launched that broadened the business and increased sales.

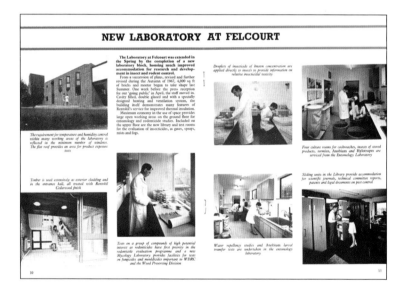

Rentokil colleagues moved into a new laboratory block at Felcourt one week before Rentokil held its press reception for going public.

SCIENTIFIC FIREPOWER ON THE RADIO

The investment in new lab facilities underlined the enviable amount of scientific firepower the company could now call upon. On 27 September 1971, producer Dilys Breese and presenter Derek Jones of the BBC Natural History Unit in Bristol came to Felcourt to record a documentary for Radio 4's popular *The Living World* series.

The episode, 'The Problem of Pests', first aired on Sunday 30 January 1972 and featured interviews with a quintet of Rentokil's finest minds: Scientific Director Norman Hickin, Chief Biologist John Bull, Director of Research Peter Cornwell, Entomologist Colin Hawkes and Mycologist David Dickinson. Jones conducted his interviews while touring the main laboratory building and the grounds, including a visit to the outdoor rat pen, which he described to listeners as being around 6oft square with ½-inch mesh netting. John Bull described some of Rentokil's pioneering experiments of the time into using ultrasonics to repel rats from buildings and explained how the 250-odd rats in the pen were prevented from burrowing through the ground to freedom by concrete to the side of, and three feet underneath, the pen.

Jones then moved from the early autumn chill to the humid conditions of the cockroach lab, where sweating copiously, he remarked that it was "darned hot". Observing that the cockroaches were kept in plastic bins, Jones wondered whether this was due to their association with food waste. With the customary precision for which he was noted, Peter Cornwell set him straight: "No, the connection here is quite fortuitous in that they [the bins] are easily cleaned for breeding purposes, and by using a material with a very high co-efficient of slip on the inside we can keep all our insects inside the bins rather than them escaping."

Suitably informed, Jones proceeded to other labs to examine wood damaged by woodworm and examples of lovingly cultivated fungus. When Dickinson waxed lyrical about samples of *Lenzites*, *Coniophora cerebella* and *Merulius lacrymans*, Radio 4 broadcast these scientific names unhesitatingly. This was not a show intent on dumbing it down.

Like all good interviewers, Jones saved his best question until last, asking Hickin whether as a published authority on wood-boring insects and wildlife conservation there was any contradiction working in the pest control business. Put on the spot, Hickin gave an answer that was an articulate, well-reasoned gem: "Neither I nor my colleagues feel there's any contradiction at all. The maintenance or the increase in the populations of desirable species of animals and plants on the one hand, or the limiting of undesirable species on the other, is in our view the management of man's biological environment and when all's said and done, this is practiced on nature reserves as well as in kitchens and grain warehouses."

Another of Rentokil's top scientific minds of this era was Robin Edwards, who finally retired as Chief Entomologist in 1991 after 31 years with the business. Edwards discovered a species of carpet beetle (*Anthrenus sarnicus*) new to science, conducted 36,000 insect identifications over the course of his career and wrote the book *Social Wasps*. He was also author and co-editor of *Termites, A World Problem*. Both titles were part of the important Rentokil Library series. Edwards was responsible for a large amount of R&D technical literature and trained countless technicians and surveyors.

Now that Rentokil was a listed company, a key objective was to extend the international presence achieved through the whirlwind of openings and acquisitions during the previous decade. Yet even though flotation meant Rentokil had at its disposal a war chest for international expansion, it was clear that there were some overseas markets that, while undoubtedly offering growth opportunities, were either too small or too risky to merit buying up a local player or bearing the costs of starting from scratch.

Books in the Rentokil Library series.

INTERNATIONAL FRANCHISING

For markets such as these, Rentokil developed a franchising model. This allowed it to enter countries such as Thailand, Argentina, Ghana, Senegal, Zaire, Iran, Kuwait, Namibia, Seychelles and St Maarten in the Netherlands Antilles. Alongside the franchising, investment in subsidiaries continued. In 1970–71, businesses were established in Finland, Belgium, Norway, Tanzania, Uganda, Zambia, Israel and Malaysia. Then in 1974, two acquisitions marked a serious move into the USA: wood-preserving company TaCo and pest control business Josephsons. In a few short years, Rentokil had transformed itself from having a predominantly UK focus into a multinational corporation with a mix of subsidiaries and national franchisees.

On the road with Hygiene services in Trinidad, 1976.

The proof of this increasingly exotic pudding came in November 1974 when the Felcourt Training Centre hosted Rentokil's first ever Overseas Managers Conference. Eighteen managers jetted in from various parts of the globe to share best practice and listen to presentations from 15 lecturers. The overarching theme of the conference was 'Doing Things the Rentokil Way'. Against a backdrop of serious shareholder scrutiny, the group was demonstrating how well it grasped the importance of delivering uniformly high standards of service and a consistent brand experience.

Life as a PLC was going well. So much so that in 1973 Sophus Berendsen followed Rentokil onto the stock market – although unsurprisingly it chose to list on the Copenhagen Stock Exchange (CSE) rather than

London. At the time, CSE still occupied the Børsen, one of Denmark's most magnificent old buildings, an ornate 17th century edifice with a fabulous spire of four intertwined dragons' tails. Forget temporary TV studio sets, this was a properly imposing dragons' den for investors.

Back in the UK, where in the early 1970s Rentokil had well over 2,000 employees, the company was showing it cared not only about revenue and performance in the job, but also about the wellbeing of the people contributing to its success. At this time Rentokil did not have a personnel department and the expectation was that Regional Managers would be responsible for recruitment, pay, training and welfare. Yet despite its lack of HR infrastructure in those days, the company was fairly progressive in terms of the benefits it offered, including a pension scheme with free life assurance cover, profit-related bonuses and up to two months' full pay for absence due to sickness.

AN EDUCATION IN PAYROLL

Gill Brown, who today is an important member of the pensions team, began her Rentokil career with a job in payroll in 1970 at the tender age of 15. At first she was based at St James Road, East Grinstead, where the payroll department was shielded from prying eyes. "I used to work right up the top in the attic of this old Victorian house with one lady who smoked – she had a cigarette hanging out the side of her mouth the whole day long. She came from Nottingham and I was from East Grinstead and she was very different from the people I had grown up with. As she was already in her 60s and I was only 15, I had my eyes opened by some of the stories she told."

Before long, payroll was relocated to a bigger building at 218 London Road, East Grinstead. The business was doing well, but this was an era when the UK was hard hit by economic instability and industrial action. When Prime Minister Ted Heath imposed emergency measures to conserve energy, including the three-day week, Brown and her colleagues gamely continued working at their desks while the electricity was turned off, feet in cardboard boxes to ward off the worst of the chilly draughts. Thick tights were *de rigueur* in the cold as the company dress code forbade women from wearing trousers unless they formed part of a trouser suit. Using the hand crank adding machine went a little way towards keeping warm, although the trick lay in not cranking it too vigorously because it had a tendency to fly off the desk.

Rentokil had become a very significant employer in the East Grinstead area and it seemed that pretty much everyone who lived locally knew somebody with a connection to the company. What the Rentokil brand stood for and how the company conducted business commanded respect.

"I started at Felcourt back in 1973," remembers research analyst David Taplin. "It was a totally different business then and I've often thought back to those days. The old grandees of the company were still there.

"Felcourt in the 60s and 70s employed a large number of secretarial staff. It was in the middle of nowhere, surrounded by farmers' fields, and in those days secretaries did not have cars. So Rentokil had a contract with a local coach company which ran coaches all around the local villages picking up staff. It picked up staff in the morning, took them to work and then in the evening it picked them up again and took them home to drop off points in various towns and villages, and it went to the accounts building at Garland Road in East Grinstead as well once that opened. In later years the company had its own coach which Robin Pocock of the maintenance department would drive doing the 'Felcourt run'.

"In my very early days I used the coach as I didn't have a car and it was the only way for me to get to work. There was one time when the coach was going back up into East Grinstead. It was a very heavy snowy winter and the coach couldn't make it up the hill. All of us on board had to get out and push. We managed to get it round the bend until it got traction and then we walked up and met it at the top."

As well as the Rentokil Library series of books, there was also a physical library in the old R&D building at Felcourt, complete with part-time librarian and proper rolling shelves. Employees were able to borrow scientific books, logging them in and out as with a public lending library by signing a little card in the front of the book. Moreover, anybody could order a scientific book on any aspect of the company's work. When it arrived it would be stamped to show it was the property of the Rentokil Library and would be catalogued with information including the date it was purchased and who ordered it. Later, with the advent of the internet, many of the books were given away to schools and the library was converted into the R&D archive, with the sliding shelves used as a repository for the department's reports, documents and workbooks.

Those more used to lean modern-day organisations that outsource non-core areas of business may be amazed at the scope of what Rentokil had in-house during this era. A printing department with its own printing press produced promotional material, technical reports and other documents for the UK and other markets. There were gardeners to tend the grounds, including the vines and kitchen garden from which fresh produce was harvested to be served in the directors' dining room. Keeping this refined eating experience going required its own skilled personnel, as did the staff canteen, which served a three-course meal every lunchtime in two sittings – with a dinner bell alerting everyone to the beginning and end of each. Even at the time, younger members of staff considered this terribly old-fashioned. A display department made perspex displays, while a maintenance department attended to running repairs and undertook tasks such as building stages for events. There was a tennis court in the grounds, a croquet lawn behind the manor house and three fields opposite the frontage of the house were also owned by the company. One of these was used as a sports field.

FILLING UP AT FELCOURT

Harking back to a time when many surveyors operated out of Felcourt, there was still a petrol tank and pump on-site, delivering cheaper fuel than could be bought from filling stations. Whenever employees wanted fuel they were allocated a numbered tag which they took to the pump at lunchtime, where the directors' chauffeur Bill Stone would fill up the car. A bill for the fuel would then appear in employees' wage packets.

Prudent savings made here for company and employee alike would have been particularly welcome at the time of the 1973 oil crisis, which as well as leading to blackouts caused a rapid escalation in petrol prices. Rising energy prices were, however, helpful for Rentokil's home insulation business. The company had exclusive UK rights to Rockwool up until 1978 and the fact that government grants were available for blown and laid insulation between 1976 and 1982 acted as a further stimulus for growth in the Property Care field, where Damp-proofing was similarly thriving due to local authority damp-proofing grants (between 1967 and 1974).

A massive wave of public sector house building during the 1960s and 1970s led to a huge increase in the number of British households living in socially rented accommodation. A peak was reached in 1981, when just under a third of British households resided in social housing and local authority business was of tremendous value to Rentokil. However, the election of Margaret Thatcher's government in 1979 and its swift introduction of a right-to-buy scheme led to a fast decline in the proportion of council houses as tenants took their chance to get on the property ladder.

The decline in council property ownership was to have an obvious impact on the Damp-proofing and Insulation businesses, but the period before this occurred was something of a golden era and work was plentiful. Although staff numbers ebbed and flowed during the 1970s and early 1980s, roughly speaking around 300 people were employed in Woodworm and Dry Rot, another 300-odd worked in Damp-proofing, with a further 100–200 in Insulation.

Local MP Geoffrey Johnson-Smith cut a ribbon to officially open the new accounts building, Rentokil House, in Garland Road, East Grinstead on 13 June 1975. The building housed 180 clerical and managerial staff and, as Rentokil proudly proclaimed at the time, "incorporates an ICL 1902A computer". Yes, just the one! Mind you, this was a mainframe computer, powerful for its time. And it should be borne in mind that the desktop computing revolution was little more than a speck on the horizon: 1975 was the year in which both Microsoft and Apple were formed, and was nine years before Facebook founder Mark Zuckerberg had even been born. Among the other technological marvels at Garland Road was a machine capable of producing 200 cheques per minute. Copies of all the 20-year guarantees issued for woodworm, dry rot, insulation and damp-proofing treatments were stored in a micro-film library. This was no small archive, given that the company had carried out around 350,000 woodworm treatments, 170,000 dry rot treatments and 150,000 damp-proofing treatments. As well as sending out 30,000 invoices and 40,000 statements every month, people at Rentokil House paid the wages of the entire UK workforce. Weekly.

"The payroll department wasn't allowed to be anywhere that people could wander in," recalls Gill Brown. "So again we had to be on the top floor and the post had to be put in this dumb waiter and go straight down to the post room."

Employees were paid weekly by giro cheque. These could only be issued for a maximum of £50, so anyone earning above this amount would receive an envelope containing more than one giro cheque each week. Brown and her colleagues became expert at tallying the amount of envelopes with the number of people on the payroll and at judging by feel alone how many cheques were in each envelope. "I had to sit and count and recount because it wasn't allowed to go in the post until it was right. There were all these manual checks and systems in place. We used to spend a lot of time calling out names to check things because we didn't have computerised systems."

Information flowed at a much slower pace than we are accustomed to today out on the frontline, too. Pest control technicians received their weekly work on a set of job cards sent through the post. At the end of his rounds, a technician would complete his job cards for the day, put them in an envelope and post them to the branch. The procedure was also to ring into the branch every day to find out if there were any problems from customers needing prompt attention. In practice, this often meant going to a phone box once a day, armed with the requisite 2p or 10p coins to make the call. All that a technician did had to be laboriously handwritten onto the job cards which were posted off daily. Carrying a sufficient supply of stamps was therefore imperative.

Pre-computerisation, everything was reliant on bits of paper – Rentokil eventually became one of the largest users of carbon paper. Branch offices featured large boards displaying information about the customers and technicians assigned to them. Making the system run smoothly required no little skill and a talent for forward planning. There were no PDAs and mobile phones to enable smooth, continual communication. Apart from the daily phone call, technicians were out on their own and branch managers had no way of knowing for sure where they were at any given point in the day. Yet there was little in the way of skiving and Rentokil technicians earned respect for their reliability and professionalism.

In 1976 after attending a three-day conference on the future of British industry at which fellow captains of industry had heaped praise on Rentokil, Group Managing Director Teddy Buchan was moved to say: "The name Rentokil stands for ability and honesty. Let us guard it to the point of jealousy, it is our property."

Both Rentokil's reputation and revenues were growing impressively. Group turnover stood at £15 million in 1970, but by 1975 had leapt to just under £40 million. In its 20-odd years in charge, the Westphal-Buchan double act had taken the business forward with great aplomb. Yet it had become apparent that a breath of fresh air was needed. In 1973 Westphal, who the previous year had been awarded an OBE for services to exports, stood down as joint Managing Director at the age of 52, leaving Buchan as sole group MD. This allowed the Australian to spend a bit more time at sea indulging a passion for sport fishing. At the Pest Control Division Managers' conference in December

1973, he was presented with a set of fishing tackle and in the same month a lavish dinner was thrown in his honour at the Savoy.

Bob Westphal, pictured on his motor cruiser The Fabricka, *retired as joint Managing Director in 1973... but was to return to a leadership role within the business.*

The entire Sophus Berendsen board flew in from Denmark for the occasion, at which to much merriment, Westphal was presented with a pink plastic telephone. The phone was not a visual gag chosen at random – it represented the ship-to-shore radio telephone the company had bought for his 48-foot ocean-going motor cruiser *The Fabricka*, which was moored at Chichester. Westphal's other passion outside Rentokil was the fledgling Penshurst vineyard at his farm in Kent, where, in a nod to his roots, he kept wallabies – they once escaped but were quickly rounded up by locals who were encouraged in their outback-style endeavours by the offer of a reward. One of the marsupials, perhaps keen to show its Aussie character, was found outside a village pub. Away from such distractions and with the help of his son David, the irrepressible Westphal was soon producing very drinkable wine for sale commercially.

One of Bob Westphal's passions was viniculture. As a reminder of his Aussie roots, he kept wallabies on his vineyard in Kent. They were known to escape, as reported in the Rentokil Review.

SUCCESSION PLANNING

Yet even with so much else to keep him occupied, he was not leaving the business entirely. The Sydney-born executive remained on the group board and continued in his role as Chairman of the company in the Pacific. His contribution to the business was far from over, but succession planning was now firmly on the agenda. An heir apparent was identified in the shape of Brian McGillivray, a bright young Scottish executive whose star was rising fast. McGillivray began his corporate career as a graduate management trainee at

Anglo-Dutch food and household goods giant Unilever. Then there was a four-year stint at management consultancy firm PA, where he gained accountancy qualifications, before a move to a board-level role at National Freight Corporation where he was responsible for international transport. After another four years he felt ready for a new challenge – just as Rentokil was looking for an infusion of fresh blood at the pinnacle of the organisation.

Brian McGillivray, Chief Executive in the late 1970s.

In May 1976, at the age of 34 and after six months finding his feet at Rentokil, McGillivray took up a Managing Director role and occupied his seat at the group boardroom table. From the outset he made it clear that while he was a fan of the methodical and considerate way Rentokil's employees went about their business, he wanted to inject greater urgency into the organisation, foster more innovation and further boost growth by attracting more people of management calibre into the business.

His strategy certainly delivered growth. Annual results for 1977 saw turnover top £50 million for the first time as the group continued an unbroken streak of setting a new profits record every year since the 1969 flotation, with an impressive £1.4 million leap in pre-tax profits to £8.5 million. In reporting the numbers, the *Financial Times* drew attention to a vast improvement in the performance of the UK business, which at this time accounted for just over half of group revenues: "After three years as a laggard, Rentokil's UK interests last year took off, increasing its profit contribution by 38.5% and accounting for all the group's 19% pre-tax profits rise."

Commenting on the results, McGillivray wrote: "We have done what British industry is always pressed to do – we have increased productivity. In doing so we have passed some of the benefits on to our customers and overall given them better value for their money." But in a somewhat less upbeat continuation of his assessment, he referred to a "mixed picture" and alluded to "difficulties" experienced by some companies in the group. Here was a sign that problems might lie ahead.

WOODWORM AT GATCOMBE

Even so, the business was picking up some noteworthy work. There was woodworm and rising damp treatment for Princess Anne's new home, Gatcombe Park, and a major heritage preservation project to save the roof vault at York Minster from collapse. Just as with Westminster Hall in the days of Maxwell-Lefroy, the culprit was deathwatch beetle. Grubs had caused serious damage to 31 of the 68 bosses studding the south transept ceiling. In addition to conventional spraying, timbers that were structurally sound enough were treated by driving small plastic injector tubes into them. This allowed for a special preservative to be pumped under pressure deep into the wood. Another of the UK's most famous and historic buildings, Banqueting House on Whitehall, scene of the execution in 1649 of King Charles I, was likewise treated for deathwatch beetle.

Cartoon from the July 1975 edition of Rentokil Review.

In Asia, there was the contract to keep one of the world's leading hotels, the Mandarin Hong Kong, free of cockroaches. Guests had been dissatisfied at the number of pests still in evidence while a local contractor fought a losing battle. Rentokil was brought in and after a three-week initial treatment by two servicemen – Yim Man Cheung and Lee Ping Kwan – it was swiftly on top of the problem. To keep it that way, Rentokil ran a hygiene education programme for hotel staff, including a series of lectures in English and Cantonese featuring slides and four colour films. Meanwhile in Belgium, Rentokil secured a three-year contract to control rats in Brussels' 300km sewer network.

Graham Foote, who was responsible for building business across Europe for four years, says that while the Rentokil Group as a whole was repeatedly hitting annual revenue growth targets of 20%, Europe was growing roughly twice as fast, although from a smaller base. Foote reported in to McGillivray and enjoyed working with his fellow Scot, as they shared a "dry sense of humour". For the first couple of years in the job, Foote continued to be based in Glasgow, though the vast majority of his time was spent travelling. For around 48 weeks of the year he would plane-hop to meetings across Europe, then end his working week by filling in his superiors at Felcourt before catching a late flight from Gatwick back up to Scotland. Several attempts were made to lure Foote down to live in the southeast of England to be based out of Felcourt. Reluctant to relocate his family because his two daughters were settled at school, he initially resisted.

"At one point Brian McGillivray said he would buy a jet plane to fly me back and forth to Europe out of Gatwick," says Foote. "That was seriously put on the table because I was covering 11 European countries at the time. And I actually said, 'This is the beginning of the end for a company, Brian, if you start talking about buying private planes'."

Eventually, Foote acquiesced to a move down south. Something had to give with his punishing schedule. There was a moment of clarity when flying to a meeting in Hamburg between Christmas and New Year. No direct flight was to be had from Glasgow, so his route necessitated transferring to a connecting flight in Amsterdam. On one leg of the journey he looked around and realised he was the only passenger on the aircraft. A move to Felcourt suddenly seemed a lot more attractive, especially as McGillivray had promised Foote that he would be first in line to take on the plum role heading up the Pest Control division once highly respected Rentokil veteran Jim McCue retired.

Jim McCue enjoyed tremendous success over many years running Rentokil's Pest Control division.

Despite occasionally indulgent ideas such as buying a private jet, financial management was generally pretty good at the company. Contemporaries speak of McGillivray's sound business knowledge, focus on results and rigorous approach to acquisitions. Investors were understandably keen to stay abreast of company performance and gain insight into likely future developments, which extended to information on R&D activities. Although the R&D function at Felcourt enjoyed a large degree of autonomy, it needed to justify its activities to external audiences as well as the board. "R&D staff had relatively little interaction with top executives," remembers Gordon Wilkinson, who worked in R&D from 1975–80. "We occasionally saw them when they brought visitors across from the main building to be shown around the R&D labs. Peter Cornwell insisted that everyone, from lab technician to PhD researcher, had a two-minute talk prepared so that they could describe what they did, how it fitted in with the work of the department and why it was important to the operating division that they supported. Investment analysts would take the trouble to travel from London to find out about the company's performance and plans."

Invariably, the analysts would depart impressed by the scale, scope and quality of the Rentokil R&D operation. They may also have admired some pristine lab coats. "Back in those days it was a much bigger research facility and we had a lady who came in and washed all our lab coats for us," says Taplin. "She washed them, starched them and ironed them. On a Monday morning you put on a clean lab coat and because it was starched you had to fight to get your way in. You ended up with wings on your arms because you just managed to squeeze your arm through the starch in the sleeves and then you really had to bang around to make it a flexible cotton lab coat."

PLATFORMS AND PINK FLARES

This being the 70s, a decade famous for questionable fashion, Taplin confesses there were times when he went to work wearing pink crushed velvet flared trousers and platform boots. Who said the lab coat look could never be funky?

Taplin began his Rentokil career in the rodent laboratory, reporting to Chief Biologist Adrian Meehan. (Incidentally, Meehan went on to author one of the acclaimed books in the Rentokil Library series, *Rats and Mice*, developed lard-based rodenticide formulations that were found to be very palatable to rats, and regularly turned out as goalkeeper for the Rentokil five-a-side football team.) One of Taplin's early tasks was restocking Felcourt's wild rat pen and he calls to mind a miserable couple of nights camped out behind bales of hay at a local farm, waiting for rats to be caught in the live traps. Still, this was a better experience than one occasion when he was tasked with collecting rats from Felcourt's large rat pen and transferring them via bucket into the four smaller pens used for different trials. Kitted out in Wellington boots, boiler suit and long thick gloves, he pulled apart the bales of straw the rats used as ground-level harbourages and scooped up his quarry. But somehow, one particularly powerful and aggressive rat managed to sink its teeth through Taplin's glove. To his horror, he found himself with a squirming rat hanging off his finger.

The bite necessitated a trip to the accident and emergency department of the nearby Queen Victoria Hospital, East Grinstead, for a tetanus injection. Expecting to be given the jab in his arm, Taplin began rolling up his sleeve. But to make a bad day worse a mischievous nurse insisted that he should have the injection in his bottom. Without any niceties, he was instructed to pull down his trousers in front of other bemused visitors to the hospital. Whether, in hindsight, this was more or less embarrassing than wearing pink crushed velvet flares is hard to say.

Fortunately for Taplin, his career was soon on an upward trajectory and he was put in charge of acquiring new equipment and introducing new techniques at Rentokil's expanding analytical facility. "In those days we were doing a big programme for validating the guarantees on our woodworm treatment. That involved treating blocks of timber and we had what's called an accelerated ageing room. Blocks of timber were placed in that room and were subjected to different wind speeds, different humidity concentrations and temperature to artificially accelerate timber. It was generally accepted that one year in the accelerated ageing room was equivalent to ten years in the loft. So if you left wood in the accelerated ageing tunnels for three years that was essentially equivalent to 30 years.

Wind tunnels in the laboratories at Felcourt were used to conduct experiments on treated timber.

"Timber was constantly being put in there and then being cut up into 1mm layers so we could do a chemical profile of the insecticide through the timber. And the entomologists knew the lethal concentration of the insecticides to wood-boring beetles. I did the analysis and found out the concentration in parts per million of insecticide through the timber. What you could show was immediately after treatment, and after 30 years, the profile as the insecticide moved through the timber. The profile changed. As a result, the company was able to increase its guarantee from 20 to 30 years. And we looked at new potential insecticides as well." The new 30-year guarantee, which was well-received by mortgage lenders as well as homeowners, was introduced in 1976. It made the lead story in the June issue of *Rentokil Review* under the headline 'Guaranteed to 2006 AD', which lent an almost sci-fi quality to the year in question.

Meanwhile, outside in the grounds, timber was under scrutiny as well. In an area that with morbid humour came to be known as the graveyard site, pre-treated timber posts were put into the ground to observe the rate at which they rotted. As Rentokil had a subsidiary in Fiji, pre-treated posts were also shipped out there to be exposed to tropical conditions and then sent back again when it was time for analysis. As Rentokil owned the pre-treatment business Celcure – a specialist in the copper-chrome-arsenic (CCA) process to improve the durability of timber for external use – being timber-proofed against decay was often referred to as being "Celcurised". The All England Show Jumping Course at Hickstead was among the customers to invest in Celcurised wood for its grandstand and members' stand. Among the other materials regularly tested at Felcourt in the 1970s was cavity wall insulation. One such test involved building a double-leaf brick wall in a lab. The wall would be jointed with lime mortar, calibrated to allow water penetration, sealed and the cavity filled with an insulant. Then rain showers of increasing severity were simulated in the lab, culminating in a six-hour storm with 60mph gale-force winds. Afterwards, insulants were examined to find out which were best at preventing water from crossing the cavity.

Wood from Fiji was by no means the only 'import' at Felcourt. The English country pile was home to a population of black rats (*Rattus rattus*) in addition to its stock of the more common brown rat. Black rats are notoriously difficult to breed in captivity as they have a nasty habit of eating their offspring if disturbed, but Rentokil enjoyed considerable breeding success and held a back-up colony for London Zoo in case its black rats were ever wiped out. They lived in the 'rat house', which before the arrival of mains electricity at Felcourt had been the shed for the generator that provided power for the main house.

RENTOKIL FILM UNIT

It's important not to overlook the huge contribution towards embedding expertise within the business made by the Rentokil Film Unit at this time. Its corporate educational films were made to exacting standards and imparted technical knowledge quite brilliantly. The British Film Institute has catalogued these documentaries, although sadly many of the original films themselves now appear to be lost. Back in the 1970s, long before moving images were easily shareable and accessible online, Rentokil put a huge amount of effort into distributing and showing its documentaries. Company figures reveal that in 1977 there were 7,365 showings of Film Unit documentaries, up more than a thousand on the previous year. This meant that on average 27 films were shown every working day!

While in cinemas *Star Wars* was the undisputed blockbuster smash of the year, Rentokil's most popular film was *Of Mice and Men*, which was shown 774 times. It may not have had Darth Vader, light sabre battles or the Death Star, but it did describe the very real health dangers posed by mice in catering facilities and hospitals. *The Intruders*, a classic early 1960s documentary on cockroaches, was the second most widely shown Rentokil film that year. Newer work matched these high standards, however. The film *Biology of Termites* picked up a Gold Award at the 1980 British Sponsored Film Festival.

Although film showings continued on an upward curve for several more years, the age of video had arrived and Rentokil was not slow off the mark in exploiting this new medium. In 1977, Tony Bye was hired as A/V Manager with a brief to set up a new Video Unit. Before long he found himself planning, scripting, directing, lighting, filming, editing and distributing 20 programmes a year with the help of just two assistants. The Rentokil Video Roundabout series tackled topics as diverse as technical training, pest biology and behaviour, health and safety, sales techniques, customer relationship management and even public speaking. Professional television reporters were often hired as presenters to guarantee the quality and credibility of the output. In a 1983 interview, Bye extolled the impartiality of experienced reporters because "they can get away with asking the Chairman questions that ought to be asked". Nevertheless, Bye was careful to ensure the journalists' personalities did not get in the way of or overshadow a story. Wherever possible his aim was to present staff with people they knew or could easily relate to.

The Manx Pied Piper, a video on Rentokil's rodent control work on the Isle of Man, put a compelling case for greater use by local authorities of private pest control services – and won the International Television Association Award of Excellence. A video with outstanding footage of rats on farms was used as a key element of a drive to up the amount of work gained from the agriculture sector and there were also instructional videos giving step-by-step guidance on the right way to clean steak bar griller plates and bakery equipment. Sometimes videos were also used as a sales aide. For example, a video showing the cavity wall insulation process was played on stands at home improvement shows where Rentokil was exhibiting and was also reformatted for Fairchild Super 8mm desktop projectors so that it could be used as a selling demonstration in presentations to individual specifiers.

For several years, the Film and Video Units co-existed, the former still run out of Kirkby. Yet the convenience of video meant its days were numbered as plainly as the pages of a script.

Acquisition continued to be a fundamental dimension of the group's growth strategy and in 1978 Rentokil turned its attention to the humidity of Florida. The group bought up the imposingly named Mighty National Exterminators Inc., a Fort Lauderdale-based company that had started in business in 1939. Offering pest control and fumigation services, Mighty National had 140 employees, a turnover of US $3.7m and a reputation for dealing effectively with termites, armyworms and chinch bugs, as well as pests more familiar to those in less sultry climes.

But expansion in the US at this point did not go as smoothly as Rentokil would have hoped and was one of a number of problems causing tension in the boardroom. A loss-making venture in the security market, plus concerns raised by some executives as to McGillivray's style of leadership, ratcheted up the misgivings. Added to this, McGillivray did not always see eye-to-eye with Bob Westphal, who in 1978 had returned to a more central role in the business as Group Chairman. An uneasy situation eventually became untenable. All of which was a great shame, as McGillivray was widely respected and many colleagues admired the way he worked.

"Brian had been instructed by the board to personally investigate what had gone wrong in the States and what should be done to put matters right," recalls Ken Bridgman, who was on the board at the time. "Brian wouldn't do that – he sent one of his lieutenants to produce the required report. I think that decided the board that Brian couldn't be controlled and it would be best if he left. A pity, because he was a clever man."

Long-serving executive Ken Bridgman joined the group board in 1964.

McGillivray departed in 1981, as the official line had it: "by mutual agreement following difference of opinion on policy". Bridgman was appointed Managing Director on a temporary basis with a brief to dispose of some poorly performing businesses and recruit a replacement for McGillivray. Westphal affixed the role of CEO to his position as Chairman, likewise with half an eye on identifying a successor.

Disagreements notwithstanding, McGillivray had done the business proud. In the last year of the 1970s, Rentokil's worldwide sales were £73.2m, up 21% on 1978. The majority of revenue still came from the UK, but Europe – which employed around 680 people, and where the Netherlands was the largest market – contributed 21.5%. Australia and the Pacific accounted for 8.5%, America 6.5%, Africa 4% and Asia 2%. Among notable international highlights was a major AUS $600,000 contract to fumigate Parliament House in Brisbane; a strong performance from Sweden in industrial wood preservative and timber treatment plants; a contract to treat stations on Hong Kong's new Mass Transit Railway against cockroaches one month before opening; and healthy growth in export sales of wood preservative products from Celcure Malaysia.

This 1978 press advert for Rodine C by the Product division appeared in British national newspapers in a £20,000 campaign.

In the UK, the Pest Control, Hygiene and Sanitact businesses all posted record figures in terms of both sales and profits. On the building services side, the Woodworm and Dry Rot and Insulation divisions were also buoyant but Damp-proofing struggled due to "poor quality of enquiries". Meanwhile in the Products division, national and trade press advertising campaigns were launched to support sales of Woodworm Fluid and Rodine C to wholesalers, hardware stores and other retailers, while the national sales team dealt both with Rentokil-branded products and the Tutor range of fire blankets and protective clothing. CCA-based wood-preserving products, of which Celcure A and Boliden K33 were the leading examples, were sold in over 25 countries for use in vacuum pressure impregnation plants. Many of these were constructed at a factory in Oxfordshire controlled by the Wood-preserving division. It was estimated that the Wood-preserving division was selling enough wood preservative each year to pre-treat all the timber needed to build 220,000 three-bedroom houses or 100,000km of 1m high interwoven fencing panels.

YEW LODGE

At this time, Rentokil showed how seriously it was taking staff development and its ability to provide customers with unmatched expertise by purchasing at auction a site for use as a residential training centre. Yew Lodge was located close to Felcourt. Back in the days when Henry VIII appropriated vast swathes of land from the church, it was part of the manor of Felcourt granted to Sir John Gresham. For most of the 19th century, the site was referred to as Little Felcourt Farm but it was eventually renamed in honour of the vigorous yew tree in its grounds, thought to be over 500 years old. It was incontestably a magnificent place to come for training. Entering through a dark oak door, visitors would walk across the mosaic tiled floor of the entrance lobby into ground floor rooms panelled with golden oak that gave the feel of a Jacobean interior, a retro style in fashion in the Edwardian era. Contemporary art nouveau elements and motifs were also to be found in the designs of the fireplaces.

Despite all the growth and forward-looking investment in training, at the outset of the 1980s the culture of Rentokil and its approach to conducting business would still have been recognisable to previous generations of employees. UK Technical Services Manager Nicholas Donnithorne paints a vivid picture of what it was like when he came to the business in June 1980. "When you joined R&D you would be taken round and introduced to everybody. You were taken upstairs to be welcomed by Doctor Cornwell. I can still remember his words to me which were: 'Right Nicholas, you will hear me called many things – Doc, White Death, White Mischief etcetera. You will call me Dr Cornwell.' I could live with that because you know where you stand." In Cornwell's case, that was not always at Felcourt. In addition to his role as Director of R&D, the no-nonsense scientist with his distinctive shock of white hair travelled frequently because he was responsible for Rentokil businesses in the Caribbean, Asia and Africa (except South Africa), parts of the world where he had conducted entomological research prior to joining Rentokil in 1963.

A good proportion of employees at this time had a military background and wore shoes that were immaculately shiny thanks to traditional spit and polish. Even without catching sight of the shoes, their bearing was usually a giveaway. There were also a few people with experience in the plantation business, among them Adrian Tyrer, who became one of the Managing Directors of group subsidiary Rentokil Limited in 1973, with responsibility for Pest Control, Hygiene, Wood-preserving, Products and Exports – while Vernon Hancock oversaw Damp-proofing, Woodworm and Dry Rot, and Insulation. Tyrer, who arrived at the company in 1955, had previously spent eight years running a tea plantation in Ceylon, now the independent nation Sri Lanka.

Meanwhile, the car park at Felcourt was a sea of white Vauxhall Chevettes. A popular prank was to hand some car keys to a new recruit and send them off on a spurious mission to retrieve something from a white Chevette, without telling them the registration. Of course, the company joke went that you could have a Chevette in any colour... as long as it was white. This echoed another old quip from the British Ratin days: you could have a suit in any colour, as long as it was grey!

Newcomers to clerical jobs at head office were still taken by colleagues to see the rat pens in the grounds as part of an informal initiation. There were also beehives, which remained in place until some suffered a direct hit from trees felled by the great storm of 1987. And to enhance the buzz, colourful characters were not in short supply. Jo Ward of the rodent unit, who gloried in the nickname Ratty Mouse, was known for joyfully riding her horse into the grounds of Felcourt from time to time.

"We had a proper old-fashioned switchboard with long wires," says Donnithorne. "Three ladies sat there and I knew them all very well. If you wanted to make a personal phone call, what you used to do was ring up the switchboard and say, 'I'd like to make a call'. They'd say: 'Rightco, when you dial the number we'll put the stop-clock on for you'. And it was about 2p a minute, a sensible fee. When you'd finished your call you left your desk, walked down to the ladies and paid them your money. It was amazing to watch them connecting and disconnecting the cables to put people through."

The technology may sound quaint, but Rentokil was now a fairly big business. Lying just around the corner, the appointment of a new CEO with a seemingly insatiable appetite for delivering growth on a major scale meant it was going to get a whole lot bigger.

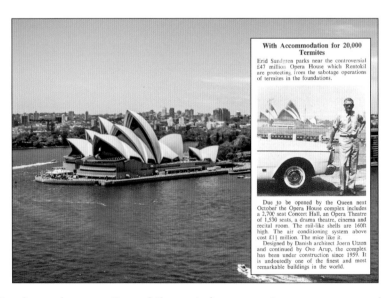

In the early 1970s Rentokil carried out termite treatment at the iconic new Sydney Opera House.

A JAK cartoon in which Rentokil is a vehicle for political satire.

Cartoon by JAK (Raymond Jackson), published in the Evening Standard on 27 September 1974. Courtesy of the
British Cartoon Archive, University of Kent, www.cartoons.ac.uk.

LUDVIG AND SARA ELSASS FOUNDATION

The flotation in 1969 of Rentokil Group – and Sophus Berendsen several years later – brought huge financial rewards to the Elsass family. A lot of that money has been put to extremely good use.

During his long entrepreneurial career, Ludvig Elsass worked hard to provide for his children. One of his main aims was to ensure that his daughter, Helene, would be able to live in comfort. Helene Elsass (1921–2003) was born with cerebral palsy (CP) and her severe physical disabilities meant she needed a wheelchair her entire life. As the business thrived, Helene's father made provisions for her future.

By the early 1970s, Helene found herself sitting on a fortune and decided that she wanted to spend it on helping others with CP. With that purpose in mind, in 1975 she set up a foundation bearing her parents' names.

"My grandfather decided that my aunt should never be in need of care," says Helene's nephew Nick Elsass. "When she died she left nearly £200 million to the foundation."

Today, Nick Elsass is Chairman of the foundation, which funds research, provides support and campaigns on behalf of people with CP. Its biggest spending commitment is the Helene Elsass Centre, opened in Charlottenlund, north of Copenhagen in 2007. This centre of excellence offers a wide range of services, from courses for parents whose children are newly diagnosed with CP, to occupational therapy and research into the impact tailored exercise programmes and special diets have on the condition.

HEC also works with hospitals and municipalities on developing best practice in relation to CP and collaborates closely with the University of Copenhagen in areas such as neuroscience.

"I tell everybody who wants to know about this fantastic story where some commercial money has been put into use in a philanthropic charity way," says Nick Elsass. "Rentokil was such a big part of our family life. I was brought up with it. My father [Adam Elsass] said in one of his many farewell speeches that Rentokil was his fifth child. Also, my mother's brother-in-law was Teddy Buchan, who used to be the Rentokil Managing Director. I even worked there for a while in the 1970s, selling pest control in the southeast of England, and it was a wonderful experience. So all my life I've heard about it, lived with it and now through the foundation we can help people with cerebral palsy to a better life."

Portrait of Ludvig Elsass by Testrup Boysen.

Courtesy of Elsass Foundation.

THE ESSENTIALS

1969 – Rentokil Group floats on the London Stock Exchange.

1970 – Boosts Hygiene capabilities with two acquisitions: Thames Service and Hygiene Services (Scotland).

1973 – Termite treatment to the foundations of the newly completed Sydney Opera House as guided tours and test performances take place ahead of its official opening.

1974 – First Overseas Managers Conference on 'doing things the Rentokil way' held at Felcourt.

1975 – Oil giant Shell's London headquarters, Shell Centre, treated for a biscuit beetle plague.

1977 – Group turnover tops £50m.

1979 – Pest control contract for new 52-storey NatWest Tower, at the time Britain's tallest solid structure.

CHAPTER
SIX
Aiming High

In the mid-1980s, Rentokil was involved in a landmark project in Norway that was of immense cultural significance.

Norway is the only country in Northern Europe where medieval wooden churches survive in significant numbers. Its magnificent stave churches (*stavkirke*), built in the 12th and 13th centuries, are rightly seen as national treasures. The grandest of all, Urnes Stave Church, was constructed in circa 1150 and is lavishly decorated with intricate wooden carvings depicting a variety of real and mythical creatures in a style that draws on both Nordic and Celtic traditions. Indeed its historical significance and exceptional craftsmanship is so great that it features on the UNESCO list of world heritage sites.

Of course, the wooden construction of these churches means they are vulnerable to damage. When the threat posed by wood-boring insects became evident, the Norwegian authorities acted. In August 1985 Rentokil was commissioned by Norway's Cultural Heritage Department to rid three stave churches on Sogn og Fjordane on the country's west coast of house longhorn beetles (*Hylotrupes bajulus*). The magnificent Urnes was one of the trio of treasures to be treated, together with Hopperstad and Undredal. All dated back to the 1100s. A team led by technical expert Colin Smith worked with extreme caution to play its part in preserving these unique Scandinavian architectural masterpieces.

"The stave churches and the Viking ships are among the most important historical monuments in Norway," says Dr Jørgen H. Jensenius, an architect who specialises in surveying and documenting Norway's medieval wooden churches and who previously worked for the Norwegian Institute for Cultural Heritage Research in Oslo. "If something happens to them, many Norwegians will feel that it affects their very identity. When Fantoft Stave Church was burned down by Satanists, local people stood crying outside the fence for weeks." Arsonists had destroyed Fantoft in 1992; its reconstruction was completed in 1997.

A Norwegian stave church wrapped in plastic for a week-long fumigation.

The 1980s assignment involved a team of eight people who spent eight weeks travelling around the stave churches in camper vans. The treatment method was gassing with phostoxin, a gas now forbidden in Norway. Each stave church was wrapped entirely in plastic and fumigated for one week. "It was important to pack the church well enough in order to keep the gas sealed inside the building," says Rentokil Initial Norway Managing Director Espen Agnalt.

As the house longhorn beetle can be difficult to destroy, Rentokil placed different pieces of wood throughout the sealed buildings. Radiographic techniques had previously been used to establish that these pieces of wood contained live beetles. After the fumigation, this 'indicator' wood was sent to the UK for analysis, which confirmed that all the insects had been killed. Then the stave churches were treated with woodworm fluid to prevent further infestation.

Great care was taken in executing the complicated preservation work on Norway's stave churches because these buildings are such an important part of the country's cultural heritage.

As this was late summer, many tourists came to watch the work in progress. Others had travelled to see the stave churches unaware that restoration work was being carried out and were disappointed to find these buildings under wraps. One member of the Rentokil team, Jan-Erik Glæsel, couldn't resist giving a misleading answer when an American tourist asked him why the monuments had been wrapped in plastic. He told the curious onlooker that the stave churches were always wrapped up before wintertime because monuments in Norway had to be protected before the cold set in. The tourist thought this perfectly logical.

MR 20 PER CENT

It wasn't only vertiginous wooden church spires that were aiming high. As the 'can-do' decade of the 1980s got into its business-friendly stride, changes were taking place at the top of Rentokil.

CEO Sir Clive Thompson oversaw an era of rapid expansion.

Clive Thompson arrived as a director in 1982, stepping up to the role of CEO the following year. Thompson had begun his corporate career in

1964 as a marketing trainee at Anglo-Dutch oil giant Shell. After a stint in pharmaceuticals as General Manager at Boots East Africa, he was running Jeyes' successful aerosol-packing business before he turned 30. By the age of 35, the high-flying businessman was on the board of Cadbury Schweppes, eager for ever bigger challenges and confident he could deliver eye-catching growth for Rentokil year after year.

Thompson would go on to spend over 20 years at the helm of the business and delivered growth on an unprecedented scale. A probing *Management Today* profile described his style as "methodical, disciplined, exact, the sort of man who worries at an answer like a dog gnaws at a bone, constantly coming back to it, making sure he has covered all the right points". He was certainly direct, and his hunger for scaling up the business was impossible to ignore.

Of his time running Rentokil he says: "I took the company, as Chief Executive and with personally a strong marketing pedigree, from being a predominantly UK business in woodworm, dry rot, insulation and timber preserving with £100 million sales employing about 5,000 people in 1982 to a company, 20 years later, with leading businesses in security, hygiene, facilities management and parcel delivery through over 400 acquisitions, employing 100,000 people in all the major developed economies of the world, with a consistent use of the Rentokil and Initial brands worldwide and with sales approaching £3 billion."

There's no contesting the scale of change that took place during the Thompson era. He was given the nickname "Mr 20 Per Cent" by the media after he set Rentokil the target of increasing company profits by 20% every year. During the 80s and much of the 90s, Rentokil enjoyed huge success and high regard while riding a wave of expansion.

TV botanist David Bellamy with Rentokil's former Scientific
Director Dr Norman Hickin at the Interbuild show in 1983.

Despite Thompson's massive influence, Rentokil was in no way a one-man show. The group's UK operations were restructured into three divisions in 1983: Contract Services, under Managing Director Graham Foote; Property Care, run by David Chenery; and Timber Preserving and Products, headed up by Mike Waddell. As well as Pest Control, Rentokil's Contract Services Division included Office Cleaning, sanitary disposal specialist Sanitact, and Hygiene. The latter, headed up by General Manager Doug Manning, was a well-established business long before Initial came into the group. It employed around 240 staff who worked across three main areas: catering hygiene business Catercleanse; washrooms; and the supply of electrostatic air filters. Beyond these core areas, the business would take on a variety of other jobs, small and not so small, from shampooing carpets to cleaning silos.

Property Care was created on 1 April 1984 by amalgamating Woodworm and Dry rot, Damp-proofing and Insulation. The thinking behind the move was to put in place a more integrated, easier-to-access offering for customers and keep a lid on costs by avoiding duplication of roles, for example by having one surveyor who could cover both Woodworm/Dry Rot and Damp-proofing. Some staff were laid off because of a cross-over in roles but there was also an expansion in sales and management staff. Unfortunately the timing was not the best. "There was the mid-80s downturn," says UK Technical Services Manager Nicholas Donnithorne. "It also became apparent that having both survey and sales teams was wrong."

DIY woodworm products piled high at the warehouse in Kirkby, June 1981.

The Property Care side of the Rentokil business, such a powerhouse over the previous 20 years, was finding life in the 1980s a whole lot tougher. "Come 1986 we had a combination of a drop to 20 branches, redundancies, the slow loss of two-man teams and surprisingly large retirements as the pioneer staff reached retirement age," says Donnithorne. "Plus of course the start of more competition of new firms mostly staffed by our redundant but highly trained staff." In late 88/89 more rationalisation was required to stay afloat and Property Care was further pruned back to five service centres, with additional losses of staff.

Despite the setbacks and downsizing, Property Care continued to deliver a first-rate service and received plenty of support from Rentokil Group both in terms of driving performance and safeguarding the wellbeing of employees. "With Property Care I got involved when our technicians were spraying woodworm fluids which were organic solvent-based," says Rentokil analyst David Taplin. "I could actually measure the concentration of organic solvent in the air that our technicians were exposed to. We even took samples from within their respirators to confirm that what they were breathing in was safe." Taplin also provided technical service back-up for commercial customers such as timber yards that were using Celcure pre-treatment products. For example, deploying air-sampling equipment to show there was no danger to workers from the arsenic used as the main constituent in the CCA process and writing reports containing best practice and safety recommendations.

As it happened, Rentokil had become an innovator in the field of arsenic acid production. In 1979, when a shortage of supply drove up costs, a decision was made to look into the feasibility of Rentokil developing its own arsenic plant. In conjunction with academics at Liverpool University, Rentokil carried out a series of laboratory trials and plant pilots, all the time mindful of the significant health and safety concerns of working with arsenic. A safe new process of producing arsenic acid was pioneered and within two years and at a capital cost of under £500,000 a plant at Kirby was producing 3,000 tons of arsenic acid annually – nearly all of which went into making 6,000 tons of CCA paste. This impressive scientific and commercial feat was recognised in 1983 when Rentokil was presented with the Queen's Award to Industry for Technological Achievement.

Colourful Rentokil Review *cover celebrating the company's international footprint, Christmas 1983.*

Across the group there were lots of other positives to report. The overarching theme of the 1984 annual sales conference was 'customer care'. Almost 800 staff attended the event at Harrogate Conference Centre at which the Rentokil Customer Care Campaign was launched. Its key messages were that everyone across the business had to put more effort into giving customers a better deal and that from the first point of contact to the last, quality of service should be worthy of the Rentokil name.

HOSPITALS CAN DAMAGE YOUR HEALTH

US operations, which early in the decade were racking up a significant loss, were back in the black by 1985 and delivering annual profits of over $1m. In the UK, Rentokil was actively campaigning for legislative change. When 19 elderly patients at Stanley Royd Hospital, Wakefield, died following a salmonella outbreak due to failures in basic food hygiene, Rentokil was one of the driving forces behind a successful campaign by the British Pest Control Association (BPCA) and other bodies to abolish crown immunity, which had prevented hospitals and other public buildings from being prosecuted. Lifting crown immunity ensured that hospitals were legally obliged to implement the requirements of environmental health officers. The 1985 BPCA report, *Hospitals Can Damage Your Health*, provided specific examples of failings and gave details of the sort of pests that were causing serious problems.

Speaking in the House of Commons in support of the campaign, Labour MP Anne Clwyd said, "The British Pest Control Association, in its report, asks: Would anyone with any sense serve a sick patient food that has already been contaminated with organisms that cause food poisoning, boils, abscesses, typhoid, pneumonia, dysentery, worms or jaundice? Would that sensible person bandage a wound with material exposed to contamination from the contents of drains, sinks and sewers? Sensible or not, this is what is happening in hospitals up and down the country. The Association also drew attention to a survey of 360 nurses conducted by *Nursing Mirror* last year, which showed that 88% had seen cockroaches in their hospitals, 53% had seen rats or dead mice, and 51% considered their hospital unclean. That is the evidence of people working in those hospitals. It is clear that hundreds of NHS hospitals fail to meet accepted hygiene standards, and pose serious hazards to patients and staff."

Crown immunity was lifted from UK hospital sites in 1986 and the Department of Health introduced a model contract for pest control. Rentokil's work through the BPCA was a huge contributory factor in bringing about these changes. The *Hospitals Can Damage Your Health* campaign was honoured as winner in the public affairs category in the Institute of Public Relations Sword of Excellence Awards. The award was presented to Rentokil's longstanding Director of Public Relations, Peter Bateman, immediate past President of the BPCA, who had personally played a major role in the report and the wider lobbying activity.

Meanwhile, as the company continued to grow, the need to manage the Rentokil brand carefully became ever more apparent. Charles Grimaldi, who started as Marketing Manager for Woodworm in 1982, set about making sure that branch managers were provided with consistent presentation materials for use when talking to building society managers, solicitors, estate agents, surveyors and other key stakeholders. Previously, Grimaldi recalls, it had been "completely uncontrolled" with branch managers making use of a ragbag of different materials for their presentations, "as likely to be granny's projector as anything sensibly designed". Concerned that different parts of the company were ploughing their own furrow in terms of how they presented the Rentokil brand, Grimaldi plucked up the courage to raise the issue with Clive Thompson, even though they had barely spoken before. To his relief, Thompson was receptive to his ideas and soon Grimaldi found himself reporting directly to the CEO in a group-wide marketing position – charged with ensuring brand coordination and consistency. Thompson, a knowledgeable marketer himself, was "a very good mentor and tutor," says Grimaldi.

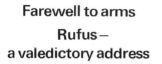

(Left) A farewell to arms. Rufus, the knight who served valiantly as Rentokil's brand icon for many years, is retired from active service. (Right) New logo, April 1980

To reinforce the quality of Rentokil's service and the prestige of its name, Thompson and Grimaldi decided to incorporate the Royal warrant into a redesigned company logo. For obvious reasons, tremendous sensitivity was required. Making a royal endorsement seem shabby was not an option. Working with designers, 'mood boards' were used to fine tune the typography and achieve the right balance between the Rentokil name and Royal warrant symbol. An underline was introduced to add substance and ensure the logo didn't seem too 'floaty'. New corporate identity guidelines were drafted to make consistent implementation as straightforward as possible. Due to his rigid enforcement of the logo guidelines, Grimaldi came to be affectionately known as 'LogoCop'.

Meanwhile, the spirit of intra-company sporting rivalry that had been a feature of the 60s and 70s was still going strong. On a scorching Sunday afternoon in 1984, a Rentokil staff XI played cricket against Clive Thompson's XI, comprising senior figures from the group including Graham Foote, Doug Manning and David Chenery. The staff XI, captained by the head of Rentokil's Video Unit, Tony Bye (a fine name for a cricketer!), prevailed by 65 runs to earn the Ted Buchan Trophy. Thompson was reportedly "brilliantly caught out" for 15 and overall his team had no answer to the accuracy of Tim Dighton, who ended the match with impressive bowling figures of four for six.

Playing on Thompson's team that day were the head of Rentokil's South Africa business, Ed Meyer, and his boss Jim Morton, the Regional Managing Director responsible for the USA, Australia, New Zealand, South Africa and Fiji. In February 1986, Morton had the pleasure of presenting Meyer with the "Rentokil £1m flag" at a celebratory dinner dance at the Belmont Hotel in the Western Cape town of Ceres, awarded in recognition of Rentokil South Africa breaking the £1m profit barrier in 1985. To mark the achievement, Rentokil Group sponsored a weekend of festivities for South African employees, including a bus tour through the winelands of the Cape, with a stop-off for wine-tasting at the Blaauwklippen estate and a picnic lunch at the 300-year-old Boschendal vineyard. A highlight of the dinner dance was a song written for the occasion by Sales and Marketing Services Manager, Vince Angus-Leppan, who sang it, accompanied on guitar by colleague Ruth Kritzinger, to a jovial black-tie-wearing audience. One line in his catchy chorus – "We're here because we made a mil" – went down almost as well as the bottles of wine on the tables.

A keen viniculturist himself, Bob Westphal would doubtless have approved of the winelands tour. In May 1987, the charismatic Australian retired as Chairman after 37 years with the company. Unlike his earlier 'retirement' in the 1970s, this time it was for good. Back in 1968, Westphal was interviewed for a Central Office of Information film. Asked to define the secret of growth, he had replied: "Firstly, hard work. Secondly, a good team of people who enjoy doing their work. And finally, a commitment to doing a really first-class job for the customer."

It's a fair encapsulation of his philosophy and at the same time a convincing rationale for Rentokil's ongoing success. The Rentokil brand was now famous internationally and often cited as a synonym for pest control by commentators, cartoonists, comedians, politicians and ordinary members of the public in snappy remarks and biting witticisms. At the Nelson Mandela 70th birthday concert staged at Wembley Stadium in 1988, reggae act UB40 performed 'Rat in mi Kitchen', leading compere Lenny Henry to quip, "If I had rats in my kitchen, I'd call in Rentokil." A nice gag, and further brilliant exposure for Rentokil – considering the Mandela concert attracted a worldwide TV audience estimated at 600 million viewers.

GENUINE CAMARADERIE

As the 1990s dawned, the culture and spirit of previous decades was still very much in evidence. Rentokil Senior Legal Counsel Yvonne McCabe, who came to the company in 1990, was struck by the camaraderie and sense of fun of the time. Managers used to sneak wine and stilton out of the annual executive Christmas lunch at Yew Lodge for more junior members of staff to enjoy at the payroll Christmas party. Adding to the amusement, Head of Payroll Maureen Collins and Sarah Steer of the credit control team would write a satirical festive pantomime every year that was staged at Garland Road.

"Senior managers like Graham Foote came out and made idiots of themselves, either dressing up as women or whatever," says McCabe. "There were numbers like 'The Felcourt Walk', which was a bastardisation of 'The Lambeth Walk'. It was done in the canteen so they were all being made up in the kitchen. Some of them seemed to really enjoy getting made up. It was good that you could laugh at the senior managers who took part. That was largely down to Maureen and Sarah, who would start writing it in October. My boss Gareth Brown played Rab C. Nesbitt one year. It was very tongue in cheek." Perhaps Brown brought more allure to the role than is commonly associated with the slovenly, opinionated Scottish character, or indeed pantomimes in general: several years later he and Sarah Steer got married.

Despite the example set by Bessie Eades, in the early 90s the upper echelons of management were male-dominated, as were many of the frontline services such as Pest Control. There were exceptions, including at least one family where both husband and wife worked as Rentokil pest controllers, with his and hers matching vans parked side by side on their drive at home. It was in the higher ranks of the organisation where the shortage of women was more evident.

Yvonne McCabe joined as a B-grade Manager, but promotion to A-grade status in 1993 meant that as part of the senior management team she was permitted to use the directors' dining room at Felcourt by right, even though she was based at another building. This raised the hackles of one chauvinistic senior executive who preferred the testosterone-heavy status quo. When McCabe got wind that this rather unreconstructed senior colleague had threatened to walk out of the dining room if she were to go there, she and some of her senior colleagues, including her boss Gareth Brown and his boss Robert Ward Jones, made a point of going to Felcourt for lunch. In the event, the sexist dinosaur lacked the confidence to make good on his threat and lunch for McCabe and her supportive entourage was very satisfying. All good fun but also emblematic of a long outdated culture that prevailed in the company at the time of separate dining rooms segregating bosses from other employees.

Away from gender politics, the 1993 hostile takeover of Securiguard for £75.2m took Rentokil into the UK and US manned guarding business. By the end of the year, group turnover had risen above £600m for the first time (up almost 27%) and profits were up 20% to £147m. The UK was still Rentokil's largest market by far. While margins were improving at mature UK businesses and turnover growth was certainly decent – up 8.2% in UK Pest Control, 10.6% in Hygiene – it was not rising as fast as elsewhere in the group. In part fuelled by acquisitions, turnover shot up 93% to £91m in North America and rose 27% to £109m in the combined Asia Pacific and Africa region.

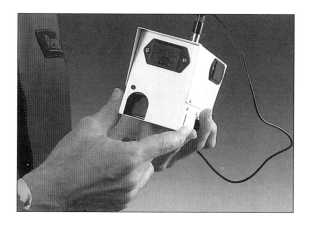

Launch in 1992 of Mouse Alert, the 'ultimate' in mousetraps. The most up-to-date mousetrap of its time was able to radio a control centre, set off a flashing beeper and dial the pest controller's phone.

Michael Gibbes, Regional Managing Director of Asia Pacific and Africa, congratulates Bill Crosby, Managing Director Rentokil Australia, for winning the Rentokil International Trophy, awarded to the overseas company with highest profit in the group, in 1992... for the fourth time in succession.

MULTI-STEP REBRANDING

Diversification and geographic expansion was part of a strategy articulated as developing Rentokil as an "environmental service company to industrial and commercial customers" in the major economic groupings of Europe, North America and Asia Pacific.

With new businesses joining the group thick and fast, a multi-step rebranding strategy was devised to integrate them under the banner of the Rentokil name. "We tried to do it in a manner that was considerate, to bring people in rather than keep them apart from us," says Grimaldi. The progression went: Company X, acquired by Rentokil; Company X, part of Rentokil; Rentokil, previously Company X. From the outset it was made clear to the former owners and senior managers of incoming businesses that this would be the formula. What was up for discussion, dependent on the circumstances and depth of culture at acquired companies, was the time frame for each transition.

As acquisitions took Rentokil into new areas and the nature of the group's business became more diverse, inevitably it became harder to explain what the company did. At financial presentations, questions were frequently asked about the group's traditional businesses such as Pest Control and Property Care. Grimaldi helped Thompson rehearse answering these questions in a way that opened the door to talking about other areas of the business that were less familiar to the investment community "without appearing impolite". Another subtle investor relations technique was to position tropical plants all around the venue to plant the seed (as it were) in analysts' minds that they should be asking questions about the Tropical Plants part of the business.

The mood throughout the company was buoyant, although one legal issue was causing concern. A man called William Gaskill initiated litigation in which he alleged that Rentokil's use of the chemical lindane in woodworm treatment at his home caused him to develop aplastic anaemia. This is a rare but potentially fatal blood disorder which the plaintiff developed during childhood, though by the time of his action he had been free of the condition for over five years. Rentokil opted to fight the lawsuit and vindication came when the high court ruled in its favour. In a nutshell, the plaintiff was unable to show that his exposure to lindane had caused aplastic anaemia.

WINNING ADMIRATION

For Rentokil, 1994 was to prove a year in which its reputation was burnished. The December 1994 issue of *Management Today* named Rentokil Britain's most admired company. Glaxo and Marks & Spencer occupied second and third spot.

Rentokil topples Glaxo to become Britain's most admired company, in rankings published by Management Today.

"Rentokil's place at the top of the table seems well-deserved," wrote the magazine. "Its financial virtues are by now renowned; phenomenal long-term growth in profits and earnings per share, strong cash flow and, despite an almost constant stream of acquisitions, a never-depleted store of cash."

Needless to say, Rentokil exploited the 'Most Admired' title in its marketing and staff communications throughout 1995.

"We produced a button badge for every member of staff in the UK which caused enormous interest," says Grimaldi. "The beauty of it was that those service guys who liked the badge wore it every day. And those guys who didn't like it would tell everybody they got this pathetic metal badge. But in the process they were reinforcing the message about us being the best company. So we didn't care either way."

The 'Voted Britain's Most Admired Company' message was painted on every van in the fleet – and stayed there for three years!

In the mid-1990s, the accolade of being Britain's most admired company was put on prominent display as part of Rentokil's van livery.

Not only did the endorsement act as a powerful marketing message, it also worked as a psychological reminder to technicians that their customer service was now being judged against the highest standards. Meanwhile, the company continued its growth march, with turnover for 1995 up 18% to £860m and pre-tax profits up 21% to £214 million. It was in good shape to maintain the acquisition spree that had seen 200 companies snapped up in a decade.

IN PURSUIT OF BET

However, the next significant acquisition Thompson had in mind was considerably bigger than any company Rentokil had bought before. In fact, the target was far bigger than Rentokil itself. Roughly three times the size of Rentokil, business services company BET was a competitor across a number of markets.

Originally called British Electric Traction, BET could trace its roots back to the late 19th century and was once a major player in public transport. It was involved in the electrification of tramways in British city centres before moving into operating bus and tram services. After divesting itself of its public transport interests, BET transformed itself into a conglomerate made up of over 50 businesses spanning cleaning, personnel services, catering, textiles services, electronic security, plant services, education and training and leisure services. One of its outstanding brands was Initial, which it acquired in the 1980s, although it had previously had a minority shareholding in the business stretching back to the 1950s. Initial began trading in 1903 when American entrepreneur A.P. Bigelow started a towel-rental service for London businesses. Initial Towel Supply Company was so-called for the simple reason that towels were embroidered with customers' initials – personalised service. Over the years, the business grew and diversified into broader washroom and hygiene services.

When in February 1996 Rentokil's overture for a takeover at 190p per share was rebuffed by the BET board, the bid turned hostile. Rentokil's strategy was to talk up the good fit between the businesses and present the takeover as an earnings enhancing move that would not rack up enormous rationalisation costs. At the same time, it accused BET's management of failed strategies and destroying shareholder value. The cover of the document outlining Rentokil's 'Increased and Final Offer for BET' twisted the knife, showing the BET share price standing at 167p on 2 April 1991 but languishing at 139p on 13 February 1996. Rentokil prevailed. BET was successfully acquired on 26 April 1996 for £2.2 billion.

Cartoon satirising the hostile takeover battle for BET.

The acquisition was a coup for Rentokil. It should not be forgotten that although Rentokil was a PLC with a tremendous degree of autonomy, in the run-up to the deal it was still majority owned by Sophus Berendsen. Although the Danish parent was seen very much as a sleeping partner and was wholeheartedly supportive of the takeover in its public utterances, behind the scenes there were some misgivings about the scale of the transaction. "When Rentokil acquired BET there was a big uproar in Denmark because in Denmark and Scandinavia one cannot buy a company and get a net negative capital, which Rentokil had the first year when they acquired BET," says Nick Elsass, who was on the Sophus Berendsen board from 1990–2002. "We spent a lot of time, Clive [Thompson] and I, trying to make the Danish board understand that of course you could do it if you had a plan and the back-up from banks and from the old BET."

One of the largest takeovers in British corporate history was completed, leading to the creation of the world's leading business services company with annual turnover above £3 billion and a workforce of 150,000 employees.

May 1996 issue of Rentokil Review, *celebrating the £2.2bn acquisition of BET.*

In the wake of the deal, Thompson wrote to staff: "During the 80s and 90s the Rentokil brand name has been very successfully transferred to stand for quality service in such areas as Tropical Plants, Office Machine Maintenance, Healthcare and Medical services and Security. However, despite our belief in Rentokil as a great brand name, even we have to reluctantly accept that it could be inapplicable in some areas and that it might be difficult to use it for catering, for example. The Initial brand name therefore provides exciting opportunities to develop two brands, Rentokil and Initial internationally."

In retrospect, it's probably fair to say that the Rentokil brand had already been stretched too far. Heritage, familiarity and relevance made it a perfect brand for pest control and a good fit in the field of Property Care; but while there was a smattering of logic in applying the 'protective' aspect of its values to sectors such as security, common sense should have prevailed to put the brakes on such a move. Was Rentokil really a good name for a team of armed guards? Did it shout tropical plants likely to remain in the best of health? Even the strongest brands can appear absurd if extended too far. That's why toothpaste brand Colgate's foray into ready meals was doomed to failure. And why Coors mineral water, Bic disposable underwear, Cosmopolitan yoghurt and Harley Davidson perfume, despite being genuine, real-life brand extensions, seem utterly ridiculous.

At a group level, the BET deal led to the creation of the Rentokil Initial corporate name still in place today. The logo, which has since been reworked into a simplified double-decker, displayed the Rentokil name in red while Initial was rendered in blue. A red/blue virtuous circle appeared in front of the names which were underlined in their opposite colours. Clearly, the thinking was to demonstrate that these two parts of the enhanced business were being treated as equals.

Rentokil Tropical Plants' first Chelsea Flower Show gold medal, 2001. Rentokil enjoyed considerable success at the RHS Chelsea and Hampton Court shows and BBC Gardeners' World Live over the following years.

ATLANTA OLYMPICS

While getting the corporate identity straight was important, what really mattered was serving customers. And there were plenty of achievements out on the frontline.

Rentokil became an official supplier to the Atlanta 1996 Olympic Games. USA Pest Control secured the contract to keep the 80,000-capacity Olympic stadium free of rodents, cockroaches and ants, while Tropical Plants as sole provider of interior landscape services had the job of supplying and maintaining almost 20,000 plants and flowers. Separately, there was work specifying and servicing plants for giant cruise liners such as the *Oriana* and *Sun Princess*.

In Australia a pest control contract was picked up for the iconic Sydney Harbour Bridge. The pylons at each end, used by the Roads and Traffic Authority, provided a refuge for rats and cockroaches. Cate Philp, who secured the contract, had the dubious pleasure of an awkward site inspection. "Believe me, you haven't really lived until you've experienced crawling between steel girders, with a railway line a few inches above your head and a 70-metre drop to the water below," she told colleagues.

Over in Guyana, South America, Rentokil faced the tricky task of treating the high court building in the capital Georgetown for a termite infestation. The entire exterior wall of this historic 19th century wooden building required treatment, and to make the job more challenging it was not possible to do any work when the court was in session. Consequently, sub-slab drilling and injecting was carried out after hours and on Sundays. There was no way Rentokil was going to let the termites get away with it – although perhaps the insects might have done had they retained the services of Guyanese lawyer Lionel Luckhoo, who in 1990 made it into the *Guinness Book of Records* as the world's most successful lawyer after securing a scarcely credible 245 consecutive murder acquittals as a defence barrister.

To add to his enormous satisfaction at completing the BET acquisition, Thompson was knighted by the Queen for services to industry. Then in 1998 he took on one of the most prestigious roles in the business world as President of employers' body the Confederation of British Industry (CBI). Truly, his career had hit a highpoint. Yet trouble was approaching. "The BET acquisition was more than we were able to absorb, to be truthful," concedes former Rentokil Director Graham Foote, who retired from the business in 1998. Thompson's remarkable 16-year run of achieving profit rises of 20% or more had hit the buffers.

The Right Honourable Michael Portillo MP, at the time Secretary of State for Defence, sitting between receptionists Dawn Lucas and Clare Stevens while visiting Felcourt in the mid-1990s to attend a CBI luncheon hosted by Clive Thompson.

An August 1999 headline in *The Economist* expressed the state of affairs succinctly: 'Missed the 20%'. Having been forced to issue its first ever profits warning in May 1999, alerting investors to the fact that the company would not hit the magical 20% mark long taken for granted, Rentokil Initial's share price took a beating.

"In retrospect," wrote *The Economist*, "Sir Clive should have dropped his 20% target sooner. His defence is that, 'inevitably, you had to carry on until you failed.' But the suspicion is that Rentokil increasingly substituted a target for a strategy." After years as a City darling, the criticism was painful to take. Hindsight is a marvellous thing, but clearly it would have been better had some of the non-core businesses that came as part of the BET acquisition been sold off sooner.

A new era of retrenchment and corporate belt-tightening had arrived. In certain parts of the business, this was taken to extremes. Ronan

Greany was bemused by the local take on keeping costs firmly under control when he arrived in Asia to manage the Philippines office. "There was a General Manager's personal stock of toilet paper in the Philippines; everyone else had to bring their own except for me. And the roll of toilet paper was duly presented to me on arrival. Austerity was taken to mean that the company wouldn't provide drinking water, so they would boil water on the stove. That was the local interpretation of the austerity measures. They wouldn't buy pencils for the people to work with but they'd buy the lead for the pencil as long as the colleague brought his own pencil in. There was stuff that was unbelievably extreme. I said: 'Stop! Let's have water, this is ridiculous.'"

With the arrival of the new millennium, Rentokil Initial decided to right the ship by slimming down and concentrating on seven businesses: Security Services, Facilities Management, Hygiene Services, Pest Control and Property Care, Parcels Delivery, Conferencing and Tropical Plants. Businesses in sectors such as Temporary Help, Bulk and Liquid Haulage and Construction Plant Rental were sold off. This large-scale restructuring involved the disposal of roughly one third of the company's business activities by turnover. "There were a number of businesses [that came with the acquisition of BET] that we had no experience of at all," says Charles Grimaldi. "We were jolly good at organising thousands of people, blue collar workers; very good at that. Now a trucking business or a crane business is more about the hardware you've got than lots and lots of people. Therefore we should have shed those much faster."

Disposals at this time included the sale of the British timber-preserving business to American group Osmose for £4.2m. Rentokil Initial also conducted a massive share buyback programme. This included purchasing Danish company Ratin A/S, which held 32% of its shares. Ratin A/S was spun out of Sophus Berendsen in 1998 purely as an investment holding company for equity in Rentokil Initial. The long years of Danish ownership that had delivered so much in terms of growth and financial stability were conclusively at an end. From March 2000 through to the end of 2003, Rentokil Initial spent almost £1.9 billion buying back shares. All such share buyback purchases, said the 2003 annual report, were "earnings per share enhancing."

In January 2003, James Wilde succeeded Thompson as CEO, with Thompson assuming the position of Chairman. The slimmed-down group now employed around 93,000 people and remained profitable. Yet the 1.7% rise in pre-tax profits achieved in 2003 was a long way short of what investors desired. And given his 20 years at the top of the organisation, it was no surprise that Thompson's influence remained strong. Murmurings of discontent became harder to ignore. Whether it was time for change at the top was becoming an increasingly frequent topic of conversation.

Matters came to a head in May 2004 and news of Thompson's departure was released at the same time as a profits warning that indicated profits would be coming in at under £350m rather than the £408m analysts had been expecting. Deputy Chairman Brian McGowan replaced Thompson as Chairman with immediate effect. In its story headlined 'Rentokil's Thompson toppled in board coup', *The Daily Telegraph* quoted McGowan on Thompson's reaction to the fait accompli: "I think he was astonished. He said he admired our courage, which I thought was pretty good stuff."

This was by no means the end of the boardroom blood-letting. Two months later CEO James Wilde was also asked to 'fall on his sword', with McGowan asserting that the business was in need of a fresh pair of eyes. That fresh pair of eyes came in the shape of Doug Flynn, an Australian who had held senior roles at media companies News International and Aegis. Flynn arrived as CEO in April 2005.

Doug Flynn was appointed CEO in 2005.

IN A BUBBLE

Despite the boardroom upheavals, Rentokil was still delivering work to the highest standards.

In 2005, the Norwegian Royal Family discovered an infestation of clothes moths at the Stiftsgården Royal Palace in Trondheim. The palace, built in 1774, is both a museum and an official royal residence, containing irreplaceable royal coronation chairs and crowning relics. These were under threat from the ravenous insects. The State Facilities Management Company and Norwegian conservation experts agreed that Rentokil Pest Control was the only company with the reputation and technical knowledge to take on such an important project.

Colin Smith, International Technical Director at Pest Control, flew to Norway to carry out a survey at the palace. He decided that Rentokil's unique controlled atmosphere technology (CAT) would be the best way to eradicate the insects without damaging the antique furniture. CAT is an environmentally-friendly method of pest treatment, using either nitrogen or carbon dioxide. Infested items are placed into airtight, laminated aluminium bubbles into which one of the gases is pumped. In this instance, Rentokil used five nitrogen CAT bubbles, each measuring approximately 60 cubic metres, to treat over 300 items of furniture. The furniture was then returned to public display in the palace. As with the stave churches 20 years earlier, Rentokil was playing a vital role in preserving Norway's heritage. Shortly afterwards CAT was used to treat furniture at UK stately home Longleat House, near Warminster, Bath. Only this time the culprits were common furniture beetle (*Anobium punctatum*) and Australian spider beetle (*Ptinus tectus*).

Other earlier uses of the CAT bubble technique included treating 43,000 museum artefacts stored in the Jurong Repository in Singapore – among them rickshaws, delicate linen, wooden statuary, books and furniture – and preservation of a masterpiece by the tempestuous Italian artist Michelangelo Merisi da Caravaggio.

The Taking of Christ (1602) is one of the great oil paintings by the exponent of the *chiaroscuro* style, the most famous artist of his time in Italy who became notorious for the violence of his life as much as for his eye for composition and the finesse of his brushwork. The multi-million pound painting is one of the great works on display at the National Gallery of Ireland in Dublin. But it was at risk of damage when it was found that biscuit beetles had got into the glue at the edges of the canvas.

Thankfully, experts from Rentokil in Ireland were able to remove the threat without harming Caravaggio's beautiful painting in any way – killing off all stages of the pest by sealing the masterpiece in a nitrogen-filled CAT bubble for a month.

The whereabouts of this great artwork had been unknown for around 200 years until in 1990 it was recognised in the Dublin Jesuits' dining room. In 2010, *The Taking of Christ* was put on temporary display in Rome as part of a major retrospective exhibition at the Quirinale to mark the 400th anniversary of Caravaggio's death. In the *New York Times*, under the headline 'An Italian Anti-Hero's Time to Shine', Michael Kimmelman wrote of the glorious paintings and "mobbed" galleries due to an outbreak of *Caravaggio-mania*.

The threat of biscuit beetle damage is one thing, opportunistic assaults by leading business figures quite another.

After only four months as Rentokil CEO, Doug Flynn found himself having to defend a takeover approach fronted by Gerry Robinson, the high-profile former boss of Granada, through his takeover vehicle Raphoe Management. It was claimed that Robinson stood to gain £55m over five years had his move been successful, but while the financial media lapped it up and speculated gleefully, a lack of detail about his intentions led the Takeover Panel to set a one-month deadline. As a report in *Forbes* magazine put it, "Quit playing games, UK Takeover Panel Tells Robinson." The deadline arrived with no sign of a proposal.

The 'will-he, won't-he' shenanigans of Robinson's posturing had been an unwelcome distraction for Rentokil Initial at a time when confidence was at a low ebb.

Flynn set about making changes, further focusing the company with the sale of guarding and electronic security businesses, and the sale of Felcourt, replacing it with a modern head office in London, shared with Google – a company with which Rentokil would work closely in the not-too-distant future. For many employees past and present, waving goodbye to Felcourt and all it signified was an emotional wrench.

"The last morning we worked there I was in before it was daylight – this was April time," recalls Gill Brown, who was based at Felcourt for eight years. "I went in really early and the whole house was moon-lit. I could see the moon and hear an owl and it was lovely. I just stood and admired the house."

Much as Karl Gustav Anker-Petersen and so many others had done.

It was time to modernise and move on.

THE ESSENTIALS

1983 – Clive Thompson appointed CEO.

1985 – Fumigation of the stave churches in Norway.

1986 – Moves into 'office horticulture' with purchase of Plants at Work.

1993 – Acquisition of Securiguard Group for £75m.

1994 – Treats soil around the new Petronas Twin Towers, Kuala Lumpur, to keep what was then the world's tallest building free of termites.

1995 – Britain's Most Admired Company, according to *Management Today*.

1996 – £2.2 billion acquisition of BET brings the Initial business under Rentokil ownership.

1998 – Major three-year mosquito control contract for the Maremma region of Italy.

2000–2001 – Group slimmed down with former BET businesses sold representing a third of group turnover.

2003 – Rentokil Tropical Plants wins gold medals at Hampton Court Flower Show and BBC Gardeners' World Live, and a silver gilt at Chelsea Flower Show.

2004 – Deputy Chairman Brian McGowan replaces Sir Clive Thompson as Chairman.

2005 – Called in to protect 300 items of priceless antique furniture threatened by clothes moths at Norwegian royal residence Stiftsgården.

2005 – Doug Flynn appointed CEO.

2006 – Felcourt is sold.

CHAPTER
SEVEN
Renewed Focus

I n 2006, Rentokil returned to the acquisition trail in a major way for the first time since the BET deal a decade earlier. This time, however, the move was highly focused – in terms of both the geographical and business fields of operation. The target company was Pennsylvania-based family-owned pest control business JC Ehrlich, the fourth largest pest control company in North America.

An Ehrlich vehicle.

The business was set up in 1928 by insecticide salesman Julius Ehrlich after he moved to Reading, Pennsylvania. Over the years the company grew its footprint to the point where at the time of the acquisition it had 42 branches across seven East Coast states, dealing with rodents, termites and carpenter ants. It posted sales of US $124m in 2005 – more than four times the level of Rentokil's existing North American pest control business. Rentokil paid $142m (£80m) to buy the business, run by two of Julius Ehrlich's great grandsons, Victor Hammel and his brother Bobby.

The 2006 purchase of US pest control business JC Ehrlich marked a return to major acquisitions for the first time in a decade.

Rentokil Initial Director of Marketing & Innovation Stewart Power joined the company just weeks before the deal was finalised and happened to be in the US at the time the transaction was completed – earlier than originally expected in order to prevent news leaking out. "I was in the really privileged position of being invited to join Victor and Bobby Hammel for dinner in a restaurant the night the deal was hopefully going through. And the phone call came through to say the money has been wired: millions and millions of dollars wired across to the two of them. Neither of them drink and it was a dry restaurant. We were sitting there and it was a case of them raising a glass of sparkling water and saying, 'Good, we're part of Rentokil, let's carry on now.' They were absolutely not fazed by the money at all.

"Next morning the news broke and there was a whole series of things going on in their office about the announcement. But I was the only person from Rentokil in the country at that point and they invited me to come in. As I pulled up they had the Union Jack flying on a flag pole – they had two flag poles and had the Stars and Stripes at the same height, which apparently they shouldn't have done. I was welcomed in by Victor and got the red carpet treatment. I was made to feel so welcome. Being the first Rentokil person entering what became the head office of Rentokil North America and everything that acquisition offered to the group was incredibly special. That was our foundation for what has now become our biggest pest control operation with a lot more scope to become bigger still."

Hot on the heels of the Ehrlich deal came the $38m (£19m) purchase of Presto-X, a business covering the central US States. Further acquisitions, small and large, have added scale and breadth to the North American Pest Control operation in recent years, notably a first-time entry into Mexico with the 2011 acquisition of Tetengo – headquartered in Monterey, but with a network of 15 branches across the country – and the 2012 purchase of a high-quality business in California, Western Exterminator Company. In the case of the latter, Rentokil stumped up $93m for the pest control company to Hollywood stars which had revenues of $149m per annum.

The upshot of this busy deal-making has been the utter transformation of Rentokil's pest business in North America – the world's largest pest control market. Whereas in 2005 it was a relatively small player with 16 branches, 300 employees and annual revenue of $27m, today the picture is different. In 2014 it was operating out of over 200 branches, employed 3,500 people and delivered $468m in revenue. More than 17 times the revenue of ten years earlier.

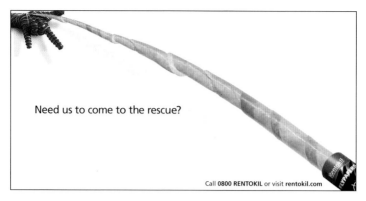

Need us to come to the rescue?

Call **0800 RENTOKIL** or visit **rentokil.com**

Who needs Spider-Man when you can call on the Pestbusters? A billboard campaign pays homage to the web-slinging superhero.

While smaller acquisitions in the US and the businesses in Canada and Mexico have been rebranded as Rentokil, the strength of reputation and recognition enjoyed by Ehrlich, Presto-X and Western in their regional markets means they still trade under their historic brand names – while the Rentokil name is used for national accounts and as the overarching brand for colleagues internally. For instance, in consumers' eyes Western is strongly associated with its famous top-hatted Little Man with a hammer logo.

Rentokil Vice President, Human Resources for the Americas, Scott Cook, says that what the company looks for in acquisitions – and what those businesses that are already part of the group share – is the loyalty of their employees and a willingness to go the extra mile on behalf of customers. "Part of what makes people stick here is that they genuinely believe in serving customers and what has kept them from going somewhere else is maybe that other companies don't value service in the same way," he says. "It's not about what the management says and expects; it's in the DNA of the folks that are doing it."

While acquisitions continued, Doug Flynn's strategy to re-focus the group was also underway. In 2006, manned guarding and a number of smaller businesses were exited, generating disposal proceeds of £144 million, while the sale of the Initial conferencing and electronic security businesses for over £600m were to follow not long after.

TAKING LESSONS INTO OTHER MARKETS

The scale and international reach of Rentokil means it is able to bring a huge amount to the businesses it buys in terms of systems, expertise and career development. But it is also very much a two-way street. Countries in which termites are a problem, such as the US and Australia, present significantly bigger residential pest control opportunities than those that do not, such as markets in Northern Europe.

America's termites, you don't stand a chance.

"We're learning from our US and Australian colleagues about how to do a better job of delivering consumer pest control," says Stewart Power. "That's a positive. Some of it has come out of Australia, but it's only been since 2006 when we got up to scale in the US that we suddenly realised what an opportunity there is to learn in that way. Taking those lessons back to other markets, even if we are not applying them in the termite space, means we have a more approachable brand and have learnt how to approach our residential customers a bit better."

Eye-catching outdoor advertising in New Zealand created by Auckland agency Republik. Special reflective inks became visible at night when illuminated by car headlights and streetlights, cleverly 'highlighting' the campaign message.

More innovative advertising from Auckland, which is breezily nicknamed 'The City of Sails'.

Australian colleagues helping Rainforest Rescue to protect the natural habitat in Queensland.

That said, Rentokil has always been a market-leader at giving customers what they need. In Hong Kong, where it has been operating since 1964, Rentokil signed a two-year contract in 2007 with the government of the Hong Kong Special Administrative Region (HKSAR) to provide pest control technologies and services. Valued at HK $280 million (£17.9m), it was the highest value contract of its kind ever signed by the government of the HKSAR. In the same year, Rentokil significantly boosted its presence in China through the purchase of a majority stake in Beijing Taiming Technology, which was renamed Rentokil Taiming.

With the Beijing 2008 Olympic Games looming, China was in the eyes of the world as never before. The games saw 10,500 athletes compete in 28 summer sports spread across 37 different competition venues. Over 28,000 journalists descended on the Chinese capital and more than 100,000 volunteers helped out as the games trumped expectations and billions of viewers watched on TV or digital media. But beyond athletic achievements and wall-to-wall media coverage, a fascinating behind-the-scenes story was unfolding. Hosting the games was not only a catalyst for investment in sport and transportation infrastructure, it also delivered a boost for public health as the Chinese authorities took steps to improve food and water safety. According to the IOC, a new disease prevention and control system was implemented in Beijing, 100,000 Chinese chefs took food cleanliness classes and 200,000 additional food inspectors were hired.

Technicians at the Beijing Olympics, with the landmark 'Bird's Nest' national stadium in the background.

Rentokil played its part as one of the 'preferred suppliers' of pest control around the city of Beijing. Key services provided by Rentokil included managing pest-related issues during the peak breeding season for cockroaches, flies, mosquitoes and rodents as part of the Beijing Pest Control Emergency Support Team. One hundred and fifty Rentokil pest-control technicians provided daily inspections and treatments where necessary. The company also evaluated over 800 technicians and assisted in the development of a series of pest control technician training courses for the Beijing Pest Management

Association as part of its role as the only foreign pest control company to be one of the master training instructors.

The Beijing team ready for action.

Beijing has been described as the first "social media Olympic games" and in line with growing expectations for fast, tech-driven solutions, Rentokil deployed some formidable technology of its own, including the PestNetOnline reporting system designed to manage pest control for any organisation, highlight pest control risks and provide effective pest-prevention recommendations. The system enables customers to view total pest control coverage across their estate and monitor activity at individual pest detectors. Barcodes are allocated on the basis of risk and when data is uploaded, for example when a technician visits, customers receive an instant email report. In this age of accountability, the system provides an audit trail for regulatory bodies. By identifying any problems or weak spots, customers can be more proactive in their pest control management, cutting out unnecessary site visits.

Rentokil's new smart mousetrap RADAR (Rodent Activated Detection And Riddance) was also used in Beijing, integrated with PestNetOnline.

RADAR uses innovative technology to deal with mice in a humane and eco-friendly way. Two entrances – one at each end of the unit – allow mice to run through its passageway. When a mouse breaks two consecutive infrared beams, it trips a circuit that immediately closes both entrances, and carbon dioxide is released. Carbon dioxide use is recognised as one of the most humane ways to kill a mouse, and Rentokil is one of the few companies in the world allowed to use it as a rodenticide.

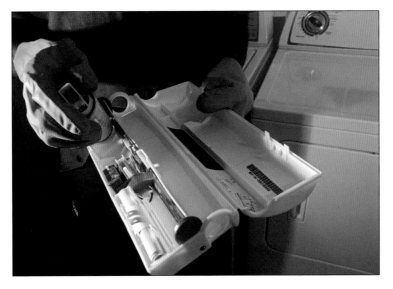

The innovative RADAR trap.

Unobtrusive, effective and with a simple design, RADAR exemplifies high-quality innovation. Yet even with RADAR's many obvious virtues, the pest control regulatory environment is so stringent that it took three years of hard work making a case to the authorities to secure approval for this revolutionary product. Few rivals would stand much chance of bringing a product of this kind to market. And no other company in the pest control sector can rival Rentokil in terms of know-how. That is why in 2008 when, as part of a brand refresh, the company asked its customers what

Rentokil meant to them, the answer came back loud and clear: experts in pest control.

This hardly came as a surprise. In the previous year, the decision had been taken to rebrand Rentokil Tropical Plants as Ambius. The new name, derived from the word 'ambience', was designed to reflect the fact that the world's largest provider of plants for commercial spaces had a mission to create the best possible environments in which people can work and relax. Undeniably, it's a far more appropriate name for a business of this kind than Rentokil. Shedding the association with an area of business in which it had never sat comfortably tightened up the focus of the Rentokil brand and brought more clarity to the marketing around it.

At a group level Rentokil Initial had problems. A £27m swing from profit to loss at the City Link courier business and a series of profits warnings triggered what the *Daily Mail* termed a "night of the long knives" in the boardroom, led by Senior Independent Director, Peter Long. On 20 March 2008, CEO Doug Flynn was ousted. A new senior leadership team had been lined up and so, at the same time, it was announced that the triumvirate of executives who had succeeded at ICI would take the helm: Dr John McAdam as Chairman (subject to shareholder approval at the next AGM), Alan Brown as CEO and Andy Ransom as Executive Director, Corporate Development. Brian McGowan, the Chairman, had already announced his intention to step down no later than the annual general meeting and also resigned on 19 March. He had been Director for 11 years and Chairman for four.

Despite facing the challenge of the global economic downturn, the revamped executive team brought stability and continuity back to the business by executing a turnaround programme that once again placed greater emphasis on core route-based categories such as Pest Control, Hygiene and Workwear.

Alan Brown served as CEO of Rentokil Initial from 2008–13.

PROUD TO WEAR THE SHIRT

But strategy is nothing without delivery. And there were signs that the Pest Control business could perform much better in its traditional UK heartland, and indeed elsewhere, if some underlying issues were addressed. Phill Wood, who in 2009 took on the Area Managing Director job for UK, Ireland and the Baltics after three years in a European region role, held the view that the business had to an extent lost touch with what had made it great in the first place: frontline technicians and surveyors.

"The years between 2000 and 2005 in the UK were a fantastic era for product innovation," says Wood. "That's where mouse RADAR came from, that's where PestNetOnline came from, the first websites

– it was an incredibly strong period for hard-edged development. But somewhere along the line, the organisation lost something. It probably became too product-centric. Our products and services were so much better than anybody else's that I think we drifted into a view that that in itself would solve things."

Wood resolved to address the situation by stepping up training and restoring pride in the job. An after-dinner speech by New Zealand rugby union legend Sean Fitzpatrick provided inspiration for the latter. Fitzpatrick, one of the All Blacks' greatest ever players and team captain for five years, spoke of the enormous sense of belonging and pressure to do well that comes with pulling on the famous international shirt. Sportswear brand Adidas encapsulated that pride in a commercial called *Captains*, which featured one famous former All Black captain after another donning the iconic shirt and ends with the resonant line: "The legacy is more intimidating than any opposition."

It occurred to Wood that Rentokil's long track record and reputation as an academy for the best technicians in its field was similarly worthy of great respect. He launched the 'Proud to Wear the Shirt' campaign to focus attention on the pride technicians and other employees should feel about the job they do – making sure that he too proudly sported a Rentokil shirt. Other managers followed suit. "We should respect the fact that it is our technicians who actually make this company great. Rentokil is about frontline technicians and surveyors."

But there was much more to it than symbolism. The technician manual, for a long time regarded as sacrosanct, was rewritten to better reflect the demands of the 21st century. And in response to feedback from frontline staff that they wanted better training and more professionalism, the structure of training was systematically reformed. "We revisited all of our training," says Wood. "We introduced four levels of training in the UK that are third-party certified and then we tied that up with the money. So if you pass the exams, you get more money. We ended up putting thousands of training days into the business, taking Rentokil back to this era of technical expertise and making it an academy company once again. And we started investing big time in field biologists: my Rentokil business in the UK has more qualified field biologists then every other pest control company added together."

This drive to professionalism is increasingly leading major customers to specify minimum qualification standards – which is good news all round. The Rentokil Guild of Technicians Award was revived to further celebrate achievement. And in an additional development, Rentokil launched a graduate scheme in 2011, with 50 science graduates recruited in the first few years. Graduate entrants are given a thorough grounding in the business, spending one year as a technician and the second as a surveyor. The first graduate trainee to have made it to branch manager level is a woman and around one third of graduate scheme members are female. The business also proactively looks to hire ex-military personnel, who are valued for their discipline, smartness, good communication skills and experience of dealing with stressful situations. Here, at least, there is little difference between Rentokil today and the business of previous generations.

IN TRIBUTE TO MATT WOOD

It should have been just another normal day at work in central London. But for colleagues at Rentokil's Wendle Court office in Vauxhall, and many others besides, Wednesday 16 January 2013 became something altogether sadder and more traumatic. Shortly after 8am in poor visibility, a helicopter collided with a construction crane and plummeted onto the street below, outside Rentokil's office. The helicopter pilot, Pete Barnes, was killed instantly. So too was an unlucky commuter on the ground who was simply making his way into work.

Shocked employees at Wendle Court swung into action and conducted a head count. It soon became apparent that every member of staff was accounted for bar one: Matt Wood. When he wasn't reachable on his mobile, it was at first presumed he was on the Tube, on his way to work. But as the morning wore on, with calls to Matt still going unanswered, the worst fears of colleagues and family were confirmed.

Matt's brother Darren also works for Rentokil, but at a different location. A few days after the crash, he paid a moving tribute to his sibling on BBC Radio 2's *Jeremy Vine Show*. On the morning of the disaster, he told listeners, he had received a text message from Matt just before 6.00am. Matt wanted to know how Darren's 11-month-old son Flynn, who was in hospital at the time, was doing. Darren was touched, though not at all surprised, that his brother was so concerned and had taken the trouble to get in touch early in the day. Fortunately, he was able to reassure Matt, who was a doting uncle, that his nephew was fine. The brothers agreed to speak later. Tragically, it was not to be.

As Alan Brown, CEO of Rentokil Initial said at the time: "We can confirm that our colleague, Matt Wood, was fatally injured in the helicopter crash as he was walking to our office in Vauxhall. Matt was well known to all of us who visit the Vauxhall office, including myself.

He was in every respect a warm and generous man and a cornerstone of our team in Vauxhall. We extend our deepest sympathy to Matt's family and to our colleagues in Vauxhall who, though safely evacuated, will be deeply affected by this tragic accident."

The boardroom at the Camberley head office was renamed in Matt Wood's honour. Gone far too soon, but certainly not forgotten.

WELL-MANAGED TRANSITION

When Alan Brown stood down as Rentokil Initial CEO in 2013, a rigorous succession planning process was undertaken and the board decided that Andy Ransom, one of the three former ICI executives who'd joined the company in 2008, was the right person for the job. He knew the company well and had extensive international business experience. This transition was a welcome improvement on the boardroom upheavals that had seen previous CEOs reluctantly deposed against a backdrop of investor unease.

During his tenure as CEO, Brown succeeded in laying solid foundations for future success. His focus on customer service and operational excellence was accomplished in highly challenging circumstances, coinciding as it did with the Great Recession and financial market turmoil. Brown was a popular figure amongst staff, known for his quick wit and passion for success. Once market conditions improved, City Link – which had struggled to hold on to customers – was sold. The so-called 'problem child' had been offloaded. On his departure the company praised Brown's "significant transformation" of Rentokil, particularly growing its international presence in such countries as Brazil, China and India.

Rentokil Initial Chairman John McAdam and Chief Executive Officer Andy Ransom.

Andy Ransom took charge of a company with a solid platform to build upon but still with much to do. His plan was to focus the company on its core categories and to introduce a simpler geographical business structure. He introduced a differentiated approach with every operation mapped to one of four 'quadrants', each with its own strategies to maximise growth. The aim was simple – grow the business in faster-growing countries such as Asia, Latin America, the UK and North America, while reducing exposure in tougher markets. The days of large-scale restructuring were over. It was time to deliver and to do so at pace.

In his first two years, the company made good progress, including the disposal of the site-based facilities management business, Initial Facilities. This was not a great fit for a business pursuing a route-based strategy – moreover, it occasionally presented an obstacle to other parts of the group in terms of winning business from rival facilities management companies. Its £250m sale in 2014 was an eminently sensible move. There then followed a series of acquisitions across growing economies. In 2012 the business had less than a third of its sales coming from growth or emerging markets; by the middle of 2015 over 60% of sales were coming from these faster-growing economies. The pace at Rentokil was hotting up.

Just as in the early days, Pest Control was again the biggest part of the business and a key cornerstone of the growth strategy, generating 41% of group revenue (£740m) and 44% of group profit in 2014. After cutting debt by £260m, the figures for 2014 showed the business with its lowest net debt for 15 years.

Also in line with decades past, Rentokil was continually applying its expertise to assignments of huge national or even international significance.

A case in point was vital work on clipper ship the *City of Adelaide*, launched in 1864. The only other clipper ship of its kind in existence is the famous *Cutty Sark*. But while the *Cutty Sark* has been a major London tourist attraction on display in a purpose-built dry dock in Greenwich since the 1950s, the *City of Adelaide* spent many years lying in disrepair on the banks of the River Clyde in Glasgow. This was despite the fact that around 250,000 Australians can trace an ancestor who migrated to the country on the passenger ship during the 25 years it sailed between European ports and South Australia. In light of the significant part the ship played in Australian history, a 'Bring Her Back' campaign gained enough support to secure the clipper's return to Australia to become a visitor attraction. However, given that the ship was filthy, in poor condition and being used as a roost by pigeons, there was a huge amount of work to be done before it could be moved and meet Australia's stringent bio-security requirements.

A team of Rentokil experts removed the birds and their droppings from the clipper. Galvanised steel mesh and 19mm polypropylene netting were used to prevent the pigeons from re-entering. Taking a systematic approach to the cleaning operation, the team cleaned and disinfected the main deck, bottom deck and top deck quarters. The hull and other parts of the exterior were cleaned with pressure washers and sterilised to prevent any organic material from reforming. Pest control steps were also taken, from spraying with insecticide to putting down bait boxes right the way through – following stringent biosecurity procedures to make sure that the *City of Adelaide* would not be carrying any undesirable passengers to Australia.

Rentokil's work passed inspection by an official from the Australian government's Department of Agriculture, Fisheries and Forestry (DAFF) with flying colours. A metal cage was then built around the clipper so that it could be loaded onto a barge for its long journey to the other side of the world.

PROJECT SPEED

For colleagues working inside Rentokil, one of the stand-out changes of recent years has been the process of transforming Rentokil into one of the world's largest users of Google technologies (social media, video calls and apps), which began with the widespread adoption of Google's suite of online tools and the launch of what internally was given the code-name Project Speed.

Today, many employees are based at home, hot-desking or out on the road. Virtual communities are used to share knowledge and best practice.

Sales leads are posted on Google+ social media community boards along with actions pursued. Managers can post out daily updates, highlighting star performers and providing relevant information. It is also a far more transparent process.

Technicians now post pictures of issues they face such as pest identifications, either to seek advice or to gain further information. In the past, they may have had to return to the office or ring the technical desk to ask for help in identifying, for example, a spider found in a supermarket. It could be time consuming as descriptions were read over the phone and databases consulted. Today, they can post the high-quality picture or stream images and receive responses almost in real-time. Lessons can be shared immediately.

When technicians were first given Gmail addresses, there were compatibility problems with their PDAs and usage was fairly low. But when a smartphone trial was conducted with a branch in 2012, it was an entirely different story.

"Myself and Operations Director Dave Hall gave out smartphones to 50-odd technicians when we were touring the branches," recalls Phill Wood, MD for the UK and rest of the world region. "The next day, one of the technicians came back to Dave and said, 'I spent all night on this smartphone and I found an app that allows us to count flies in a catch tray.' Over breakfast on the next leg of the tour, Dave and I had a discussion that went, 'So normally we spend four or five years screaming at people to get this stuff implemented and this guy has spent all night doing it in his own time.'

"I said to Dave, 'I think we are on to a winner here.' That day we decided to extend our pilot to the whole UK. We put 650 smartphones into the business for all technicians. That technician influenced our investment."

Google Hangouts (video calls amongst up to ten people) have also transformed the way colleagues interact. Time, money and energy are saved because the need for physical meetings of colleagues located across the country or around the world has been reduced. For instance, it's not unusual for virtual training sessions to take place involving employees in South Africa and the UK.

They are used in other ways, too. Technicians now have on-site consultations with their line managers via Hangouts, seeking advice on difficult issues they face. By sharing images and videos from a job, the technician can tap into a manager's years of experience. It's like having a virtual manager by your side. The following statistic might be surprising: Rentokil is the second biggest user of Hangouts in the UK after Google itself.

One of the most visible ways in which Speed has changed working practices has been through the introduction of apps, such as Speed Mapper. Prior to its introduction, technicians in UK Pest Control would often plot their working week using filing systems that contained details of their customers, their service-level agreements and their immediate requirements, and a series of physical maps to find their way around the country.

But if they were called out to an emergency, there was no way to check if there were other customers in the vicinity to ensure that the rest of the day was not wasted. Rentokil has service-level agreements with key clients, such as leading supermarkets, restaurants and retailers, specifying terms such as the number of visits per month and the time between an emergency call-out and a return visit.

Speed Mapper brings up a Google Map of the neighbourhood, with coloured icons marking the location of every client and their current status, demonstrated by the numbers 0, 1 and 2, highlighting those that need to be visited that week. It allows technicians to check the locations of key customers and the terms of their service level agreements. They can plan their days more efficiently, by focusing their attention on certain postcodes, for example, or by checking out the locations of other key customers after an emergency call-out or follow up visits that could be made on the return journey.

Speed Mapper also provides an up-to-date traffic map, indicating the expected time it will take to travel to each customer. It has reduced drive time and means that technicians can spend more time looking after customers than stuck in their vans. Rentokil runs a £50 'find an app' scheme that offers a cash incentive to colleagues to share apps that they have found useful in their day-to-day work. To date, 18 apps have been shared, including a document scanner, WhatsApp and Evernote, which organises all notes and documents, and Skitch, which allows users to mark-up documents and share them.

Through initiatives such as Project Speed, Rentokil is using new technology to improve the efficiency of its route-based services.

A company that had been among the largest users of carbon paper has come a long way. Embedding technology in this way not only allows technicians to do their jobs more efficiently but is also helping build bonds by sharing special moments. A great example of this was a recent Guild of Technicians dinner held at the Football Association's national training centre at Burton upon Trent. Football superstar Kevin Keegan was guest speaker and very gracious with his time, happily posing for photos with each technician as they came up to collect their certificates. All of these photos were posted on Google+ and excitement spread quickly. Within just 24 hours there were 60,000 page views.

WORLD CUP IN BRAZIL

Little in the way of scene-setting is required for the massive sporting event that was the 2014 FIFA World Cup in Brazil. As fans, players, officials and the media converged on the football-loving South American country, Rentokil was busily providing services to team hotels, stadiums, restaurants, shopping centres and airports.

Germany might have emerged worthy tournament winners, trouncing the host nation en route to the title in a one-sided semi-final, but Rentokil's Brazilian employees could at least take comfort from the fact that they were clear winners in their match-up against an array of pests. Among the contracts related to the World Cup were: major transport hub São Paulo International Airport; Hotel Accor Caesar Guarulhos, which hosted a delegation from Iran; São Paulo Futebol Clube (Cotia e Barra Funda), the football training centre for the USA and Columbia teams; Hotel Renaissance Marriot São Paulo, for bed bug inspection ahead of the arrival of a FIFA delegation; Horii Empreendimentos Resort Paradise, which hosted a delegation from Belgium; and Arena da Baixada, the main football stadium in Curitiba which staged four matches and for which Rentokil provided pest control services, with spraying and baiting conducted in all areas of the stadium including changing rooms, administrative offices, bathrooms, media room, bars and coffee shops.

One of the most significant tournament-related contracts was for the Royal Palm Plaza Resort Hotel in Campinas where Cristiano Ronaldo and the rest of the Portuguese team were staying. Ahead of the World Cup the local municipal health authority reported the largest dengue fever outbreak ever recorded in the Campinas area, with 21,967 confirmed cases and one death. Dengue is a mosquito-borne tropical disease and people can be infected through a single bite. To reduce the risk of dengue, Rentokil upped its fogging of the Royal Palm's green areas from once a week to twice weekly. The hotel took the added precaution of changing its garden flowers to ones that do not accumulate water, reducing the risk of providing an attractive home for mosquitoes.

While the pests have hardly altered since Brazil previously hosted the World Cup in 1950, the way people live their lives has changed considerably. Digital technology has come to the fore. Globally, more than 3 billion people are now internet users. Business customers and consumers now expect a rapid response and slick digital communications alongside an excellent service from technicians and others they encounter face-to-face.

By investing in extranet technology and providing access to remote monitoring support for customers who need to protect a hard-won reputation, Rentokil is leading the way in its field. An array of useful smartphone apps has been developed. And a lot of effort is also going into optimising websites so that they appear at the top of search engine rankings. Rentokil's vans are easily spotted on the streets but the business enjoys far greater visibility online. The brand has always been accomplished at generating buzz through marketing and PR, as shown by that headline-grabbing campaign in Hamelin during the 1960s. These skills remain very much in evidence.

PESTAURANT – A TASTY CONCEPT

On Thursday 15 August 2013, at the One New Change office and retail development in the City of London, Rentokil grabbed the attention of passers-by and triggered plenty of online chatter by unveiling the world's first pop-up 'Pestaurant'.

A Pestaurant chef is imaginative with his seasoning.

Sweet chilli pigeon burgers and a range of sweet and savoury edible insects were served free of charge to inquisitive Londoners – some delighted, others disgusted. Further pop-up Pestaurants followed at different locations and went down so well that the concept was rolled out internationally with a Global Pestaurant Day taking place on 4

June 2014, with pop-up venues synchronised across 12 countries to a great reception. In Writer's Square, Belfast, visitors consumed three quarters of a kilo of edible insects, from cheddar cheese mealworms and curry crickets to plain roasted locusts, together with 880 sweet chilli pigeon burger tasters. Pestaurant has also been taken on tour to schools across the UK, in support of Rentokil's chosen charity Malaria No More and its 'Miles for Malaria' fundraising campaign.

A pop-up Pestaurant, 2013. St Paul's Cathedral provides a magnificent backdrop.

Lining up to try the food in the City of London.

Across the Atlantic in Washington DC, Rentokil company JC Ehrlich teamed up with DC Capital Kitchen, which provides 25 million meals to low-income families in the US capital. The charity promoted the Pestaurant event to its 20,000 Twitter and Facebook followers. In return, Rentokil donated $5 for everyone adventurous enough to try an insect meal and $20 for each brave soul who entered the 'eat as many bugs as you can' contest. Crickets were the delicacy of the day. Further Pestaurant events are in the pipeline internationally.

Bug delicacies on offer from a Pestaurant in Edinburgh's Grassmarket.

To date, over 20,000 people have visited Rentokil's Pestaurant, PR coverage has included over 70 TV and radio interviews and 1,200 newspaper articles. The campaign won a series of PR industry awards including the Best Consumer PR Campaign 2014.

"Pestaurant captured the public's imagination," says Malcolm Padley, Communications Director at Rentokil Initial. "It gave us a creative platform to demonstrate our expertise, drive digital traffic and build brand awareness. It showed that there's a fun side to a serious business that protects people and enhances people's lives. In the spirit of the Rentokil Film and Video Units of the past, much of the success was captured on camera – though hosted digitally on sites such as YouTube and Instagram."

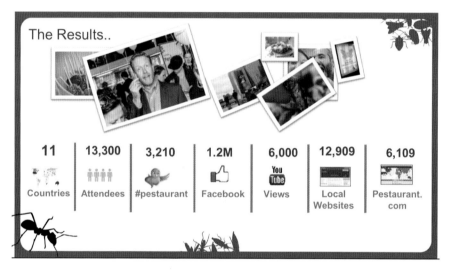

The international Pestaurant campaign of 2014 caused a big stir (and not just to a pan of crickets).

Beyond the fantastic publicity Pestaurant has generated for the Rentokil brand, there's a serious side to the bug-crunching. Chowing down on critters need not be a revolting *I'm A Celebrity...* bush tucker trial-style culinary ordeal. When nicely prepared, insects taste good. Moreover, the consumption of insects, or entomophagy to use the technical term, can have a positive impact on the environment. Crickets, for example, need 12 times less feed than cattle, four times less feed than sheep, and half as much feed as pigs and broiler chickens to produce the same amount of protein. As well as being a good source of protein, insects are high in B vitamins and minerals like iron and zinc, while being low in fat. So they're a healthy option too. Diners are spoilt for choice: it's estimated that more than 1,900 species of insect have been used as food.

Bow down to the biggest buzz about bugs in Washington DC since Watergate. A 2014 Pestaurant event delivers a ten-out-of-ten culinary thrill near Capitol Hill.

Queuing for the Pestaurant in Trinidad (left), this adventurous consumer (right) chooses a light bite here instead of a visit to KFC.

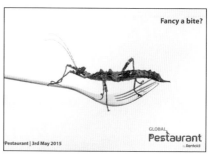

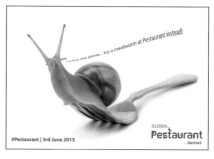

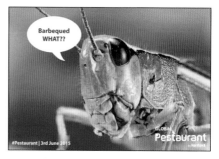

Putting the RT (Retweet) into Rentokil. Smart digital marketing campaigns on social media platforms such as Twitter help keep the Rentokil name top of mind. #Pestaurant

EXPANDING THE RENTOKIL BRAND THROUGH ACQUISITIONS

As this book makes clear, acquisitions figure prominently in the history of Rentokil – playing a significant part in making the Rentokil brand what it is today by bringing great people, new customer relationships and new ideas into the company.

At the beginning of this decade, when the group still faced some difficult financial challenges and financial markets were effectively closed due to the global recession, acquisitions were understandably thin on the ground. However, as the benefits of a more focused strategy kicked in and the financial position improved, the M&A taps were turned back on. Nine acquisitions were made in 2012. The following year this rose to 16. And in 2014 £68m was spent on making 30 acquisitions (23 of which were in Pest Control, underlining the renewed focus in the business). This included pest control market entries in Chile, Colombia and Mozambique and the purchase of UK business Peter Cox Property Care, a market-leading specialist in wood-boring insects and damp-proofing, which is being partnered with Rentokil's existing Property Care business. By the same token, the acquisition of EcoTime Pest Control, based in Milan, represents an important density building opportunity in northern Italy.

In recent years, there has also been a push into the newer EU member states in Eastern Europe, beginning with the acquisition of Pest Protection Services in Estonia. PPS was set up by Scottish businessman Iain Lawson, who cut his teeth working for Rentokil early in his career. Lawson, a passionate fan of the Scottish national football team, had known little about Estonia until travelling to a Scotland away match as part of the Tartan Army. But Lawson was so impressed with what he found when visiting the capital, Tallinn, that he invested in a local pest control business. In short order, Rentokil followed up the PPS acquisition with a move into the Lithuanian market by buying Dezinfa, which is run by Managing Director Margarita Kutkaike. The late Bessie Eades would surely have been delighted to see a woman running a national pest control business. And with a substantial number of women joining Rentokil's graduate programme, there's every likelihood that there will be far more female faces in senior roles within the business in coming years.

A fine illustration of Rentokil's commitment to ensuring its businesses meet consistently high standards across the globe is the acquisition in late 2014 of Tropical Exterminators in the Bahamas. Mark Lanford was transferred from the Ehrlich operation in the US to take charge of integration as Bahamas Country Manager. Although Tropical is a high-quality business with an excellent track record, some immediate improvements had to be made to meet Rentokil's more demanding requirements.

"In the Bahamas, there is very little in the way of regulatory standards governing the use and transport of pesticides and fumigants," says Lanford. "There is no licensing to speak of, so the barriers to entry to this business are very low. There are plenty of 'mom and pop' competitors who work out of the back of their cars and do pest control."

The first thing Rentokil did when it took over was to provide safety training and upgrade equipment that had fallen behind in repairs. Trucks were modernised, for example by installing fumigant racks. In a short space of time, around US$100,000 was spent on fumigation tools and general safety improvements in order to bring the business into line with Rentokil's own high standards. International consistency is increasingly important.

Another example of this can be seen with the recent acquisition made in Mozambique. Armand Bruneau, Regional Business Manager Kwa-Zulu Natal and Mozambique region, says the acquired company had previously dealt with snakes by killing them. This was not compatible with the Rentokil way of doing things, so a snake specialist from Johannesburg was brought in to teach the Mozambique technicians how to handle snakes safely. Now the Mozambique business offers hotels and other customers a service where a technician is sent out to catch a snake without injuring it, put it in a snake tube and relocate it in the bush away from populated areas. The discovery of huge natural gas reserves in Mozambique has put the country in the spotlight and is helping attract overseas investment, which means Rentokil's growth prospects in the country look very promising.

In 2015, Rentokil continued its expansion in the Americas with its first entry into the main cities of Guatemala and El Salvador as the company continued its push into higher-growth and emerging markets. While relatively small markets, the news of Rentokil's expansion here caught the media's imagination. As well as extensive news coverage there was even a newspaper cartoon depicting a poor Rentokil technician with a rather large snake curled around him.

Over the years, Rentokil's international expansion has given the cartoonists plenty of ammunition. Take the acquisition of Western Exterminator in the US. This spawned the publication of a cartoon showing rats wearing ten gallon hats. It's "a ten gallon rat" ran the punch line. While the global banking crisis saw a cartoon published with a sardonic observation from a rat's point of view.

'It's true – apparently you are never more than ten feet from a banker'

Even rats have their phobias, according to one satirist.

Cartoon by Mac (Stan McMurtry), published in the Daily Mail on 11 February 2009. Courtesy of the British Cartoon Archive, University of Kent, www.cartoons.ac.uk.

Amid the celebrations of Rentokil's 90th anniversary year, important strategic acquisitions continued. August 2015 saw the purchase of Chicago-based Anderson Pest Solutions, which has annual revenues of $21m. Then on 1 September 2015 came news of a bigger takeover. Steritech Group, one of the largest pest control companies in North America, with operations in the US and Canada and a great reputation for customer service and client retention, was snapped up for $425 million in cash. The company is also a leading provider of auditing services across food hygiene compliance, workplace safety, customer experience and other areas of operation that businesses need to get right to preserve trust in their brand names. The acquisitions have further strengthened Rentokil's position as the number three pest control business in North America, a market which accounts for roughly half of all spending on pest control services globally. With annual revenues of around $0.8 billion, Rentokil's US business is now its largest single country operation.

What would Harold Maxwell-Lefroy have made of it all?

"And what subtle flavour are we pushing this month?"
"Something festive I hope."

THE ESSENTIALS

2006 – Acquisition of JC Ehrlich.

2007 – Launch of hi-tech trap RADAR (Rodent Activated Detection And Riddance) which combines infrared sensor and CO_2.

2008 – Preferred supplier of pest control services and products to Beijing Olympics.

2009 – Agreement with Google to standardise company email globally and make use of other communication tools via Google Apps.

2011 – Entry into Mexican pest control market with acquisition of Tetengo.

2012 – Project Speed underway to introduce Google's collaboration suite of tools, changing the way that Rentokil operates through smartphones and apps.

2013 – World's first pop-up Pestaurant.

2014 – 23 pest control acquisitions and a flurry of work relating to FIFA World Cup in Brazil.

2015 – Acquisition of Anderson Pest Solutions and the Steritech Group Inc.

CHAPTER
EIGHT
Tales from the Frontline

Rentokil employees are renowned for being able to think on their feet. It's a quality that has proved useful time after time. All the more so when unusual, bizarre or particularly testing situations arise.

Weird events seemed to happen more frequently in days gone by and the need to make it up as you went along was all the greater. Partly that's because technology and business practices were more rudimentary, while far less prominence was given to health and safety concerns.

Here are some personal recollections that paint a vivid picture of what life at Rentokil used to be like from the late 1940s through to the approach of the new millennium. Some of the anecdotes are hilarious, others more reflective. Each storyteller's voice is unique. Combined, their perspectives provide a warm, personal history of Rentokil. The grit and gumption in the face of a challenge, sense of humour and quick-thinking of these talented individuals explain why the company has enjoyed such longevity. Without the commitment, character and problem-solving skills of these and other amazing employees, there would be no Rentokil.

STUCK IN THE MUCK

Bob Wood (Rentokil pest control 1963–2003) joined the company seven years after the death of Karl Gustav Anker-Petersen and soon found himself in a sticky situation with the founder's son.

"After I had been with the company for about a year, working as a pest control serviceman as we were then called, I was told one morning that I was to take a young man out with me and 'show him the ropes'. I was understandably apprehensive when informed that the young man was none other than Eric Anker-Petersen, the adopted son of Karl Gustav. He had spent a short time in the armed services, was the heir to a considerable fortune, and was now to work in the business.

"I decided to show Eric one of the worst rat infestations I had seen. It was on a chicken farm in Kent. The chicken sheds were about 50 metres long and ten metres wide. The chickens walked around on slats about four feet off a concrete floor. Their droppings accumulated in the space under the slats and remained there until the chickens were cleared out at yearly intervals.

"So at the end of a year the space would be more or less full of droppings, plus spilled food, the odd chicken carcass and in this case hundreds of rats.

"I met up with Eric at our office and was amused to see he was dressed in an expensive blue suit, even though he knew we were going to a farm to treat for rats. I had timed the visit to coincide with the annual removal of the chickens, so that we could kill as many rats as possible before the droppings were removed and the rats scattered to other sheds. On arrival we armed ourselves with stout batons of wood and I told Eric to be prepared when I flung open the shed doors. I knew there were always half a dozen or so rats sheltering just inside and if we were quick we could kill a few with hefty blows from our clubs. Rats move very quickly but we still managed to dispatch one or two.

"Having got the doors open, I noticed that the slats had already been removed in preparation for the removal of the droppings. I decided that we would use a large quantity of quick acting rodenticide, reckoning that with chicken feed no longer available the rats would readily scoff my toxic concoction. Back at the van I set to mixing up a brew of bread, chocolate flavouring and zinc phosphide.

"Just a few minutes later, whilst still preparing the special mix, I heard desperate cries for help from Eric. When I looked up I saw that he had ventured into the shed and was now about a third of the way along, but only visible from the waist up! On the upper surface the chicken droppings formed a hard crust; below the constituency was more like porridge. Eric had obviously assumed he could walk over the surface, and he could up to the point where it gave way and he sank into the glutinous, stinking mess.

"I wasn't about to go in after him and suffer the same fate. Anyway, he had reached the bottom and could sink no further. I suggested he manoeuvre himself to the edge and use the sides of the shed to haul himself back to the entrance. What a mess! What a terrible smell! What a ruined suit!"

BANKING ON TROUBLE IN BELGIUM

In the mid-1970s, pest control surveyor Walter Spruyt was looking over a famous bank in Ghent to see if it had pigeon problems.

At 6ft 4in. the imposing figure of Spruyt was hard to miss. The amount of attention he was giving the bank raised the suspicions of a plucky old lady who convinced herself he must be up to no good. Throwing caution to the wind, she strode up to the man she supposed to be a criminal slyly casing the joint and warned: "Don't try it, I shall call the police!" A surprised Spruyt protested that his business was winged pests and he had no intention of taking flight with other people's money.

AND YOU THOUGHT POSTAGE STAMPS WERE ADHESIVE

After leaving the Royal Navy in 1946, Maurice Herring worked for a while as a coal delivery driver. That job was dirty, physically demanding and poorly paid. So when the opportunity to move into pest control came up, he leapt at the chance.

"I saw an advert in the paper for a pest control operator at £4 per week with a car supplied. I answered the advert and was granted an interview with Mr Blenkinsop, the TGM in Newcastle in May 1948. I was successful and started with the company working for British Ratin and Chelsea Insecticides.

"I was required to stay away from home three nights per week at places such as Scarborough, Whitby, Middlesbrough, Leyburn and Richmond. I was given a float of £5 by the company, which at that time easily covered the expense of petrol, B&B, meals and phone calls. Unbelievable!

"The late Bill Allison was the only operative in Hull at the time and I accompanied him for the first two weeks of my training. One Saturday morning we were called to an existing customer at the village post office and stores at Sigglesthorne.

"They had a reoccurrence of rats. In those pre-warfarin days our armoury was very limited. We had Ratin, which was a culture. Although it was effective for a while, I'm sorry to say that the rats built up an immunity to it. We also had No. 2s, which was red squill – a powerful emetic that needed flavouring for the rats to take it readily. We also had thallium sulphate which was not suitable for food premises.

"Ratin and No. 2 had been used extensively at the shop. Some dead rats were found but there is always one rogue. This one had found a hole opposite the till. As the shop was closed on the Sunday, Mr Allison in his wisdom considered that we should lay a sticky board around the hole. This was a very sticky material called DAK, which needed heating and spreading onto cardboard and shaping around the hole. This we did and arranged to call back first thing on Monday.

"The shop was run by an 85-year-old lady and her spinster daughter. Unfortunately, when we arrived on the Monday morning, the daughter had gone to the wholesalers and in spite of many warnings, the old lady was stuck on the DAK board with a rat between her feet. We soon released her."

TIMBER!

After a demanding induction course in which he tried his hand on the frontline in all areas of the Rentokil business, Technical Writer Gordon Wilkinson should have known that authoring a 500-page book on timber preservation wouldn't be as easy as falling off a log.

"Following completion of a PhD in chemistry at the University of Leicester and a short time in publishing in London, I joined Rentokil in 1975 as a Technical Writer to produce articles for academic publications based on research from the R&D laboratories. The job involved working with R&D managers to transform material from laboratory reports into publication format and get the articles to press, allowing them to focus on managing their research teams.

"My line manager at Rentokil was Dr Peter Cornwell, an entomologist with a special interest in cockroaches. He had a keen interest in ensuring that the results of the research in the R&D division were published in professional journals and that, where possible, those articles could provide the basis for press stories.

"Peter organised an induction course for my first three months, which involved working with each of the company's divisions – at that time, Pest Control, Timber Preservation, Damp-proofing and Hygiene. This was a great opportunity to get to know how the business was organised and how the developments from the R&D division improved technical operations. I was able to get involved in the Pest Control division by helping to deal with a black rat infestation on a ship in the London Docks, clearing a mouse infestation at a grain silo, eradicating cockroaches from a famous London hotel and fumigating spices to eliminate insect pests. At the Timber Preservation division, I was able to see how timber was treated for use in different applications and how the chemical formulations were developed and manufactured. Perhaps the most memorable was helping out in Hygiene division, where I really got 'hands on' by steam cleaning the men's toilets at Victoria Station – perhaps the first and only time someone with a PhD in chemistry was doing the job.

"After a few years as Technical Writer I was asked to take on a management role and became Head of the Timber Preservation section, which allowed me to build a knowledge of that industry sector.

"In my final role as Head of Communications, in 1979 I produced a 530-page book, *Industrial Timber Preservation*, for the Rentokil Library series, which for many years was the standard textbook for the industry. During the course of writing the book I sometimes worked at home and sat on an old chair given to us years earlier by an elderly aunt. One day I was leaning back on the chair and it collapsed. The reason quickly became clear: woodworm!"

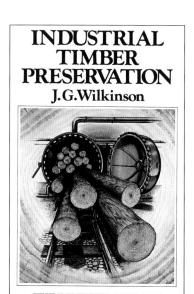

TO THE BAHAMAS WITH A CHIHUAHUA

Over the course of 36 years with Rentokil, Graham Foote progressed to senior national and international management positions. But a posting to the Bahamas early in his career felt like a hardship until changes were made.

"I started as a serviceman on the west coast of Scotland, Glasgow area, in 1962. I worked there for approximately 18 months and helped set up the first official training – getting a lot of the lads to go to night school in Glasgow on a pest control training course.

"I'd only been doing the job for around 19 or 20 months when I was asked if I was interested in moving to the Bahamas. I was contacted on the Monday and my wife and I went down to Felcourt for an interview on the Friday, with Bob Westphal and Teddy Buchan, the two chief executives at the time. It was strange for a 21-year-old kid not long out of the air force to be interviewed by people at that level. I said, 'My wife's a probationary teacher and really she needs to give at least a month's notice' and they said, 'A month from today is when you go out then.'

"We went in February 1964. It was amazing. Rentokil had built a house in the service area of the island which measured 20ft by 20ft. That included a store room, a little office which led from the store room, a door from the office through the toilet and out the other side into an L-shaped room which was a kitchen and living accommodation. Very tiny. It was in the middle of a quarter-acre site full of rubble from other contractors and there was rubbish lying on the ground. There was also a Commer van. The first thing my wife Margaret did was burst into tears. We'd come away from a large tenement in Glasgow that had a room that was bigger than the whole of this property.

"We'd been there four months when Teddy Buchan came out. I remember my wife attacking him about the conditions and how poorly paid I was at the time. We got on to a better footing after that. It was agreed I'd get 5% of turnover, once it reached £16,000 a year. I then spent the next three and a half years building turnover, while making sure it was profitable.

"I'd joke that Bob Westphal would have been a pirate if he'd lived hundreds of years ago; while Teddy Buchan was a Scot who was very much a gentleman. They were different types entirely which is why it was a very good combination, the two of them running the business.

"Bob would come to the Bahamas and I'd introduce him to all the clients I had – I didn't have that many of them! He'd only be there for two or three days and he'd want me to take him out deep sea fishing like he used to do in Australia. Teddy would come out, I'd meet him at the airport for his annual visit and, unlike Bob, he would want to sit in the office to tell me all that was happening with businesses around the world. And he'd put me through a test on what he'd told me last time he was out.

"I had dogs before I joined Rentokil [a passion throughout his career: Graham Foote is a renowned breeder of chihuahuas and chairman of the British Chihuahua Club] and we took a chihuahua and a Pomeranian to the Bahamas with us and later brought them back to Scotland."

A MILLION MILES ON THE ROAD

Henry Trewren, a former Rentokil Regional Manager, recalls a career packed with laughter, loyalty and variety – in which he certainly clocked up the miles.

"I had just left the RAF as a newlywed and was looking for work. My wife Cynthia and I decided to move from Liverpool to Bristol. The local Bristol paper had an advert from a company called Woodworm and Dry Rot Control for a job as a technician which had further prospects. Their office in Bristol was the first branch office outside the London headquarters in Baker Street.

"My Rentokil career started on 10 October 1960. Bill Mynall, the branch manager, acted as a father figure for all levels of staff. The branch in those days covered Cornwall, Devon, Somerset, Bristol, Wiltshire and Jersey.

"Expansion allowed me to work in the Woodworm and Dry Rot division, Rentokil Insurance, the Insulation division and finally the Damp-proofing division. Promotions allowed me to work in various branches throughout the country.

"Rentokil always had a national sales conference in Harrogate. A formal dinner was part of the proceedings and a household name such as Ken Dodd, Harry Secombe, Jim Davidson and Bob Monkhouse entertained us.

"Twenty-eight and a half years passed – as did one million miles driving numerous types of vehicle – providing memories of a company that was simply the best. It was not a job; it was a way of life!"

THE MAGGOT ON THE PATH TO WISDOM

Jürgen Althoff, who retired as Technical Director at Rentokil Germany in 2013, recalls his visit to Felcourt in 1980 for an arduous and at times hilarious training course that made a deep impression.

"As a young German biologist, just engaged by Rentokil Germany, I was sent out 35 years ago to the 'UK mothership'. I was to learn about pest control via a training course at Yew Lodge, Felcourt – by the way, a wonderful place. The breath of scientific pest control was alive in those walls. After that my job would be to train the German organisation technically, passing on the genes from the centre.

"At that time, every UK employee had to pass the examinations on this course. Coincidentally, with me were 15 biologists, ten salesmen, two branch managers and the future Division Manager, Michael Gibbs. All were native English speakers.

"Of course I felt a connection with the other biologists. But in the previous months they had had time enough to learn the 400-page technical handbook and on the first day of the course they were already prepared for the examinations. So they spent every night in the bar, drinking, laughing and playing snooker. Meanwhile, I sat in my room, not drinking, not laughing but learning about pests in a foreign language with thoughts like: am I in the right company?

"On the fourth day we had the session 'Flies – Lifecycles and treatment methods'. The trainer was John Bull – a great man, a real scientific and practical expert – but in a way his name was his concept. Shortly before noon he suddenly asked the question: 'How many hooks does the maggot of a shit-fly have at the front of its body that enable it to crawl forward?' My answer, 'Who cares?' got a big laugh in the auditorium. But my neighbour whispered to me, 'Jürgen – such comments are not helpful for your career.'

"Nevertheless, the ice was broken and Michael Gibbs asked, 'Is there any advantage to me in knowing this in my future job as Division Manager where my focus will be on driving a pest control organisation and earning profit?'

"John Bull left the room and then came back with a big jar full of maggots that he'd retrieved from the laboratory. He put a piece of the jar contents on everyone's desks and said: 'Use your ten-times lens to find out'.

"Then, like a Buddha, he said: 'Whatever you do, love the details of pest control so that you are recognised by clients as a knowledgeable, authentic pest controller.' His message was, dig deep into pest control matters, whatever the matter is, because that's where the quality service starts.

"After dinner that day he said to us all: 'Come and see me in the library, I will show you some videos about rats, mice and other night-shifters'. One course participant precociously wanted to know whether this was voluntary or a duty. He answered: 'On my training day, nothing is voluntary.' At 11 o'clock that night after six videos, he said: 'I have another one about the corn weevil!' Now half of our group was ready to kill him.

"Nevertheless, this Hogwarts-like place in our company was the source and root of our understanding that later allowed us to conquer the German pest control market. In my duties as biologist, branch manager, Division Manager and Technical Director, I have never forgotten the ambition John Bull presented at this time."

THE BIRDS THAT STOPPED TIME

Bob Crawford joined the Belfast office of what was then British Ratin in 1956, working for Rentokil in Northern Ireland during a difficult period in the history of the province before retirement in 1988. Here he recalls an early adventure.

"In the 1950s Belfast was still one of the top locations in the world for shipbuilding and the shipyards were an important source of pest control business. They were building Royal Navy frigates. Once one was launched, the keel of the next one was put down. But this time it was something different. The metal plates for the side of the ship were treated with something. I think that they were trying to build a ship that was less magnetic – so many were sunk by magnetic mines during the war. But that was all hush-hush. I took some photos but was ordered to burn them and the negatives. And I did.

"We were asked to chase the starlings out of that yard. The acid from their droppings was damaging the plates. Four of us went down every evening at dusk when the birds were coming in – in their thousands! We were armed with two scarecrow guns like the farmers use to frighten the birds away after planting their seeds, a revolver from which we fired blanks to make them think they were being shot at, rockets to fire up among them and an iron bar to bang against the gantries and make them echo from one end to the other: about 200 yards long. Each night the starlings became fewer. The thing is to break their habit of roosting in a location and make them go somewhere else.

"The next thing is the city fathers are wondering where this sudden influx of starlings has come from. There are that many of them that they are even seen fighting for roosting places around the centre of town and the city hall.

"A week later the headline on the front page of the *Belfast Telegraph* is that the birds have stopped the Albert Memorial Clock. They could roost on the big hand from 10 past the hour to 20 past, and then on again at 20 to and off at 10 to. The small hand was too close to the dial, so they couldn't roost on that.

"Now there was another task for Rentokil: hiring out the fire brigade turntable ladder, the only thing that would reach high enough to put bird repellent on each side of the big hands. Jim Peters went up and did a very successful job.

"In those days we could hire the turntable ladder and driver. Six pounds for the first hour and three pounds an hour after that – but with no promise it would be staying with you!"

THROUGH DUSTY DUCTS ON A JOURNEY OF DISCOVERY

Trevor de Silvia, General Manager at Rentokil Initial (Barbados), remembers an inspection at a bank headquarters on the Caribbean island that turned up previously unknown termite behaviour.

"Back in the early 80s, I had to survey the multi-storey regional headquarters of Barclays Bank, which operated in Barbados at the time, for termite activity. These premises continued to experience termite activity after Rentokil had provided a treatment against termites.

"Part of the survey involved inspection of the horizontal air conditioning ducts on the roof of the building which only had enough space to travel in a forward direction by crawling 'commando style'. As the duct had never been cleaned, a 'dust storm' was generated as I moved through it, significantly reducing visibility. After approximately 40 feet, this horizontal duct ended at a vertical duct feeding the lower floors. Fortunately I could feel the opening ahead of me.

"Having inspected the building and not found the source of activity, I noticed that there was a 500-gallon water cooler tank used to recirculate cool air throughout the building: this was the first air-conditioned building on the Island. To insulate the water tank it was covered in cork, which I noticed had some holes.

"Upon probing the cork insulation, live winged reproductives started to swarm out. Having found the source of infestation, which was related to an aerial infestation by *Coptotermes havilandi sp.*, the cork insulation was injected. It took 200 gallons of termiticide; the cork had been converted into a colony of termites.

"After destruction, a one foot by one foot section of the colony was removed and an image of this appeared in our termite handbook. Before my discovery, the ability of this species to establish colonies via aerial infestation was unknown."

BUTTERFLY CHASERS AND GIGANTIC BEETLES

Alan (F.K.) Deutsch worked at Rentokil for more than a quarter of a century, first as a chemist, eventually as Production Director.

"In 1958 I lived in Sanderstead, near Croydon, and worked as the Development Chemist for Adhesive and Allied Products in Barking. An advertisement in the *Daily Telegraph* for a Works Manager/Chief Chemist caught my eye. I applied and was invited for an interview with Dr Norman Hickin, Technical Director at Rentokil, Fetcham.

"The interview seemed to go quite well and Dr Hickin said that I would have to attend another interview with Ted (E.M.) Buchan, joint chief executive. Two weeks later I returned to Fetcham for the second interview. The only thing I remember from that occasion was that Mr Buchan arrived about three quarters of an hour late and was surprised to see me. He said that no one had told him about the interview and apologised; he had been having his hair cut. He asked me if I would be happy to be a pebble in a small pond rather than the large pond of working for ICI. At the end of November 1958 I received a letter offering me the job at £1,000 per annum.

"On my first day I met Charles Nichols and for the next six months I shared an office with him and learnt the various aspects of the job. At the same time I worked through the various departments and intricacies of the work in the factory. This included purchasing raw materials and containers, processing fluids and powders and filling into tins and other containers, decanting into drums and into other packaging materials, quality control, organising the despatch of orders by rail and by our own lorry fleet.

"Soon after I had arrived, I noted a certain amount of celebration going on due to the turnover of the Group having reached £¼ million. After about six months I was told that the research centre at Felcourt wanted to start a research and development section for the Timber Preservation division. At the research centre there was one other chemist, Bryan Eastwood (responsible for the Pest Control division's technical development) and three biologists. Bryan and I christened these entomologists 'butterfly catchers'.

The available laboratory was so small that Brian and I had to take it in turns to use it. I found out that I was also responsible for technical service work and this meant I was out and about quite a bit of my time. After starting at Felcourt, the Retail Sales Manager gave me a pass for the Ideal Homes Exhibition at Olympia in London. He suggested I should have a look at our stand and see if I could assist with any enquiries that might arise. On arrival at a very crowded hall, I fought my way towards the stand. I found myself behind a couple of elderly ladies and heard one of them say: 'Mabel, see that one over there. Well we've got them in our loft… twice that size'.

"'I know,' said the other. 'We have them as well.'

"I was astonished to see them looking at a model of the common furniture beetle, the normal insect that we know as woodworm. The model was beautifully made. And was about two feet in length and one foot in height."

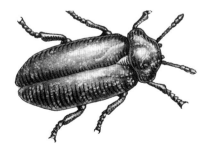

POIGNANT SECRETS OF A 'MANOIR' IN BRITTANY

In 1974, Gerald Moores returned to the UK with his family after 20 years serving in the police force of what is now Zimbabwe. While pondering his next career move, fate intervened – in the shape of problems with his home. Yet these problems paled in comparison with later discoveries in France.

"I had no idea what I was going to do for a living but the rising damp and insect infestation at the property where I still live actually changed my life. I contacted Rentokil and arranged surveys with a view to solving the problems in this 1897 terraced house. I immediately hit it off with the damp-proofing surveyor, Clive Gainard. When he learned that I was temporarily unemployed, he mentioned there was a vacancy for a surveyor and if I was interested I should contact his manager, Mike Hawkes, at the Bristol office.

"I did as he suggested and, despite my total lack of knowledge of the building industry, Mike Hawkes took a chance on me and I started my training in November 1974. I immediately felt at home in the company and became impressed by the high standards of technical excellence in all the divisions.

"In 1990 I was a Development Manager with the Property Care division and Bob Hanney was my immediate supervisor. We were developing 'greener' and 'safer' treatments for the treatment of wood-boring insects and fungal decay in timbers, involving new chemical combinations and delivery systems. Bob and the division's Marketing Manager, Guy Henshall, negotiated a reciprocal arrangement with Alan Mason, a top landscape gardener and garden designer who had purchased an old *manoir* in Brittany which had eight-plus acres of land. He intended to create a typical English garden within six months, filming the transformation in collaboration with his partner Marylyn Webb – a producer and presenter – who subsequently became his wife. This would eventually become a TV series, *Le Manoir*, which was shown on Channel 4. Bob and I – especially Bob with a live deathwatch beetle running across his hand – made brief appearances in the TV series, our overalls clearly showing us to be Rentokil employees.

"The reciprocal arrangement was that Rentokil would survey the property and carry out all the necessary treatments for common furniture beetle and deathwatch beetle in return for a professionally produced training film covering our new treatment methods and materials.

"I shall always remember my arrival in the Breton village of Port de Roche and my first impressions of the memorial that dominated a small triangle of grass at a minor road junction. The memorial honoured 11 men of the village, executed by the Gestapo in 1944 for alleged involvement with the local Resistance.

"Shortly after our arrival we were told of the direct connection between the manoir and the memorial. The manoir's 19-year-old gardener had been one of the men executed, shot against the main south-facing wall of the house.

"During our April inspection we were examining exposed roof timbers in one of the larger attics – using powerful torches and mirrors to examine inaccessible areas – when we made our first discovery. Fixed to the blind side of a main structural beam was what remained of an aerial system for an old-type radio transmitter – undisturbed and apparently undetected for almost 50 years. The rubber components had mostly perished, but what appeared to be the radio connectors were still identifiable.

"The manoir had probably been used as a safe house or local Resistance HQ during the German occupation. This belief was confirmed when we made a more startling discovery.

"Whilst lifting floor boarding in one of the smaller, more inaccessible attic rooms – preparatory to carrying out woodworm treatment – we saw what at first glance seemed to be some metal piping lying between the joists. Further exposure revealed plumbing of a more lethal kind. A wartime British sten-gun and an old pattern American army rifle lay side by side in the dusty space between the timber joists. The young gardener was probably the only person who knew where the arms cache had been concealed.

"The local gendarmerie were visibly surprised when handed two potentially lethal museum pieces in apparent working order. In my view, the hidden firearms and radio transmitter provided a more poignant remembrance of the brave young Breton patriot than the formal stone monolith."

WHEN CORRUPTION IN NYC WAS RIFE

Max Lewis, a young Corporate Planner at Felcourt, was sent to New York in 1974 to run the Josephsons acquisition and became the very first employee of Rentokil Inc., bringing his wife and ten-day-old baby with him to the Big Apple. He recalls it as a "baptism of fire" – very different from the way business is conducted today.

"The office was at 555 Grand Concourse in the Bronx and the police used to sit on the top of the building to watch drug deals," remembers Lewis. "I realised something was wrong when immigration raided us a few weeks after we got control and half the staff ran down the back stairs. I realised that something was very wrong when the $10 a month we were paid to do pest control in a tenement flat turned out to be not for one flat but the whole building, with often 50 flats in the building.

"Bribes were expected in exchange for certificates with minimal pest control work being done – which led to Rentokil resigning such tenement building accounts. Getting guidance on these things as a 24-year-old innocent from Felcourt was a non-starter, and we had no email in those days. That year the city was in chaos. It was broke and the teachers and public service workers were paid their salaries only because the teachers' pension fund lent the city money. There was rubbish in the streets but my immediate problem was the office manager who phoned to say his wife had taken away all his clothes and he could not come to work unless I bought him some clothes."

TEENAGE ANGST IN THE BEDROOM

Rentokil's resident entomologist, Matt Green, was exposed to more domestic drama than he bargained for when accompanying a technician on a job in Brighton.

"We went out to a bed bug survey in Brighton in a flat in an old art deco building. It was myself and the technician on a first visit. The lady of the house had three teenage sons and had subdivided the rooms in the flat with plasterboard.

"We'd been round most of the rooms in the house and we'd sprayed up one of them and looked at where the bed bugs were. The rooms had not been decorated and there were joints in the plasterboard everywhere, so it was quite difficult to chase all the bed bugs out of all the joints and treat them all. When we got to the final room, we couldn't get in. The lady said, 'Oh, it's OK' and she knocked on the door and said, 'Stephen, Rentokil want to get in and spray for the bed bugs.'

"There was a shriek and Stephen's girlfriend, who'd apparently been staying the night, flung the door open naked, ran past us into the bathroom and then sat in the shower for the remainder of the survey, screaming that she was filthy, was never going to be staying there again and that their relationship was over – while Stephen was in his bedroom crying into his hands about the impending destruction of his social life. But the technician I was with didn't bat an eyelid and carried on with the spraying. To him, it was a standard Tuesday morning and he was already planning to move ahead to the next job – calm professionalism!"

The Bed Bug Bandits characters created by Rentokil to highlight pest problems feature in digital marketing campaigns.

CHAPTER NINE

Going the Extra Mile

It's often said that great brands are built from the inside out. There's no organisation for which that statement rings truer than Rentokil. That Rentokil is an outstanding 21st century brand is not down to its logo or advertising but due to the commitment and consistent excellence of its people. Customers trust Rentokil to deliver. And Rentokil *does* deliver, because its employees around the world put customer service at the heart of what they do. Time and time again, they are willing to go the extra mile, often in extremely demanding circumstances.

The fantastic teamwork and relationship-building skills of its people are what makes Rentokil such a special business and respected brand. That's not meaningless corporate waffle. These are the values Rentokil employees live and work by. Here, in their own words, are some stories about challenges they have faced in recent times. The challenges are diverse, yet what shines through all the stories is how much Rentokil's people care about their clients and colleagues. Never more so than when the going gets tough.

AFTERMATH OF THE 7/7 LONDON BOMBINGS

On the morning of Thursday 7 July 2005, four British Islamist extremists carried out the first ever suicide bombings in the UK, detonating their devices on three London Underground trains and a bus. The attack

caused carnage, leaving 52 civilians dead and more than 700 injured. Rentokil stepped up to the mark, taking on the arduous three-week biohazard clean-up operation on the Tube. Emma Robinson, Senior Hygiene Account Manager at Rentokil Specialist Hygiene Services, takes up the story.

"It's certainly one of the most horrendous things I've dealt with. I've been in the job for 20 years and over the years we've built good relationships with Network Rail and various other rail companies. When news broke it was obvious that there were sites that were going to need specialist cleaning support. And of course that's what we do. Within 48 hours, on a Sunday, they were on the phone saying, 'We need your services'. It really was as simple as that.

"The job grew and it was an ever-changing job. You'd do risk assessments and method statements and things like that and then within 30 minutes it could all change again. We ran it with two teams of 12 people per team and we were working 24 hours a day. One team would start at seven in the morning and they would take over from the team that had worked the previous 12-hour shift. I had a supervisor, Roger Goode, who went to the last part of the shift and would then stay into the first part of the next shift to make sure everything was running as it needed to. It made me think about how it must have been in the war because everybody just came together.

"We didn't have enough staff in our depot to provide that many people, so we enlisted resources from other branches of Hygiene. We had people from Birmingham, Preston, Leeds, Bristol and everyone came together with a kind of camaraderie. It was an incredibly difficult working environment. But I went to some of the sites, and it wasn't how it read in the papers – bits of bodies everywhere and rats and mice – it wasn't like that at all. But because the ventilation systems weren't working in the Underground, it was incredibly hot. The guys were working in ridiculous temperatures [60 degrees Celsius] and as a result were having to drink copious quantities of water all the time. Because they had to wear steel-toe-capped wellingtons they were sweating profusely to the point where they were emptying the wellingtons every couple of hours because they were just dripping with sweat.

"My days were never far short of 20 hours. There were so many demands and ever-changing elements to the job. One minute you thought it would be safe to work on a carriage and then it would be, 'No, actually you can't enter from that access point – this is going to have to happen, that's going to have to happen'. Quite a large amount of time was spent changing things to make it safer.

"We had to put the guys up in hotels because with them working 12-hour shifts we didn't want them to have two or three hours' travel back home. We were getting them meals from places like McDonald's and Burger King. Initially they were keeping a tally of what we owed them and we agreed we'd settle it all at the end – but because they saw what work the guys were doing and how hard they were working, every single one of the restaurants that we used throughout the duration waived our bills.

"No other contractors could start working on the lines or doing any repairs until we'd made it safe from a biohazard point of view. And we were in constant contact with the rail company because they had to approve all of the working methods to ensure that there wasn't another catastrophe. Our clients really appreciated the effort that went into it and it was incredibly short notice. On that first Sunday when they called me, we had people on site that day – I mustered about 11 people before we knew what the demands of the job were going to be. We dropped everything to accommodate this.

"I contacted our MD before I contacted anyone else and he said to me, 'You need to make sure that the guys are comfortable with it and their families are comfortable with it,' which is equally as important. So I had the conversation with everyone on that Sunday and said, 'Don't give me an answer immediately, speak with your families', because there was a risk that there could quite easily be more issues while the guys were working there. And in fact, when they were working on one of the lines, they got locked in on site because there was a security threat. They were trapped and that was a massive concern to me because it was completely on my shoulders as I'd asked them all to work there.

"They were offered counselling, none of them took it and none has since needed any form of counselling. A large part of that is because they deal with horrific situations every day. They deal with fatalities, suicides, road traffic accidents, all sorts of things. But because there were so many of them, and because they all came together to put London back on its feet, they were really proud to be involved. That helped take away the horrible side of it.

"At the end of the day, somebody had to do that job. All of us would say we're proud. We wouldn't want to have to do it again, but that's simply because we wouldn't want that to happen again. But if it did, a lot of these guys still work here, and I know that if something similar happened tomorrow, each and every one of them would put their hands up."

BUBONIC PLAGUE AND LANDMINES

In 2009, Rentokil flew a team of 32 experts from the UK to Libya to deal with the major public health problem of diseases spread by rats, including the nasty leishmaniasis, which comes from the protozoan-infected parasitical sandflies carried by the fat sand rat (*Psammomys obesus*). Richard Jones, Regional Managing Director Middle East, North Africa and Turkey, recounts what happened in the baking heat.

"Libya certainly was a bit of a challenge. I guess the biggest issue we had to overcome was logistics. Apart from a few main roads, there were no street names and no postcode system and we had circa 100,000 bait points to install across the three main cities – Tripoli, Mistratah and Benghazi – so establishing where we'd placed them and finding our way back was a headache.

Rentokil vehicles and equipment had to be shipped to Tobruk by military transport plane in an emergency response to an outbreak of bubonic plague.

"In the end we divided each city up into 1km by 1km squares on Google Earth then wrote software for our PDAs which allowed us to pinpoint where we had placed the rodent bait units and provided route guidance to technicians to get them back there each time, recognising which square they were in in that city automatically.

"This was a major public health programme for the country and the people in the cities in Libya thought it was fantastic because they were sick of seeing rats everywhere.

Meeting the challenges of a major threat to public health in the intense desert heat of Libya.

"One day I got a call in the early hours of the morning about an outbreak of bubonic blague in Tobruk. Within five or six hours we were driving onto military air transporters with our vans and gear. It was the weekend so I had to track down colleagues in the UK to flag up what was happening and seek advice. I remember getting hold of our Chief Scientific Officer, Peter Whittall, on the Saturday morning and asking him for assistance in getting advice from the London School of Hygiene & Tropical Medicine. I also asked whether he thought working in an area where bubonic plague had broken out or stepping on landmines from the second world war was the biggest risk for our risk assessment form!

"The Libyan army were helping us avoid the landmines; when they found anything they put wooden stakes in the ground and taped the area off. One morning we came back and the villagers had taken all the wooden stakes to build animal shelters!

"It was a brilliant team effort that was massively appreciated by the people of Libya and helped protect them from disease and plague."

TRANS-SHIPMENT... AND PESKY MONGOOSE IMPORTS

Rentokil Initial Jamaica Managing Director, Maurice Goldson, a 16-year veteran of the company, says the Caribbean island's greater focus on exports is delivering exciting growth opportunities for his business.

"The business in Jamaica started with an acquisition in 1968 and was at first just in pest control. We service right through the island. There are around 40 persons working in the business and we are still seeking to grow. Our head office is in Kingston, we have another office in Mandeville in the middle of Jamaica and then there's a depot in Montego Bay which was opened two years ago.

"The big opportunities for us really are in export, agri-export and tourism. In terms of major business opportunities, Jamaica is planning a huge trans-shipment development. We're not far from the Panama Canal and the country is setting itself up to grasp more export business. Due to the standards that are required overseas now – ISO 9000 or 22000 [quality and food safety management standards] – there is a need for proper pest control and hygiene in various locations. People are becoming more aware of the importance of hygiene, of hand care, whereas before it was less of an issue.

"We have a lot of mountain ranges in the middle of Jamaica. It's said that when Christopher Columbus wanted to describe the island he took a piece of paper, crushed it, threw it down and said, 'That's Jamaica', because it's so steep in the middle. We have clients who are deep in the hills; sometimes, when the weather is bad, it's challenging for our technicians to get to them across rivers and on narrow roads. But our response time is crucial to us and our technicians always go the extra mile because there's a certain level of pride in the quality of service and quality of product.

Although not indigenous to the country, mongooses have established themselves in Jamaica.

"Beyond traditional pests like rats and mice, we are now catching mongooses, which we have never caught before. They were brought into Jamaica way back because there was a belief there were snakes on the island. But the few snakes that there were, they dealt with. Once they'd dispensed with the snakes it meant they had to find something else to eat – things like chickens. It's not an overrun situation but one particular factory had a fair amount hiding on their property. We set up huge traps that are sometimes used to catch cats and baited them with raw meat – nicely placed, nicely dripping – or eggs, because they like that sort of thing. And we checked them daily. We're not the kind to kill the mongoose, so we carried them to a distant place and let them loose in the hills.

"We deal with pigeons in the cities, but out in the countryside we get calls for bats. We don't kill them either. We try to find a way to drive them out by making the area they live in uncomfortable. If they live in the roof of a house we put things inside there which cause them to leave. We don't seal the area where they exit: we put a bit of mesh over it so if any young ones are left behind they are still able to exit, but those outside can't come back in. Bats really are significant in terms of ecological balance because of the amount of insects they eat in the night-time."

CORPORATE SNAKE REMOVAL

Rentokil Initial India Managing Director, Sam Easaw, reveals that dealing with snakes safely and educating children about hygiene are both issues that really matter.

"The Indian cobra, common krait, Russell's viper and the saw-scaled viper are among the common species of dangerous snake indigenous to India. They have to be controlled in populated areas and at industrial sites to minimise death due to snake bites. To many people, their mere presence is simply frightening.

"Not everyone, of course. India is famed for its ancient tradition of snake charming. *Saperas*, to give snake charmers their correct name, used to be a common sight across the country – holding snakes and fostering the illusion that they were hypnotising the reptiles by playing a wind instrument called the *pungi*. In fact, the snakes only appear to dance. What they are actually doing is following the movement of the snake charmer's *pungi* with their heads. They consider the person and instrument a threat, responding by movement as if confronted by a predator.

"Snake charming was a common practice until changes to the law in the early 1970s. The charmers would take enough measures to keep themselves out of danger, like maintaining a safe distance from the snake, removing the fangs – or worse, sewing the snake's mouth shut. But as part of their training snake charmers are taught how to handle snakes adeptly and what to do in the event of a snake bite. They also help people get rid of serpents from their homes.

Indian snake charmers give the illusion of hypnotising serpents while playing a woodwind instrument called a pungi.

"The Indian government has permitted a few snake charmers to perform at specified tourist sites to save the art. But at Rentokil we are utilising some of these traditional skills as part of a modern approach to pest control. Not only have Rentokil technicians received some training from the Irula tribal group renowned for its expertise in snake and rat catching, a few of our technicians actually belong to that tribe. These days when seizing snakes they use all the necessary safety gadgets, including gum boots, snake catching sticks and specialised leather gloves as well as the normal PPEs (personal protective equipment). The technicians also exercise the Irula way of treating snakebites with tree barks at the work site as an alternative to anti-venom.

"A lot of our work with corporate clients in sectors such as food processing, pharmaceutical, industrial and manufacturing is about reducing the risk of snakes getting on site in the first place. We identify the entry points and help clients rectify the issue, using repellents to keep snakes away. If required, we plan a fortnightly or monthly snake-catching session at the client location. We work with the Forest Service to release captured snakes back into their natural habitat. They also help us in combing the areas that are prone to snakes five to ten times in a year."

CHAPTER
TEN
Reinventing Rentokil

When celebrating a landmark birthday, the tendency is to look back at past achievements, as has been the case with much of this book. Yet great brands only become great brands by remaining relevant, sustaining high standards and keeping one eye on the future. Although nine-tenths of a century is a long time by anybody's reckoning, there's every reason to be confident that the Rentokil brand will still be in rude health another 90 years from now. A lot of the work going on today in product and service innovation is laying down firm foundations for the years ahead. Rentokil is being reinvented.

Who knows whether technicians in the faraway year 2105 will be travelling to meet customers on hoverboards or teleporting to appointments – improbable as it may sound? Perhaps they will be working from home, directing pest management drones or remotely controlling a posse of robotic rodent wranglers to hunt down the most cunning pests. But if that's the way the industry has moved, the likelihood is that Rentokil will have led the way.

Through innovation and improvement, invention and reinvention; through fostering great values and building on them; by pushing the boundaries with new products, new services, new ways of solving problems for customers; by being unafraid to question the norm and where necessary disrupt tired old models, Rentokil Initial is making sure it has the agility to keep ahead of the competition. There's plenty to be proud of in the company's rich heritage, but how it is preparing for the future counts for considerably more.

At the heart of the reinvention of Rentokil is the work of the Global Science Centre in the UK. If the company has a James Bond 'Q' figure, it is surely the Director of Service and Science Innovation, Savvas Othon.

Othon first joined the business as a technician in 1994 after completing a degree in environmental biology and says his early days in the field have proved invaluable. "All the crazy ideas that you have as a technician when you're walking around on the streets, my role now has allowed me to make some of these dreams come true. All of it's wacky. That's my job, isn't it? I need to experiment and discover things that people haven't discovered."

In terms of pest control, Othon is frustrated by how much of a technician's time is wasted checking bait boxes. He believes that if the company develops better ways of detecting pests it will be a win-win scenario: higher job satisfaction for employees and a more tailored, cost-effective service for clients. As a result, interesting new avenues for pest detection are being explored. And the source of inspiration can be surprising.

POPPING CANDY

"One night I was sitting at home with my young daughter and she had popping candy in her mouth," says Othon. "She's eating it and it's noisy. So I started thinking, if you could detect the popping candy you could detect where it was coming from. If you put it in rat bait you could detect that – then you've got smart rat bait. So I got ten kilos of popping candy delivered and I said to the scientists, 'Make me a popping candy bait'. They all looked horrified – *What's going on? The lunatic's taken over the asylum.* But it worked. We got lots of popping noises from rats and cockroaches. It was the most palatable bait that we've ever formulated. But it still relied on the mouse or rat interacting with that bait. As we were going down that road, we thought about detecting ultrasound, because it's the secret language of rodents. They talk in ultrasound."

While humans can perceive sounds in a range up to 20 kilohertz, rats and mice are able to communicate using sounds at far higher frequencies than can be heard by the human ear. Research into the effects of ultrasound on rodents is far from new. Indeed, Rentokil itself conducted some ultrasonic experiments in the outdoor rat pen at Felcourt in the early 1970s. The results proved inconclusive. A device emitting high frequency noise was placed next to an established feeding point in the pen. Food consumption immediately dropped by 30% but soon returned to normal levels. Given the huge advances in technology since then, Rentokil is taking a fresh look at the possibilities.

One of the key players in what is referred to as the ultrasonic vocalisation (USV) programme is Andy Brigham, General Technical Manager, Business Support, at the Global Science Centre. Brigham came to Rentokil, also in 1994, after completing a PhD in wild rat feeding behaviour with a particular focus on neophobia – fear of the new. He was instrumental in the development of Rentokil's hi-tech RADAR mousetrap, which uses carbon dioxide to kill mice humanely. RADAR is a wonderful illustration of the unique edge Rentokil has over its rivals. It took three years of persistence to gain regulatory approval for RADAR and Rentokil remains one of only a few companies in the world able to use CO_2 gas in pest control.

"We constantly look for better methods of detection," says Brigham. "Looking at the ultrasound has certainly been interesting. You have to start by having a bit of a play – and this is one of the great things about working at Rentokil – we have licence to innovate. Maybe some things don't work but then you get to the point where there might be something useful. How rodents make use of ultrasound is fascinating because some of the predators of rats and mice won't be able to hear that noise. What you've got is a bit like an encrypted military communication channel. This is a way for rodents to talk to each other without it being picked up. It's really quite smart when you start thinking about it."

Dr Andy Brigham MSB CBiol, General Technical Manager, Science and Service, at the Global Science Centre.

WAKE UP AND SMELL THE COFFEE

Detection is the main focus of Rentokil's experiments with ultrasound at the moment. Yet, as in the 1970s, there is also some investigation into its use as a repellent and even as a means of encouraging pests to approach.

Research is being carried out into whether domesticated mice have the same language as wild mice, and whether wild mice in one region have the same language as mice living somewhere else. It may be that mice in Yorkshire differ in how they communicate from those found in Cornwall, and that Italian field mice squeak a different language to those from Sweden. Recordings captured using specialist equipment are being analysed in the search for answers.

Tighter restrictions on pest control chemicals, for example through EU Biocidal Products Regulations (BPR), provides a spur for innovation.

More environmentally friendly alternatives to poisonous bait are being developed. RADAR has proven so effective at trapping and killing mice using CO_2 that it is increasingly being deployed as a pest control solution, as well as for the monitoring and detection job for which it was originally envisaged. A multi-catch rat trap, which likewise kills quickly and contains, is at the prototype stage.

Additionally, Rentokil is experimenting with essential oils to create scents that are particularly attractive to rodents and to artificially replicate 'fear scents' that could be used to drive them away. There's mounting evidence from the high street that mice are attracted to the smell of coffee, making cafes particularly vulnerable to infestation. As many a human with a fondness for lattes or Americanos will agree, the aroma of good coffee can be pretty beguiling.

SMARTER RODENT CONTROL

It looks like an ordinary doll's house standing at the edge of a children's bedroom but the little grey faces of mice peeking out through the windows and the tails pushing through the crevices between the roof and the walls tell a different story. The colourful wooden doll's house is just one of the features of a penned area specially created at Rentokil's Global Technical Centre to monitor the behaviour of mice.

"Understanding their behaviour helps us to do a better job for customers," says Stewart Power, Marketing & Innovation Director. "It emphasises the need for a three-dimensional approach to pest control. The mice do not stay on one level or one location, but scatter across to explore every corner and crevice in the pen. Activity levels are heightened the darker the environment."

Behavioural insights are already emerging. The mice have not reached the surface of a kitchen cabinet because their claws are unable to gain purchase on certain types of smooth materials. By contrast, the top shelves of a wooden bookcase are littered with droppings – evidence that mice have been exploring. Some have climbed the unit by wrapping their legs around an electrical wire flex that dangles through a hole between shelves. Others have managed to grip their claws on the wood's chinks and cracks. "They've edged up, resting their back against the wall to help them," Power adds. Others have easily mastered a racking frame. On one shelf, a lone mouse sits at the edge of the hole, prompting would-be intruders to peek through and scurry away. It may be a one-off event, or an indication as to how mice mark and protect their territories.

The challenge for Rentokil is to take these insights and use them to produce new solutions and better trained technicians.

CCTV cameras monitor the mice at all times. Other than providing the best food and water, the scientists do not interfere with the mice's living environment. By studying their actions and behaviour, they can create methods to prevent or deter mice from accessing properties. It is about ensuring the mice or rats do not enter certain spaces.

A baby mouse can squeeze through a gap just six millimetres across, roughly the width of a pencil, which highlights the challenges in making properties totally invasion-proof. It may be more appropriate to slow down methods of access dramatically or to identify ways to prevent mice exploring beyond the environs in which they first enter.

The solution here may lie with boards, resembling draught excluders, fitted along the base of doors. Most doors have gaps between their base and floorboards, and plugging these may help slow infestations.

A wall fitted with a plastic strip that has dense bristles along its base divides another pen. There are no obvious points of entry here. The key instead is to watch how long the mice take before they break through the excluder into the space on the other side. In the event, it took several days for the mice to gnaw through the plastic bristles of a draught excluder. As a result, new rodent-proofing products are on the way as well as technical training on the most effective places to install them.

It may resemble a dolls' house but this empty mouse house has been carefully created to study the behaviour of mice.

Mice are monitored by CCTV around the clock as they explore what The Daily Telegraph *dubbed "The Big Brother Mouse House" and other parts of the penned area.*

Scientists are also observing how mice and rats interact with bait boxes. Where once mice and rats would happily have explored bait boxes, evidence has emerged that in some areas their behaviour has changed and they will avoid the traps and move round them.

Andy Brigham takes up the story: "We actually first studied this behaviour in mice in the early 1990s. At that time the mice in an area of Birmingham were so different in their behaviour to bait boxes and traps that the first student gave up when he couldn't catch any mice to study. Finally, a colleague got his first mice when he noticed some living in the bin at the back of a famous fast food retailer – he had to negotiate with them to take the bin away and race back down to Reading with his captured mice!"

Today, there is evidence that this behaviour has been seen in other locations around the world and Rentokil's scientists are studying whether larger or smaller holes make a difference to this behaviour, where the hole should be positioned on bait boxes and what colours or aromas may lure rats and mice in.

Understanding behaviour can lead to more effective rodent traps and bait types.

RodentGate is the most recent invention to launch, initially in Germany, to great success. The unit features a 'gate' which keeps the bait safe and fresh until the mechanism is activated when rodent movements break infra-red beams. The gate then opens, allowing access to the bait. Because slugs and other creatures are stopped from accessing the bait, the unit is highly effective. It boosts technician productivity and ensures accurate bait usage within the controlled boundaries.

At a time when the EU is legislating against the use of traditional rodenticides in open areas, the now-patented RodentGate has impressed regulators and experts in the industry. Just one example of where Rentokil can use its scientific backbone to provide competitive advantage.

Alongside innovations such as this, Rentokil is campaigning for better product stewardship, again to limit instances of secondary poisoning and to ensure the appearance of poisonous residues among wildlife is kept as low as possible. The company is a member of the Campaign for Responsible Rodenticide Use (CRRU).

Protecting wildlife and the broader environment are laudable concerns. And of course Rentokil is utterly behind those aims. Yet at the same time it is vocal in championing the importance of pest control in relation to safeguarding public health.

"There is a balance that needs to be made," says Product Development Director, Nigel Cheeseright, "and at the moment the strength of the human health argument tends to get lost because people are focusing on resolving environmental impact matters. Clearly they are very important, but if you balance that against human health I know which one would win for me."

The Global Science Centre, which covers the full range of pests, not only monitors behaviour and creates units for today, but is always on the lookout for what could make a breakthrough in years to come. Currently under trial is a range of repellents which might not quite match up to the Pied Piper – but, as Rentokil carries on reinventing itself, it gets ever closer to turning myth into reality.

SMART SURFACES

Matt Green, who holds a PhD in wood-boring insects, is one of the company's entomologists. Like Brigham, his work is wide-ranging. Among the areas he is delving into are: using the principles of dazzle camouflage on warships to confuse flies by making it harder for them to identify fly killers; exploring different design options for flytraps featuring ultraviolet; making insect traps out of different materials. For example, bed bugs are averse to smooth surfaces such as plastic, so a trap made out of compressed MDF is under test. There is also testing on a recently patented bed bug detection tool. This uses conductive ink printed onto a flat surface such as a piece of card or tape. Crudely, when a bed bug goes to its natural harbourage and defecates, it completes the circuit, alerting people to an infestation. Similarly, work is underway on the delivery of insecticides through 'smart surfaces' which are activated when insects walk over or land on them.

The prevalence of bed bugs is a serious concern. In April 2015, respected science writer Brooke Borel published a new book *Infested: How the Bed Bug Infiltrated Our Bedrooms and Took Over the World*. The title says it all. Clearly, the work Rentokil is doing to combat these unwelcome insects is much needed.

COCKROACH-KILLING FUNGI

Given the level of mounting regulations surrounding chemical pesticides, the scientific team is researching effective alternatives. The agriculture sector has been utilising biopesticides for a number of years and Rentokil is taking a long hard look at how some of the lessons learnt by large-scale commercial food and plant growers can be applied to urban pest control. One such area is cockroach-killing fungi – based on a fungus that is particularly hazardous to cockroaches while being safe for most other creatures, especially for human beings. The fungus is applied and attaches itself to the cockroach, sporulates, penetrates its outer shell and starts to react chemically with the insect's system. The first wave of trials has been very promising and one major plus point is that it is self-propagating because cockroaches are cannibals. By feeding on a cockroach killed by the biopesticide, the next cockroach also becomes infected. Cockroaches have already been successfully removed from one wing of a UK jail and a housing estate in Malaysia using this method.

Dead cockroaches. Rentokil has been developing heat treatments and natural fungi for dispensing with these stubborn pests.

USING HEAT TO CONTROL INSECTS

Rentokil's Entotherm Heat Pod kills insects in environments such as hospitals, hotels and food-processing facilities. This uses controlled application of heat to kill insects at all life stages, from egg to adult, and has the great advantage of being chemical-free. Through extensive testing Rentokil has established that sustaining a temperature of 54.4°

Celsius for an hour causes denaturation: damage to the cells of both adult and egg that is irreversible.

Setting up a mobile Entotherm heat treatment pod.

Developed in partnership with Revival Environmental, Entotherm won the Best Business Award for Best Innovation in the Private Sector. It is a mobile system flexible enough to deliver dry transferable heat to any contained area, large or small, infested with insect pests. The treatment works by heating a liquid syrup and delivering it through insulated pipes to heat exchangers placed within the infested area. The heat exchangers convert heat into hot dry air. Strategically placed heat probes monitor and record the core temperature. The process is monitored remotely, producing a computer-generated graph as proof of heat exposure. The treatment area is heated to eradicate pests, but not to a temperature that causes structural damage to the objects being treated. Rentokil can run reports using the heat probes and thermal imaging technology to confirm that all target pests have been eradicated effectively.

"We've heated up entire factories," says Othon. "In the UK in 2009 we heated up a bakery that was 100,000 square metres. We heated it up and held the temperature. It took us over a weekend to heat it up because all the metallic objects took a lot of the energy. We used 11 diesel generators and each diesel generator had 50 radiators in there. We heated the entire factory: no damage, killed the cockroaches and the customer was ready to bake as soon as we packed up our stuff because there were no chemicals."

The scale is undeniably impressive, but of course there are times when smaller equals better. Currently under development is a lightweight heat pod that's sufficiently compact to fit inside a backpack. Once unpacked, it will be large enough to treat individual pieces of furniture in a hotel room. And it will allow technicians to work alone and if necessary without a vehicle – useful in busy city centres.

SOLUTIONS FOR A CONNECTED WORLD

"The sensing programme is probably the biggest area of opportunity and challenge for us over the next three to five years," says Cheeseright. "We hear people talking of the internet of things and connected cities and connected buildings. Part of the challenge for us is to figure out how our pest control products fit into that future connected world. And what that means for our business and our service to customers. We need to make sure sensing can be a competitive advantage for us."

Investment in PestConnect – a remote monitoring service – provides a shining example of Rentokil playing its part in the shift to greater connectivity. And in so doing, stealing a march on less technologically sophisticated rivals.

Rentokil's investment in remote monitoring services highlights a shift within the business to greater connectivity.

The global roll-out of the myRentokil customer extranet, together with a myRentokil app available for iOS and Android, is providing customers with more real-time information than ever before, including bill information and status updates on remote monitoring for those signed up. On top of this, there has been a major redevelopment of the company's external websites – there are approximately 150 different domains across the world – to provide a more consistent experience, improve the online customer journey and to offer greater insight into who prospective and new customers are and what they are looking for.

Customers expect services that are more immediate and comprehensive than in the past. The key going forward will be to ensure a healthy balance between smart technological and product development and the unmatchable skills and expertise of technicians in the field.

Sensing, as we have seen, offers tremendous opportunities for the future of pest control. As better means of detection emerge, the likelihood is that a multi-modal approach will come to the fore at certain sites with multiple different means of 'pest sensing' brought together and connected via extranets and apps.

THWARTING SCAMS

As well as product development, the scientists at the Global Science Centre are called into action to help customers resolve contamination problems. On occasion this can extend to thwarting scams and attempts at blackmail.

"We had a case where somebody complained to one of our customers that they had found a live rat inside a multi-bag of crisps which had then run round their kitchen before they had bashed it and killed it," Brigham recalls. "That seemed ridiculous anyway because a live rat would easily have been able to get out of the pack.

"When we got this carcass, first of all it was ringing wet, which is quite often what happens when something is decomposing, and the fur was peeling off. There were some pupal cases and dead larvae on it, so I gave that to Matt, our Entomologist. It's a bit like they can sometimes do with dead people in pathology labs – if there are certain flies, you can tell how long someone has been dead. We are not CSI but we know how long the life-stage takes and there's no way that could have happened before the rat was dead or in the space of time between this person allegedly killing it and sending it back to the manufacturer and then to our business. Most of the time it was kept refrigerated and sealed up. So this animal was somewhere

where flies would have laid eggs and they would have hatched. This person found a rat carcass and thought, I'll try it on.

"Some of these strange things do happen and they are interesting because you get the chance to piece together what you know about rats, mice and even insect biology to reveal a story which we can then use with our business to help our customer. And of course they like it if you can provide them with a letter written by a specialist."

ON COURSE FOR THE 22ND CENTURY

It's reassuring to know that a business which built its early success on the back of ground-breaking products still takes innovation so seriously. As change is inevitable, it's vital that the innovation process delivers products and solutions that help maintain the edge the business has over its competitors.

Without question, some highly sensitive, tricky issues need to be addressed. But by hiring great people, training them to be outstanding and giving them the best tools and technology to do the job, Rentokil is future-proofing itself. Right now, there's no reason at all to suppose that it won't still be leading the way around the world in the 22nd century. Probably armed with technology that today we couldn't even guess at.

Come what may, the Rentokil brand is here to stay.

RENTOKIL: EXPERTS IN INNOVATION

Rentokil Initial has stepped up its commitment to R&D in recent years. From weird science to cutting-edge design, the boffins are thinking outside the (bait) box. By experimenting with new technologies and refining existing ones, they are making sure the business stays at least one step ahead of the competition. Here's a brief guide to some of the pioneering work being coordinated out of the Global Science Centre in the UK:

- **Ultrasonic vocalisations (USVs).** Experiments in detecting, repelling and attracting rodents using ultrasound.

- **Entotherm.** Heat treatment to control insects.

- **Multi-catch RADAR.** Hi-tech rodent traps able to contain and humanely control multiple rodents at the same time.

- **Smart surfaces.** Insects walk over them and are either detected or controlled by insecticides in the materials.

- **Fungus.** Natural fungus that is deadly to cockroaches.

- **RodentGate.** Another innovation unique to Rentokil – allows only the target species to access the bait.

- **myRentokil.** App that lets customers monitor for pest activity and manage their pest control service.

CHAPTER
ELEVEN
Adapt, Change, Improve and Excel

Rentokil has many longstanding customers but the longest uninterrupted customer relationship of all stretches back 80 years. Wrekin College, a high-performing independent school in the picturesque Shropshire town of Wellington, first signed up for pest control services in 1935, the year that Stanley Baldwin became British Prime Minister.

Wrekin College in the 1920s, the decade before the school became a Rentokil client.

Nestled beneath local landmark the Wrekin, a hill offering stunning views, the school was founded by Sir John Bayley in 1880 and ever since has held fast to the philosophy that each pupil should be treated as an individual rather than taught as if Mother Nature churned out endless identikit children. Wrekin College was one of the first schools of its type to become coeducational when girls were admitted in 1975. The decision was taken purely because of the belief in its educational merits, rather than any financial considerations, and to this day the school continues to nurture innovation and cherish individualism while instilling in its pupils the importance of community. Given these values, it's no surprise that its relationship with Rentokil has been long and harmonious.

"Wrekin College is proud to have an enduring business relationship with Rentokil – being its oldest customer worldwide," says the school's Marketing Manager, Andy Nicoll. "Wrekin has the highest of expectations, striving to provide the best education for its pupils and demanding exacting standards from suppliers and contractors. There have been many changes over the decades in the world of education, with Wrekin College going from strength to strength, and we are delighted to say that Rentokil has matched Wrekin's ability to adapt, change, improve and excel."

Area Operations Manager Mark Brown handing over a certificate of recognition to Wrekin College Headmaster Dr Haydn Griffiths.

Today around 400 pupils attend Wrekin, which for many years was known locally as 'The School in the Garden' due to the extensive greenery of its 100-acre site abounding with mature trees, extensive gardens and playing fields. The relationship between Wrekin and Rentokil has blossomed for such a long time because of the continuity and quality of the pest control services.

Rentokil's local technician, Glynn Teece, has been with the business for almost 30 years – and has worked with Wrekin all that time. His primary focus is on keeping the school canteen and surrounding buildings free from rats, mice and cockroaches. He's also on call to deal with infestations of flies, ants or other pests which may present themselves in the buildings or grounds. As Teece has been coming to the school for so long, he is a popular visitor who is on first-name terms with many members of staff.

Seek and ye shall find. Rentokil technician Glynn Teece is guided by the light as he kneels in the school chapel.

Rentokil and Wrekin have in common an illustrious past, commitment to deep-seated values and an appetite for evolution. That's why both organisations are preparing for the future with well-founded optimism.

CHAPTER
TWELVE
The Pest Detectives

Sure, Hercule Poirot and Sherlock Holmes could smell a rat. But could they catch one? As pests are possessed of certain Moriarty-esque qualities such as cunning and elusiveness, it's far from easy.

Pest control is often about detective work. It requires an inquiring mind and determination to get to the answer. Where is the source of an infestation? What is causing the problem? Which are the real clues to follow up as a priority – and which are the red herrings to be dismissed? Where's the best location to lay the trap? And what sort of trap should it be?

Over the following pages we highlight some real life 'pest detectives' and how their actions have helped rid businesses around the world of their pest problems.

Ricardo Felix: Pest Control Technician
Lisbon, Portugal

LISBON'S TRICKY RATS

Controlling black rats is one of the most difficult pest problems to solve. They are much harder to catch than brown rats because they like to scurry around at height, in ceilings and on rooftops. They also refuse to eat conventional rat bait.

However, they were no match for Rentokil's man in Lisbon. Working with his colleagues in the technical department, Ricardo Felix visited his customer three times a week for a year, using a number of different fruit and liquid baits (rather than traditional ones) to catch these tricky rodents. His customers were delighted with his dedication – they had previously thought the pests would never be eradicated.

COCKROACH-ULATIONS

Barbados is home to some of the world's most beautiful beaches and the rich and famous flock to its Platinum Coast. A lot of Rentokil's work on the island involves supporting the tourism industry through services to hotels, restaurants, food manufacturers and warehouses.

Alex Kirton has been working for Rentokil for over 40 years. This may sound remarkable, but not in Barbados where half of the workforce has been with the company for over 30 years! Technicians like Alex have grown up with their customers and are now looking after their customers' children's businesses.

He started off as a Termite Control Technician before broadening out his detective work to general pests and the usual run of rats, flies and cockroaches. Mosquitoes are becoming an increasing problem in the Caribbean, in light of the recent outbreak of the chikungunya virus, which is transmitted by the insects.

Barbados was the first country in the Caribbean to introduce RADAR (the world's smartest mousetrap) and Luminos fly control units. Alex has a keen nose for detecting cockroaches as demonstrated by his visits to the cathedral in Bridgetown. In spite of regular visits, Alex was puzzled as to why the ongoing treatment of American cockroaches wasn't working effectively.

On a hunch he decided to investigate the ceiling, which was not covered by the service contract, and detected a strong roach-like odour from within. Following treatment with insecticidal misting, the customer called early the next morning to report that the cleaners were having to use wheelbarrows to get rid of all the dead cockroaches.

Another historical building had been saved!

Alex Kirton: Pest Control Technician
Bridgetown, Barbados

Rodrigo dos Santos: Pest Control Technician
São Paulo, Brazil

BRAZILIAN DEFENCE HOLDS FIRM

Rodrigo dos Santos spent over three years in the field, gaining experience in many different positions, and is now an expert in pest control in the food manufacturing industry.

His proudest achievement to date is the eradication of rats in one of the country's biggest producers of rice and bean products. Working with the customer, he managed to track down a very high rodent infestation and get rid of the problem. The customer has registered zero rodent activity for five months and counting.

Based in São Paulo, Rodrigo has been involved with many large customers – producers of snack foods, chocolates, rice, pasta, soy sauce, butter and cheese – successfully keeping insect populations and other pests under control. Top priority is always given to health and safety requirements, with potential hazards assessed continuously. Rodrigo loves his job in Pest Control because of the variety of daily challenges it provides. He has started a degree in chemical engineering.

Martin Münchau and Marco Haas: Service Manager and Service Technician
Hamburg, Germany

CRUISE CONTROL

Rentokil's Pest Control team in Hamburg showed just how organised you have to be to succeed in Pest Control, when a customer faced an outbreak of bed bugs on a cruise liner.

Within a matter of days, Service Manager Martin Münchau and Service Technician Marco Haas had boarded the passenger liner in Venice. Over the next ten days they inspected 180 cabins.

Although spending time on a cruise liner sounds like a nice perk, Martin and Marco worked day and night to identify the problem areas and then carried out a specialist heat treatment in 32 cabins. Invented by Rentokil, the heat treatment works by raising the temperature in the room to a point at which insects die, but without causing damage to property. The advantage of heat is that it works its way into every part of a room quickly and easily, including into cracks or under skirting boards.

A follow-up inspection a month later in Kiel found a re-infestation in only one passenger cabin, which was quickly eliminated using the heat treatment. On this visit, the Rentokil team also spotted a new problem with fruit flies and was able to help the customer eliminate this infestation within 24 hours.

When the vessel was reassessed six months later, the inspection confirmed that all bed bugs and fruit fly infestations had been eliminated. Job done!

Helen Theron: Group Innovation Scientist
Horsham, UK

AN EYE FOR A FLY

Helen Theron is one of Rentokil's insect experts, with a particular speciality in flies. She's counted tens of thousands of them over the years. At the Global Science Centre, Helen routinely carries out tests on the efficiency of all of the company's fly control units as well as those of competitors. Methods are rigorous and reliable – and the fly trials are certified by SINTEF, the largest independent research organisation in Scandinavia.

But Helen doesn't only have an eye for the flies.

With her colleagues in the biology laboratory, she observes all species of insects. She's even propagated two different species of ant. It takes genuine expertise to create an artificial environment that contains all the elements essential for a social ant colony to thrive.

By understanding insect behaviour, Rentokil provides the best training for Pest Control Service Technicians and supports new product development.

Mao Yonggan: Service Manager
Shanghai, China

A HUMAN ENCYCLOPAEDIA

Shanghai-based Mao Yonggan is one of the pioneers of Rentokil Initial China. He joined the organisation when it was established in 2006 and has helped it go from strength to strength. Recently he played a key role in winning business with a major retail customer after leading a specialist team in an intensive, month-long rodent control programme.

Yonggan is known to his colleagues as a walking pest control encyclopaedia – even the trickiest of critters don't stand a chance when they come to his attention. As customers in China have responded to tightened food industry regulations, Yonggan's expertise in developing comprehensive pest control plans and improving hygiene standards across outlets nationwide has increased demand for his team's services.

"We take our professional image very seriously," says Yonggan. "Awareness of the need for pest control is growing in China. At the same time we are continually strengthening our pest control skills. As the saying goes, live and learn."

Anil Kumar John: Service Supervisor
Cochin, India

PROTECTING YOUR FOOD

When a fly infestation at a customer's food-processing plant got out of hand, Anil Kumar John was the first to get to the root of the problem. Anil observed that the factory floor workers had poor hygiene practices and bad habits around improper disposal of food waste.

After raising it with the relevant authorities and getting the problem fixed, Anil went on to coordinate a series of PestAware education sessions, which not only increased health and hygiene standards but reduced the potential for future infestations.

Eddie Conklin: Bird Specialist Technician
New York, USA

REACHING NEW HEIGHTS

Eddie Conklin is an expert in bird control who works in the New York area.

He started off as a general Pest Control Technician, but his mechanical abilities and finesse with tools were quickly spotted and before long he was working with the specialised bird teams.

Eddie loves a challenge, which is handy because no two jobs he is given are the same. He enjoys working at stadiums because they have a high public profile and people immediately understand the importance of bird control.

Conversely, he relishes the challenge of doing jobs for organisations such as the Port Authority of New York and the US government. Restricted access to sites means they have to find a discreet, unique bird solution for each problem area. The fun side is seeing things like the inside of aircraft hangars, something most other people never get to do.

Eddie is qualified to do all manner of bird control work, including netting, installing electric track systems or grid systems, setup of spikes or repellents, and carrying out clean-ups.

He is often required to work up in the air – just as well he has a head for heights!

FROM COP TO DETECTIVE

Pest control is a zero tolerance issue in New Zealand given the importance of its food production industry. On the front line is Mike Parsons, who recently celebrated his 11th year with Rentokil and is a fully qualified and registered technician of the Pest Management Association of New Zealand.

Originally a police officer in England before he emigrated, Mike is a keen advocate of health and safety. It doesn't matter what the task, 'safety first' is the golden rule in Rentokil.

A thorough professional brimming with enthusiasm and experience, Mike typifies the excellence that sits at the core of Rentokil's business and shows just why Rentokil is supporting New Zealand's food export trade.

Approximately half his workload is for dairy factories. The main pests to look out for on these sites are rodents, birds and 'stored product' pests such as carpet beetle and biscuit beetle.

According to Mike, the rats in New Zealand are the same as in England. However, the cockroaches are more plentiful, with various species such as the Gisborne cockroach from the tropics.

Now you know who keeps your delicious dairy products safe – a UK cop turned NZ pest detective.

Mike Parsons: Senior High Dependency Technician
Hamilton, New Zealand

THE PESTIARY

The bestiary, an illustrated compendium of beasts, was a popular form of medieval book. These illuminated manuscripts portrayed creatures of the natural world, sometimes with impressive attention to detail. Being the Middle Ages, the purpose and characteristics of the animals were usually described in a religious context, lessons in morality abounded and some bestiaries even included imaginary beasts. One of the most famous surviving examples, the *Aberdeen Bestiary*, features the dragon and the phoenix in its pages alongside beasts with a more legitimate claim to exist, such as the horse, deer, bat and ant.

Rest assured that in this **Rentokil pestiary**, the knowledge of household pests is up to date, there's no moralising... and nothing is made up.

Ants

As the majority of ant species prefer warmer temperatures, the UK climate is unsuitable for many of them. However, the few species found here can be a nuisance when they get into your home. Garden or black ants aren't thought to carry diseases; the trouble is you don't know where they've been foraging outside, so you won't want them marching through your food cupboards. Ants will travel in a wide range searching for food, following trails they have established and clustering around sources of food, becoming a nuisance in homes, organisations and businesses. Small piles of earth around holes in soil and at the base of exterior walls indicate their origin.

Some things you can do:

- track down where they are coming in and seal off the entry point

- clear up any sticky residues on worktops, because ants are attracted to sweet things

- cover up any foodstuffs which could be a food source for ants

- DIY products may deal with small garden ant problems. However, larger or multiple infestations of pharaoh, ghost or fire ants will require professional ant control to ensure it will not reoccur. Rentokil surveyors and technicians thoroughly understand the habits of each ant species.

Bed bugs

If you have bed bugs in your house, the only thing on your mind will be getting rid of them as quickly as possible. Bed bugs stay close to a food source, so are found where people tend to rest and sleep, hence the name. The frustration they can cause is not only due to the emotional stress of dealing with parasites, but also the irritation of their bites and the potential for secondary infection from scratching.

There has been a recent resurgence of bed bugs. It is widely thought that this is related to a global increase in international travel (bed bugs are known to travel in luggage or on clothing).

Birds

Pigeons and seagulls can become a real nuisance for your business. It's not just the mess they make; they can also damage your premises by dislodging roof tiles and blocking guttering.

There are a number of other problems that mean you should adopt bird control measures sooner rather than later.

Pigeons and seagulls on your premises can:

- be a health hazard, by spreading diseases such as ornithosis, gastroenteritis and salmonellosis

- deface buildings and vehicles with their droppings and foul entrances and pavements, which can become dangerously slippery

- encourage insect infestations such as bird mites, textile beetles and fleas (these are attracted to their nests and roosting sites)

- attack customers and employees, especially during the breeding season when defending their young.

Cockroaches

Finding cockroaches can be very distressing. As known carriers of diseases such as salmonellosis, dysentery and gastroenteritis, exposure to this pest also poses significant health risks. Increases in eczema and asthma have even been linked to cockroach droppings.

Cockroaches are very tough insects and their ability to breed rapidly makes professional treatment essential to control any infestation. Only expert products and solutions are powerful enough to eliminate them at all stages of their lifecycle.

If you have noticed an unpleasant lingering odour under sinks, behind appliances or in store cupboards, it's time to check for signs of cockroaches.

Signs of infestation:

- **Unusual smell** – An established cockroach infestation produces a lingering and unpleasant odour that taints items they contact.

- **Cockroach droppings** – If little water is available, cockroaches will produce brown/black cylindrical droppings, approx. 2mm long.

- **Smear marks** – If water is abundant, cockroaches will produce brown and irregular shaped smear marks. Check for marks on horizontal surfaces and at wall-floor junctions where cockroaches scuttle.

- **Shed skin** – Cockroaches shed 'cast nymphal skins' 5–8 times as they mature to adults. These are usually found close to where they are sheltering.

- **Check bathrooms, kitchens and laundry rooms** – German cockroaches need warmth and humidity so are likely to be found in and around bathrooms, laundry rooms and kitchen areas. They are also good climbers, scaling smooth surfaces like glass and polished metal with ease, thanks to sticky pads on their feet.

- **Check your basement** – Oriental cockroaches can cope with cooler, damp conditions and are more common scuttling about in basements or drains. If conditions are tolerable they can survive outside in areas such as rubbish tips. They are not as agile as German cockroaches, but can climb a surface such as rough brickwork.

Fleas

Fleas are a common problem in homes, especially those with pets. You may discover a problem with fleas even if you do not have pets, if previous owners of your property kept cats or dogs. The eggs hatch when disturbed by footfall and the flea then latches on to a new host.

Fleas may also be carried on other – especially hairy – animals like rabbits, foxes, squirrels, rats and mice, as well as livestock such as pigs.

As parasites, the greatest concern about the presence of fleas in your home or business comes from their bites. Although these are not painful, they can result in an uncomfortable itch or rash. Pets can also develop allergies to flea saliva.

Signs of infestation:

- Can you see fleas crawling on your pet's coat? They are normally reddy-brown and about 2mm long.

- Check the hind-quarters of your dog or the head and neck of your cat. These are the areas that are targeted and where you might see signs of flea activity.

- Carefully look at your pet's skin for fine black droppings. This is 'flea dirt' or adult flea faeces and looks like ground black pepper. A good way to spot it is to use a flea comb over a sheet of white paper.

- Another sign of a problem is flea dirt on pet bedding, carpets or rugs.

- Unfortunately, flea eggs are tiny (about 0.5mm long), oval and white and easily fall off pets' bodies into carpets etc., so are difficult to spot.

Flies

There are over 120,000 species of flies worldwide. Flies are considered pests because they pose a health risk to humans, pets and livestock.

They can infest your home or business and spread disease-causing organisms like salmonella and E. coli. A few species may even bite humans and animals.

If a small fly problem is left uncontrolled, it has the potential to turn into a serious infestation. Some fly species are able to mature from eggs to adults in just seven days.

Common house flies are attracted to decaying organic waste such as faeces and rotting meat, whereas fruit flies feed on overripe fruit, spilled soft drinks and alcohol.

Mice

Mice are known to spread disease as they search for food and shelter. This poses great health risks in kitchens or where children play.

Their natural and constant gnawing habit means mice can also cause great damage to your property, furnishings and equipment. Simple measures like mouse-proofing your property can help to protect you.

Signs of infestation:

- **Droppings** – 80 droppings a night, small and dark (approx. 3–8 mm in length), scattered randomly, check inside or on cupboard tops or along skirting.

- **Grease marks** (smudges or smears) – Caused by their bodies brushing against walls, floors and skirting on regular routes, dark smears around holes or around corners.

- **Urine pillars** – In established or heavy infestations, body grease, combined with dirt and urine, builds up into small mounds, up to 1cm high and 4cm wide.

- **Scratching noises** – Often at night when mice are most active. Listen for noises between partition walls, under floorboards, in false ceilings, basements and lofts.

- **Nests** – Using easy-to-shred materials, mice then line the nest with other soft materials. Check lofts, suspended ceilings, cavity walls, under floorboards and behind fridges, under stoves and in airing cupboards.

- **Tracks (footprints)** – Dusty environments such as unused lofts and basements can show up rodent tracks and tail marks. To check for activity, sprinkle flour, talcum powder or china clay and check the next day for fresh tracks.

- **Live or dead mice** – Mice are mainly nocturnal, so spotting a mouse during the daytime can be an indication of a heavy infestation.

- **Strong smell** – Mice urinate frequently and their wee has a strong ammonia-like smell. The stronger the smell, the closer you are to mice activity. This smell can linger for a long time (even after an infestation has been removed).

Moles

European (garden) moles can do considerable damage to turf, lawns, formal gardens, fairways, greens and sports grounds with their constant digging. They can quickly establish themselves in a location due to their ability to tunnel up to four metres an hour, creating complex burrow systems. The eyesight of moles is generally poor, as is their sense of smell. They find food by their acute sense of touch and vibration.

Mole hills and ridges spoil lawns, bowling and golf greens and flower beds. Their tunnelling damages the roots of young plants and exposes stones and debris that can damage machinery. These factors

are costly to gardeners and businesses that rely on their grounds, lawns, greens or gardens.

Moles prefer to inhabit areas which are rich in insects and earthworms, which account for the majority of their diet.

Mosquitoes and midges

Everyone knows how annoying – and painful – midges and mosquitoes can be. No matter how many you manage to swat, there always seem to be some that manage to get through to give you an itchy bite or two.

Here are some facts:

- they can develop from eggs to adults in just six to ten days

- they are found close to still water, where their larvae feed and develop

- they seem to be attracted to dark colours

- they will normally bite at dawn or dusk – or if you're unlucky, both. That's when their internal clocks let them know it's feeding time.

Moths

Most moths in the UK are seen as pests due to the damage their larvae cause to materials, textiles and stored products. Unlike other pests, moths pose no health risks.

Once inside your home or business, moth caterpillars can severely damage natural fibres in carpets, clothes, fabrics, fur and even leather.

Rats

Rats can be very persistent and if they gain access to your home or business can spread diseases, cause damage and contaminate food. One pair of rats sheds more than 1 million body hairs each year and a single rat can leave up to 15,000 droppings.

Signs of infestation:

- **Rat droppings** – Rat droppings tend to be found concentrated in specific locations as rats produce up to 40 droppings per night. Brown rat droppings are dark brown in a tapered, spindle shape – resembling a large grain of rice.

- **Scratching noises** – Black rats in particular are agile climbers, earning them their common name – the roof rat. They can easily gain access into loft spaces and upper floors of buildings, so scratching noises at night may suggest their presence. Brown rats, on the other hand, are less adept climbers and more likely to be identified as they scurry under decking, sheds and floorboards.

- **Footprints (running tracks)** – Rats leave foot and tail marks in dusty, less-used areas of buildings. Shining a strong flashlight at a low angle should reveal tracks clearly. To establish if an infestation is active, sprinkle fine flour or talc along a small stretch of floor near the footprints and check for fresh tracks the next day.

- **Smear marks** – Rats use established routes along skirting boards and walls due to their poor eyesight. Grease and dirt on their bodies leave smudges and dark marks on both objects and surfaces they repeatedly brush against. These marks may indicate rodent activity, but as smears may remain for a long period of time, they are not a good gauge of an active infestation.

- **Burrows** – Brown rats are well known for digging and excavating extensive burrow systems for shelter, food storage and nesting. They build burrows next to solid objects or structures (decking, garden sheds, garages etc.) and are also found in secluded, well-vegetated areas such as gardens and wasteland.

Silverfish

More than just a nuisance in homes, silverfish are known for their destructive feeding habits and can cause a serious problem in large numbers – damaging books, photographs, paintings, plaster and other household items containing starch or cellulose.

Silverfish survive in most environments, but thrive in conditions of high humidity and can often be found in dark, damp areas such as kitchens, bathrooms, basements and attics. Characterised by a silvery-blue colour, tiny scales and wiggling movements resembling that of a fish – these pests are also commonly known as fish moths or carpet sharks.

Fixing leaks in pipework, improving ventilation, treating rising damp and using dehumidifiers can help discourage silverfish.

Snakes

Snakes tend to avoid contact with people so will steer clear of you and your pets. There are three main snake species in the UK:

- adder (common viper)

- smooth snake

- grass snake.

Although most British snakes are harmless, with the exception of the adder which can bite, for your own safety and that of the snake, you should never touch them and whenever possible, please try not to be alarmed.

Native UK snakes are protected under the Wildlife and Countryside Act 1981. It is illegal to kill, injure or sell them. Creatures such as bats, badgers, water voles and red squirrels, which in certain circumstances people may consider to be pests, are also protected by law.

Rentokil is able to offer advice on wildlife management.

As we saw in Chapter Nine, in parts of the world such as India snakes pose a far greater danger to the population. Figures reported on the World Health Organization website put the number of 'envenomings' (bites by poisonous snakes) at 421,000 a year worldwide, leading to 20,000 deaths. But as many cases go unreported, this may well be a significant underestimate. South Asia, Southeast Asia and sub-Saharan Africa are the world's deadly snakebite hotspots.

Spiders

There are more than 35,000 species of spider worldwide.

Although they are seen as beneficial to our environment, many people do have an inherent fear of spiders, known as arachnophobia. In the worst cases, feelings of uneasiness at the mere sight of spiders may trigger excessive sweating, crying and even full-blown panic attacks.

Thankfully, most species of spiders found in the UK are not considered dangerous and they rarely bite. If you do get a spider bite, it often has little effect on most people, though a few species can cause an exceptional reaction due to their venom.

Rentokil offers a range of spider control solutions.

Stink bugs

Stink bugs are small but they carry a powerful defensive weapon. They get their name from the stink glands located just under their thorax (chest), between the first and second sets of legs. They can use these glands when threatened, and they burst when the bug is crushed, releasing a powerful, stinky, chemical substance that gives them their name.

There are around 7,000 species of insect in this superfamily of bugs, the scientific name for which is *Pentatomoidea*. Because their backs form a shield-like shape, they are also commonly referred to by the secondary nickname 'shield bugs'.

Stink bugs are notorious for being great hitchers. Species that were once found only in China, Taiwan, Korea and Japan have ended up in the United States, most likely by getting a ride on shipping crates. The brown marmorated stink bug (*Halyomorpha halys*) appeared first in Pennsylvania, but quickly scattered and has now infested much of the eastern seaboard including New Jersey and New York, southern states such as Alabama, Louisiana, and midwest states like Indiana and Illinois.

Stink bugs are famous for being strong fliers that can travel up to a mile. They can hitch rides in crates and on carts to get from one place to another.

Termites

Termites are considered the most destructive insect pests in the world. Many buildings and structures are damaged by them each year, resulting in huge financial losses.

There are many different types and species of termites active in the USA, Australia and countries with tropical climates. Here are the most common types:

- **Subterranean termites** – Subterranean termites are social insects that live in colonies consisting of many individuals. They are found throughout North America and are the most common termite encountered in homes. Common indications of subterranean termites are dark areas or blisters in wood flooring. They will only eat the spring wood, leaving the grain and exterior surface intact – so the damage can go unnoticed.

- **Drywood termites** – Drywood termites are commonly found in coastal states in the south and southwest of the USA. They are not as prolific as some other species, but the damage they cause can be substantial, especially as they go undetected for a long time before they are discovered. Their diet mainly consists of house wood, utility poles, furniture and dying trees. They do not require any contact with soil and prefer areas with low moisture content.

- **Dampwood termites** – Dampwood termites typically infest damp and decaying timber. This species is commonly found in the Pacific Coast states of the USA. They live in moist wood and do not require soil contact. Dampwood termites produce faecal pellets that are an indication of infestation. Dampwood termites contain several species and swarm to set up new nests during the year from January to October.

The techniques Rentokil uses to monitor and bait termites are successful because they combine an expert eye for termite spotting with treatments that tap into the natural instincts of termites.

This helps Rentokil to deliver a service that causes almost no inconvenience to homeowners or commercial property owners.

Termites locate unobtrusive termite bait stations placed around the perimeter of a property because of their natural foraging behaviour. The termites then eat the bait and share it with other nest mates.

This gradually kills large numbers of termites in the colony, and reduces its size until it can no longer support itself and collapses.

Wasps

Wasps are most active in the summer months. In the UK, the common wasp and German wasp cause the most annoyance and painful stings.

Wasps have the potential to attack in large numbers if their nest is disturbed. It is best to treat a nest earlier in the year before numbers increase and the wasps become more aggressive, increasing the threat of stings during treatment.

Woodworm

The term 'woodworm' covers many types of wood-boring beetles, some with wonderful names like deathwatch beetle and house longhorn beetle. Whatever they are called, you'll want to say goodbye to them.

Here are some helpful facts about woodworm:

- Female furniture beetles will only lay eggs in wood where they think their larvae stand the best chance of pupating into adult insects. They tend to choose wood with moisture content of 28% or higher. The average moisture content in a house is nearer 10%, depending where it is. When the larvae hatch, it takes them between two and five years to chew enough nutrients from the timber to invest enough energy to pupate into adult beetles. All the while, the timber may be drying; the larvae can be found living in timber down to 16–18% moisture content. It gets harder for them to feed as the timber gets drier and tougher and resulting adult beetles will be smaller and less likely to produce offspring, so a female must choose a low-risk place to lay her eggs.

- Outdoors this isn't much of a problem, but inside your property they might infest floorboards, furniture, wooden beams and any other wooden objects.

- Larvae burrow into the wood where they feed – and in the process make a maze of tunnels over several years. If left untreated, larvae can seriously weaken the timbers in a building, which may lead to structural failure.

FIND OUT MORE AT:

www.rentokil.co.uk

Facebook: Rentokil

Twitter: @Rentokil

FASCINATING PEST FACTS

1. The average brown rat (*Rattus norvegicus*) consumes 30g of food per day.

2. Black rats (*Rattus rattus*) prefer to eat moist foods such as fruit rather than the dry cereals preferred by brown rats.

3. A brown rat can jump around 75cm from a standing start.

4. Mice can survive without drinking water as they can get all the water they need from food.

5. The gestation period for a rat is only three weeks.

6. Fly species can be distinguished just from their flight patterns. The common house fly (*Musca domestica*) tends to fly in straight lines while the lesser house fly (*Fannia canicularis*) flies in an angular pattern.

7. Cluster flies (*Pollenia rudis*) lay their eggs in soil. When they hatch, the parasitic maggots seek out earthworms and burrow into them to feed (the worms usually die).

8. Nests of the pharaoh ant (*Monomorium pharaonis*) may contain up to 300,000 individuals and each worker can travel over 35 metres in search of food.

9. A wasp nest can home to up to 25,000 wasps.

10. Wasp nests are made from slivers of wood which the adult wasp scrapes off fence posts, trees, etc. and mixes with its saliva before crafting them into a paper-thin structure.

11. Cockroaches produce egg capsules called oothecae. In the case of the German cockroach (*Blattella germanica*), each ootheca will hold 35–40 eggs.

12. Common clothes moths feed on a protein called keratin which is found in naturally occurring fibres such as wool and cashmere.

13. A silverfish can live for up to three years in the right conditions.

14. Bed bugs will lay 200–500 eggs in a two-month period in batches of 10–50.

15. Some birds, like jays, spread their wings on an ants' nest to get ants in their feathers. It is thought that this is because the ants squirt formic acid, which gets rid of feather parasites.

16. A female cat flea can lay between 25 and 40 eggs a day in the fur of a host animal or on its bedding and during its lifetime can produce up to 2,000 eggs.

17. Flea cocoons can remain dormant for two years, only hatching when conditions are right.

18. The deathwatch beetle makes a 'knocking' sound inside or on the surface of wooden timbers by striking its head against the surface. Occupants of medieval sick rooms often heard this sound whilst keeping watch over the dead and dying, hence the name.

RENTOKIL FIRSTS

1925 – Ground-breaking timber fluid marketed commercially to combat wood-boring beetles.

1945 – Introduction of timber fluid injector.

1951 – Central London Woodworm and Dry Rot advice bureau opens.

1958 – First company to receive Royal warrant for rodent control.

1960 – UK's first woodworm insurance policy.

1962 – Revolutionary electroosmotic (EO) damp-proofing technique brought to the UK.

1969 – First pest control business to float on UK stock market.

1974 – Inaugural Overseas Managers Training Conference held at Felcourt.

1976 – Launch of a 30-year guarantee for all woodworm, dry rot and damp-proofing treatments

1983 – Honoured with Queen's Award to Industry for Technological Achievement for developing a new production process for arsenic acid.

1987 – Introduction of 'zip-up' fumigation system, precursor to controlled atmosphere technology.

2007 – RADAR (Rodent Activated Detection And Riddance) trap pioneers use of CO_2 to kill mice humanely.

2012 – Use of heat to treat bed bugs and other insects launched.

2013 – World's first pop-up Pestaurant.

2014 – Rentokil pioneers the use of Google Apps and smartphone access to support pest control service delivery.

2015 – RodentGate launches in Europe, controlling bait access to target species only.

WHO'S WHO

Anker-Petersen, Karl Gustav Danish businessman who built the British Ratin business from scratch and died shortly before the purchase of Rentokil was completed.

Bahr, Louis Scientist whose A/S Bakteriologisk Laboratorium Ratin group began producing the Ratin bacillus in Copenhagen after acquiring the rights from Georg Neumann in 1904.

Bateman, Peter PR Manager from the mid-1960s.

Bridgman, Ken Long-serving executive who joined the finance department in 1953, was promoted to Company Secretary and joined the group board in 1964. Temporarily took on the job of Group Managing Director alongside his role as Finance Director in 1981 following the departure of Brian McGillivray.

Brown, Alan CEO of Rentokil Initial for five years until October 2013.

Burgin, Pat Rentokil Group Chairman for 21 years, stepping down in 1978.

Buchan, Teddy Urbane Scot who with Bob Westphal was joint Managing Director of Rentokil Group for two decades from 1957.

Bye, Tony Launched and ran the Rentokil Video Unit.

Cornwell, Peter Entomologist with a PhD from Oxford who joined Rentokil in 1963 as Chief Biologist and quickly rose to the position of Technical Director/Director of R&D. An eminent authority on cockroaches, Cornwell combined oversight of the laboratories at Felcourt with responsibility for the company's businesses in the Caribbean and parts of Africa.

Eades, Bessie Pioneering businesswoman who ran Rentokil from 1925 up until its sale to British Ratin in 1957.

Edwards, Robin Chief Entomologist who retired in 1991 after 31 years with Rentokil. Author of the Rentokil Library series book *Social Wasps*, Edwards carried out 36,000 identifications of insect specimens and trained generations of technicians, surveyors and managers.

Elsass, Adam Son of Ludvig, became a director of what was then British Ratin in 1949 and was long-serving Chief Executive of Sophus Berendsen, at the time Rentokil's parent company, until the mid-1970s.

Elsass, Ludvig Managing Director of Danish corporation Sophus Berendsen from 1897 onwards. Saw the commercial potential of the Ratin rodenticide.

Elsass, Nick Adam's son. Third generation of the Elsass family to play an important role in the Rentokil story. On the Sophus Berendsen board at the time of Rentokil's hostile takeover of BET.

Farmer, Bob Came to Felcourt as Laboratory Controller in 1952 having previously worked in the research department at Boots. Wrote the disinfestation training manual. In the 1960s he moved to the North West to take charge of the factory at Kirkby while simultaneously running the highly regarded Rentokil Film Unit.

Farrington, Alan Head of Marketing in the 1960s and 1970s among other senior roles.

Flynn, Doug Group CEO 2005–2008.

Foote, Graham Began as a serviceman in Scotland in 1962, took charge of the Bahamas subsidiary and worked his way up to a number of important roles, such as running Rentokil's European operations and UK Pest Control before retirement in 1998.

Gauntlett, Jeff Responsible for the West of England region from 1931. Secured regular disinfestation work from the Royal Navy during the second world war. Went on to head up the London Woodworm, Dry Rot and Pest Advisory Centre opened in Mayfair, London, in 1959.

Grimaldi, Charles Director of Corporate Affairs in the Sir Clive Thompson era.

Harris, George Former independent company auditor appointed to the British Ratin board in 1940 as part of the extraordinary changes necessitated by the German invasion of Denmark. Retired as Vice Chairman in 1965.

Hedgcock, Stewart After a stint in Paris working for Columbia Records, joined British Ratin in 1932 as Karl Gustav Anker-Petersen's right-hand man. Took charge of rodenticide production during the second world war and was entrusted to open negotiations with Norman Hickin on the acquisition of Rentokil.

Hickin, Norman Expert in wood-boring beetles and a key figure in company history. Joined Bessie Eades at Rentokil in 1944 and took charge of innovation as Scientific Director. Hickin joined the board in 1947. He was instrumental in negotiating the sale of Rentokil to British Ratin and thereafter was a prominent member of the Rentokil scientific team for many years.

Holmes, Bill Came to Rentokil in 1956 as General Manager of Woodworm and Dry Rot Control. Taught himself Hungarian in the early 1960s to really get to grips with electroosmotic damp-proofing, which he introduced to the UK.

Jefkins, Frank Rentokil's first in-house Publicity Manager, active in the late 1950s and early 1960s.

Jensen, Sophus Danish expat who headed up the British Ratin sales operation in the south of England in the early days of the business.

Langebœk, Steen Succeeded Adam Elsass as Chief Executive of Sophus Berendsen in 1975, having served on the Rentokil Group board since 1965.

Lewis, Max First employee of Rentokil Inc. who in 1974 was sent from Felcourt to take charge in New York City following the acquisition of Josephsons.

Maxwell-Lefroy, Harold Renowned entomologist and creator of the Rentokil brand.

McAdam, John Became Rentokil Initial Chairman in 2008.

McCue, Jim Caught the eye of executives at HQ in the 1950s as the enterprising Regional Manager of the Newcastle district. Went on to run the UK Pest Control business with great distinction.

McGillivray, Brian Rentokil Group Managing Director from the mid-1970s until 1981.

McGowan, Brian Chairman of Rentokil Initial 2004–2008.

McIntosh, Angus Fraser Former General Manager of rodenticide and insecticide manufacturer Thomas Harley, acquired in 1961, who went on to head up Rentokil's Products Department and earned an OBE for services to pest control due to his tireless work via British and European trade associations.

Neumann, George Danish pharmacist who at the beginning of the 20th century discovered the Ratin bacillus.

Nichols, Charles Chief Chemist at the old Rentokil Laboratories in Fetcham.

Petersen, Viggo Karl Gustav Anker-Petersen's Copenhagen-based boss.

Price, Miles Managing Director of pest control company Insecta, snapped up in 1959. Subsequently Rentokil Technical Director in the early 1960s.

Ransom, Andy Appointed CEO of Rentokil Initial in 2013.

Tenniswood, Bill (Senior and Junior) Bill Tenniswood Senior came to the business in 1929 to head up sales for east London, including the rat-infested Docklands area. His son, Bill Tenniswood Junior, followed his father into the business in 1941, eventually taking charge of the printing and stationery departments at Felcourt, where he oversaw production of 50 *Years of Service*, an earlier book on the history of Rentokil published in the 1970s.

Thompson, Sir Clive CEO of Rentokil Group for 20 years from 1983.

Tyrer, Adrian Joined the company in 1955 and by 1973 was Managing Director of group subsidiary Rentokil Limited, with responsibility for Pest Control, Hygiene, Wood-preserving, Products and Exports. Also oversaw international franchising.

Westphal, Bob Australian lawyer who with fellow joint Managing Director Teddy Buchan ran Rentokil from 1957 to the mid-1970s, finally retiring as group Chairman in 1987.

Westphal, Fred Head of Rentokil Australia from the mid-1960s until 1978. Added responsibility for New Zealand and Fiji in 1974 and further expanded his portfolio in 1975 to encompass all of Southeast Asia.

Wilde, James Came to Rentokil in 1993 with the Securiguard acquisition and was responsible for the conferencing and parcels business and group strategic development before spending 18 months as CEO from January 2003.

Wilkinson, Jim In charge of the British Ratin sales operation for the north of England and Scotland in the early days of the business. Conducted the survey leading to the major Bahrain contract in 1955.

ABOUT THE AUTHOR

Rob Gray has been a journalist since 1988. His work has appeared in a wide variety of publications, from newspapers such as *The Financial Times* and *The Guardian* through to business titles including *HR Magazine*, *The Marketer*, *Campaign*, *Broadcast* and *Management Today*. Aside from developing a healthy respect for the challenges of pest control, Rob writes about brands, marketing, corporate communications, innovation, organisational development and people.

For over a decade, Rob has worked in a part-time freelance capacity as head of editorial content at the International Public Relations Association, where he is responsible for commissioning and editing the IPRA Thought Leadership series of essays on trends in media and communications. His previous book, *Great Brand Blunders: The worst marketing and social media meltdowns of all time... and how to avoid your own* (Crimson Publishing) explores the root causes of marketing disasters, takes idiocy to task and is packed with good advice on steering clear of potentially damaging pitfalls. It attracted widespread praise: "excellent" – *Forbes*; "You simply must read this book" – *Marketing* magazine. It was also the Chartered Institute of Marketing Book of the Month.

Rob has spoken at conferences and events, including the Eurobest Festival of Creativity in Lisbon. He lives with his wife Ginny in a house on the border of Northamptonshire and Oxfordshire that is overrun by teenagers. You can follow him @RobGrayWriter on Twitter.

ACKNOWLEDGEMENTS

The story of the Rentokil brand is a fascinating one and writing it has been an absolute pleasure. I am indebted to Rentokil Initial's Malcolm Padley, who not only suggested I write this book in the first place but made sure doors were opened and gave me free rein to delve into every aspect of the brand and corporate history. I'd like to think his openness has been rewarded. In learning the insides and outs of Rentokil, I've come to the conclusion that it is one of those great brands that is enhanced, rather than diminished, by telling it exactly the way it is.

A special mention must also go to Laura Folley, Mal's colleague in the corporate communications team, who worked so hard to assist with my research: making introductions, setting up interviews, ferreting out useful background material and wisely suggesting I should remove a reference to Russell Brand made in an earlier version of the text.

Thousands of individuals have played a role in building the Rentokil brand. But in order to keep the narrative flowing it was impossible to mention a large number of people by name, or indeed address every single significant event in a history that covers the best part of a century. My humble apologies to those whose names I have omitted.

Several books have been tremendously helpful to me, most notably *Rentokil: 50 Years of Service*, an excellent earlier corporate history published by the company in the 1970s. Laurence Fleming's meticulous biography of Harold Maxwell-Lefroy, *The Entokil Man* (Dexter Haven Publishing), shed welcome light on the early days and is certainly worth reading. Two unpublished manuscripts unearthed during the course of my research also helped add valuable detail to the story: Dr Norman Hickin's brilliantly titled *My Life with Woodworm*, and what survives of Hugh Barty-King's 1974 corporate history of Rentokil. Old back issues of *Rentokil Review* also contained a treasure trove of stories.

As well as sharing her personal memories of life at Rentokil in the 1970s, Gill Brown of the pension department contacted numerous retired former employees on my behalf, whose stories add a tremendous amount of warmth, humour and enlightening individual perspectives to this book. Nicholas Donnithorne, a one-man Rentokil archive, also deserves to be singled out for assiduously collating a lot of material that might otherwise have been lost, sharing his own recollections, kindly suggesting other knowledgeable persons for me to approach and casting a keen eye over the text to help root out historical and technical errors. Others at Rentokil Initial who've spared their valuable time include: Espen Agnalt, Clara Bermingham, Andy Brigham, Mark Brown, Armand Bruneau, Nigel Cheeseright, Scott Cook, Jason Cotton, Trevor de Silvia, Sam Easaw, Barbara Fisher, Maurice Goldson, Ronan Greany, Matt Green, Chris Hunt, Richard Jones, Mark Lanford, Yvonne McCabe, Savvas Othon, Stewart Power, Emma Robinson, Ayse Sav, Amelia Shire, Stuart Stevenson, David Taplin, Tracy Williams and Phill Wood.

My appreciation also goes out to: Nick Banton at the House of Commons Information Office; Andrew Harrison at the National

Archives in Kew; Ronald Dunning for sharing his genealogical expertise on the Lefroy family tree; Robert Hastings of Dexter Haven Publishing; Alistair Moir, Archive Collections Manager at the History of Advertising Trust; Anne Barrett of the Corporate Records Unit and college archives at Imperial College of Science, Technology and Medicine; Hannah Gay, author of *The History of Imperial College London, 1907–2007: Higher education and research in science, technology and medicine* (Imperial College Press, 2007); Val McAtear, librarian at the Royal Entomological Society; Mikkel Plannthin for his knowledge of the Free Danish Council's activities during the second world war; Dr Brian Ridout for his invaluable help on the life of Dr Norman Hickin; Nick Elsass and the Ludvig and Sara Elsass Foundation; Carolyn Westphal; Dr Jørgen H. Jensenius; Steen Nottelmann of Royal Copenhagen; Dr Haydn Griffiths, headmaster and Andy Nicoll, Marketing Manager at Wrekin College; and Audrey Henderson, for information on the limited edition tea caddy presented to her late husband Alan and other Rentokil employees in October 1979 to mark the 125th anniversary of Sophus Berendsen.

Additionally, I'd like to thank former employees Jürgen Althoff, Peter Bateman, Ken Bridgman, Bob Crawford, Alan Deutsch, Graham Foote, Charles Grimaldi, Maurice Herring, Paul Hocking, Fred Hook, Gerald Moores, Walter Spruyt, Sir Clive Thompson, Henry Trewren, Gordon Wilkinson and Bob Wood.

Last but by no means least, a big hurrah to Myles Hunt and his immensely talented team at my publisher Harriman House. Chris Parker worked his socks off to make this book look good and 'debug' the manuscript of inconsistencies and errors. People able to combine a cultured eye for design with immaculate copy editing skills, as Chris does, are truly thin on the ground.

INDEX

People

Companies

THANKS
FOR READING!

Our readers mean everything to us at Harriman House. As a special thank-you for buying this book let us help you save as much as possible on your next read:

If you've never ordered from us before, get £5 off your first order at **harriman-house.com** with this code: pest541

Already a customer? Get £5 off an order of £25 or more with this code: pest222552

Get 7 days' FREE access to hundreds of our books at **volow.co** – simply head over and sign up.

Thanks again!
from the team at